THE KINGFISHER
ILLUSTRATED
DINOSAUR
ENCYCLOPEDIA

Consultant Tim Batty, Curator of The Dinosaur Museum, Dorchester, England

Managing editor Miranda Smith

Senior designer Malcolm Parchment

Picture researchers Juliet Duff, Jane Lambert

DTP manager Nicky Studdart

Production manager Caroline Hansell

Additional illustrations

Julian Baker, Richard Bonson, Mike Davis, James Field,
Chris Forsey, Ray Grinaway, Gary Hinks, David Holmes, Mark Iley, Ian Jackson,
Steve Kirk, Terrence Lambert, Bernard Long, Kevin Maddison,
Shirley Mallinson, Bernard Robinson, Tim Slade, Guy Smith, Mike Taylor

KINGFISHER

Kingfisher Publications Plc

New Penderel House

283–288 High Holborn

London WC1V 7HZ

www.kingfisherpub.com

First published by Kingfisher Publications Plc 2001

2 4 6 8 10 9 7 5 3 1

1TR/0601/CAC/CLSN/140KMA

A CIP catalogue record for this book is available
from the British Library

ISBN 0 7534 0536 9

Printed in China

THE KINGFISHER
ILLUSTRATED
DINOSAUR
ENCYCLOPEDIA

WRITTEN BY DAVID BURNIE

ILLUSTRATED BY JOHN SIBBICK

KING*f*ISHER

CONTENTS

Colony-forming graptolites
from the Silurian Period,
drifting in the sea

Eldonia ludwigi, a
primitive echinoderm
from the Burgess Shale

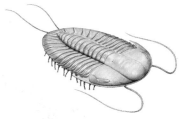

Oryctocephalus matthewi
an early trilobite from
the Burgess Shale

Aysheaia – an ancestor of velvet worms –
feeding on sponges during the Cambrian Period

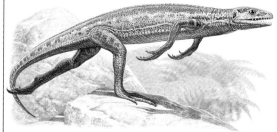

Acanthostega (left) and *Ichthyostega* (right and
above), two of the earliest four-legged vertebrates

Heleosaurus, a late Permian reptile

The fossilized
skeleton of
Parasaurolophus,
a duck-billed
dinosaur

Skeletal muscles
of the plant-eater
Brachiosaurus,
one of the tallest
sauropods

Deinosuchus, a giant crocodilian
from the late Cretaceous, attacking
Corythosaurus, a duck-billed dinosaur

FOREWORD

This book is about a group of extraordinary animals – the dinosaurs. These reptiles dominated the natural world for more than 160 million years, and from the middle of the 19th century when the first fossil skeletons were excavated, they have captured the imagination of generations of people – children and adults alike. Through the patient work of palaeontologists and other scientists, we are finding out more and more about these remarkable creatures, the continents they roamed, what they ate, the way they lived.

The work of a palaeontologist is painstaking and back-breaking, but sometimes it is unbelievably rewarding. On 12th August 1990, in the Badlands of South Dakota, many kilometres from any human habitation, I found three articulated vertebrae, some ribs and a large bone weathering out of a cliff face. I was almost certain that the bones belonged to a *Tyrannosaurus rex*, but I had no idea that the find, 'Sue', would proved a record-breaker. She is the largest and most complete skeleton of a *Tyrannosaurus* yet discovered – she is 12.8 metres long and stands 4 metres high at the hips. *And* she was not alone. She was found with the remains of other tyrannosaurs – a baby, a juvenile and a young adult.

On 17th May 2000, at the Field Museum in Chicago, Sue's mounted skeleton was unveiled to the world for the first time in 66 million years and she, like so many dinosaur fossils worldwide, has been attracting millions of visitors ever since. It has taken more than 4,500 million years for the Earth to reach its present state, and we are finding out details about its prehistoric beginnings all the time. Dinosaurs are a significant part of that prehistory. The more we discover about dinosaurs like Sue, the more we find out about the world we live in today.

Sue Hendrickson

Sue Hendrickson

LIFE IN THE DISTANT PAST

If Earth's entire history could be crammed into a single hour, animal life would not appear until the final 15 minutes was well underway. Land animals would make their entrance when the hour had just six minutes left to go, while the Age of Reptiles – one of the most dramatic periods – would run for just over two minutes, when the hour was almost at an end. This chapter looks at the first few minutes of this story, and explains some of the processes that have shaped animal life and the evidence that prehistory has left behind.

THE BEGINNING OF LIFE

WHEN THE EARTH FORMED, ABOUT 4.6 BILLION YEARS AGO, ITS AVERAGE TEMPERATURE WAS A HOT AS THE SURFACE OF THE SUN. BUT JUST 700 MILLION YEARS LATER, LIFE WAS ALREADY UNDERWAY.

The Earth is the only place where life definitely exists, although it is possible that elsewhere in the Universe, other planets have living things of their own. As far as scientists can tell, life arose on Earth through a long series of chemical 'accidents' that took place in watery surroundings. Driven by solar and chemical energy, these created the complex substances that form the machinery of all living things.

FOSSIL EVIDENCE

These rocky mounds are stromatolites growing in Shark Bay, Western Australia. They are formed by cyanobacteria (blue-green algae), which are simple microbes that collect energy from sunlight. Cyanobacteria form mounds by trapping sediment, which becomes cemented together. Shark Bay's stromatolites are several thousand years old, but some fossilized stromatolites are 3.4 billion years old – making them among the earliest signs of life on Earth.

WHAT IS LIFE?

Over 99.99999 per cent of our planet is made up by inanimate matter – matter that is not alive. Unlike living things, inanimate matter cannot grow or use energy, and it cannot respond to the world around it. Most importantly, it cannot reproduce. So how did this unpromising starting-point generate things that were alive 4 billion years ago?

The answer, most scientists believe, is by a series of random chemical reactions, that took place between carbon-containing substances dissolved in the sea. Some of these reactions formed microscopic bubbles surrounded by oily membranes, containing tiny drops of fluid shielded from the water outside. Others formed substances that could copy themselves, by attracting simpler chemicals from their surroundings.

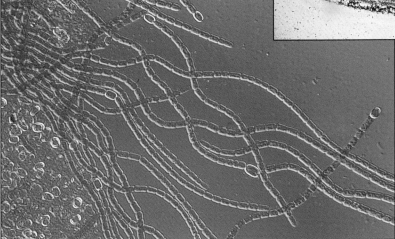

Somehow the two came together and produced the first self-copying cells. When those cells started to use energy, life began.

POWERING UP

The first living things were bacteria. These got their energy from dissolved chemicals, but as they multiplied, supplies of this chemical food dwindled, and a struggle for survival began. This struggle is a feature of life, because living things always outstrip resources. But there are hidden benefits, as this struggle also makes living things evolve.

One early result of evolution was that some bacteria evolved a new way of life three billion years ago. They developed the ability to collect energy directly from sunlight. This process, called photosynthesis, was a major step forward, because sunlight delivers energy in vast amounts.

LIFE IN THE FAST LANE

When photosynthesis began, the Earth's atmosphere contained nitrogen and carbon dioxide, but hardly any oxygen. Unlike earlier forms of life, photosynthetic bacteria

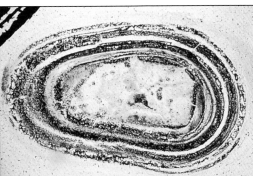

released oxygen as a waste product. The atmosphere's oxygen level began to creep up to 21 per cent – today's level.

Oxygen is a highly reactive substance – for many primitive bacteria, a deadly poison – so they had to retreat into mud and sediment where oxygen could not be found. But, as oxygen became abundant, more complex forms of life evolved that turned oxygen to their advantage. These organisms could use oxygen to 'burn' reserves of fuel stored inside their cells, which meant that they could release energy exactly when they needed it. Life was beginning to speed up.

The first of these 'aerobic' organisms were single-celled aquatic microbes, larger than bacteria and much more complex. Called protists, they teem in freshwater and the sea today. But their place at the top was not destined to last because, over a million years ago, plants and animals began to evolve.

◁ *This microscopic fossil is from a type of rock called Gunflint Chert, which is found in western Ontario, Canada. This rock layer formed about 2 billion years ago, and it contains some of the earliest known remains of microbes that lived by photosynthesis.*

◁ *The long filaments shown here are strands of Anabaena, a present-day cyanobacterium, or blue-green alga. Anabaena lives in shallow water and on damp ground, and its way of life is little different from that of the earliest photosynthetic bacteria.*

◁ *When the Earth's crust was newly formed, volcanic eruptions (far left) occurred on a colossal scale. These eruptions actually helped to create suitable conditions for life, because they gave off steam which eventually condensed to form the oceans. They also gave out minerals that early bacteria could use as sources of energy.*

EARTH'S FIRST ANIMALS

THE MOST ANCIENT TRACES OF ANIMAL LIFE ARE UP TO ONE BILLION YEARS OLD, BUT THE OLDEST FOSSILS OF ANIMALS THEMSELVES DATE FROM ABOUT 600 MILLION YEARS AGO, DURING THE VENDIAN PERIOD.

When the first animals evolved, they were soft-bodied and microscopic, and lived on or in the seabed. Creatures like these hardly ever fossilized, and the only clues they left behind were indirect ones, such as the remains of burrows and tracks. But despite their tiny size, early animals must have flourished, because they gave rise to the Earth's first visible animals: the Ediacarans.

Wilpena Pound, a giant bowl of sandstone 17km wide, lies in South Australia's Flinders Ranges – the same geological formation where the first Ediacaran fossils were found. The sandstone that makes up these hills formed over 540 million years ago, before animals with hard body parts appeared. The discovery that these rocks can contain animal fossils has changed ideas about evolution.

△ *Measuring less than 2cm across, this fossil Ediacaran,* Medusina mawsoni, *looks like the remains of a jellyfish stranded on a beach. Many think this animal, or others like it, were the direct ancestors of jellyfish that appeared during the Cambrian Period.*

A CHANCE DISCOVERY

The Ediacarans get their name from the Ediacara Hills, in South Australia. In 1946, an Australian geologist noticed some unusual fossils in slabs of ancient sandstone. Some of the fossils seemed to have been left by corals, jellyfish and worms, but others were like nothing alive today.

At first, the Ediacarans were thought to be animals from the Cambrian Period (page 28) – a time when nature produced a huge burst of animal life, starting about 540 million years ago. But a closer look showed that the Ediacaran fossils were older than this, and came from the period now known as the Vendian, immediately before the Cambrian. Until this find, the Vendian had seemed to be a biological 'black hole', containing almost no traces of animal life.

Since the 1940s, Ediacaran animals have been found in several different parts of the world, including Greenland, Russia and Namibia. As more fossils are discovered, biologists are trying to decide how these animals lived, and what happened to them when the Vendian Period came to a close.

THE EDICARAN WORLD

Unlike most of today's animals, the ones from the Ediacaran did not have heads, tails or limbs, and neither did they have mouths or organs for digesting their food. Instead of pursuing food, they probably absorbed nutrients from the water around them. Some may also have harboured algae – a living partnership that gave them a share of the energy the algae collected from sunlight. Many Ediacarans were fastened to the seabed, and looked almost like plants, but others simply lay in the shallows, waiting for nutrients to waft their way.

The plant-like species included *Charnia*, which looked like a feather made of jelly, and *Swartpuntia*, an even stranger animal with four semicircular 'combs'. But the giant of them all was *Dickinsonia*, which could grow to the size of a doormat. Like all other Ediacarans, its body was barely more than paper-thin – essential for an animal that absorbed food through its outer skin.

Compared to the animals that followed them, the Ediacarans led uneventful lives. They had no weapons or defensive armour, or any other way of resisting attack. There was no need – the Vendian sea was a safe place, because predators had not yet evolved.

A FAILED EXPERIMENT?

Over 50 years after the first Ediacarans were discovered, scientific arguments continue about their place in the animal world. Some scientists have suggested that they were not animals at all, but organisms that were more like today's lichens. Others claim that they were members of a completely separate kingdom of living things – the Vendobionts – which died out as the Cambrian Period began. Supporters of this theory point to the Ediacarans' strange body plan, which was like a fluid-filled mattress divided by partitions. They claim that Vendobionts were an evolutionary experiment, one that worked successfully until more energetic and aggressive animals appeared in the Cambrian.

MIXED FORTUNES

Because there is so little detailed evidence, neither of these theories has convinced all the experts working on ancient life. Instead, many researchers believe that the Ediacarans were genuine animals, but that they experienced very different fortunes as the Vendian Period approached its final stages. Some gave rise to more familiar animals that became widespread in Cambrian times, but others died out, and their strange features disappeared forever from the animal world.

▽ *This imaginary scene shows a collection of Ediacaran animals from different parts of the world. In the centre is* Dickinsonia, *the largest member of the group, which sometimes grew to 1m in length. To its left, three feather-like* Charnia *project from the sediment, while a trio of brick-coloured* Swartpuntia *is visible further behind.* Spriggina *– the small animal in front of* Dickinsonia *– resembled a primitive trilobite, although like all Ediacarans, it had no hard body parts.*

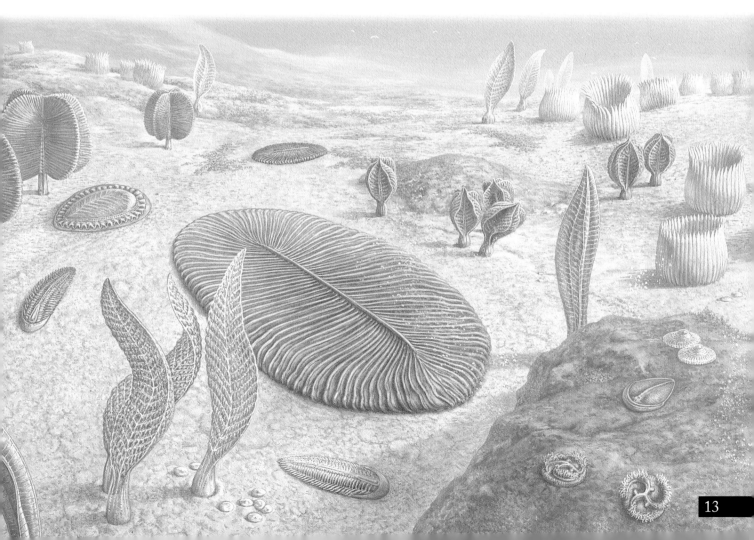

HOW ANIMALS EVOLVE

EVER SINCE SNIMALS FIRST APPEARED, THEY
HAVE GRADUALLY DEVELOPED DIFFERENT
SHAPES AND WAYS OF
LIFE. THIS PROCESS –
CALLED EVOLUTION – IS
A KEY FEATURE OF ALL
LIVING THINGS.

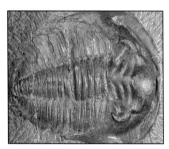
Cambrian trilobite

Ordovician trilobite

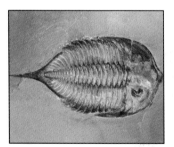
Silurian trilobite

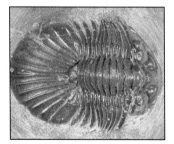
Devonian trilobite

Before the scientific study of fossils began, people believed that the world was created intact, together with all the forms of life that now exist. That would mean, for example, that the world always had two kinds of elephants, about 3,700 kinds of lizards, and about 9,450 kinds of birds. But as fossils of prehistoric animals began to surface, this idea began to look more and more improbable.

ADAPTING TO SURVIVE
Where do prehistoric aniamls fit into the living world and why do they no longer exist? Evolution provides the answers. If living things always produced young that were identical to themselves, each different kind – or

◁ *Trilobites existed for over 300 million years, and during that time, thousands of different species evolved. Each species had its own characteristic shape, with a range of adaptations that suited its particular way of life on the sea floor. Palaeontologists are often able to date rocks simply by looking at the trilobites that they contain.*

species – would never change. Young animals would grow up to be exactly the same size and shape as their parents, and they would also behave in exactly the same way. But this is not how nature works. Living things are very variable, and they pass on their variations when they breed.

These variations are often tiny, but they can have some far-reaching effects. For example, a lizard that has slightly better-than-average eyesight will be better at catching food. Compared to an 'average' lizard, it is more likely to stay well fed and healthy, which means that it is also more likely to attract a mate and breed. Because animals hand on their variations when they breed, many of its young will have better-than-average eyesight as well, and they will pass on this variation in their turn. Sharp-eyed lizards will gradually become more common, and eventually better-than-average eyesight will become a feature of the species as a whole. The species will have evolved.

The driving force behind this kind of change is called natural selection, because nature sorts out individuals that have the best features for survival. Natural selection started when life began, and has been picking out useful variations ever since.

HOW NEW SPECIES FORM
Evolution works very slowly, so it takes a long time for small variations to have any noticeable effect. (A rare exception to this rule occurs with simple organisms, such as bacteria, because these can breed extremely rapidly.) Over the long term, even the smallest variations start to add up, creating major changes in the way animals look and behave. As the generations succeed each

Phiomia

other, these changes can become so great that an entirely new species comes into being. Alternatively, differences can make the original species split into more than one line. If these lines remain separate by breeding only among themselves, two or more new species will take the original's place.

In nature, different species compete with each other for the resources that they need, such as food and space to breed. If two species have similar lifestyles, the struggle between them becomes intense. It may continue for many centuries or millennia, but the outcome is always the same: one species gets the upper hand, while the other declines, and may eventually become extinct.

Extinction is a natural feature of life. Usually it occurs very slowly, and is balanced by the new species that evolve. But extinction can also occur in sudden waves, when a sudden change in living conditions wipes out thousands or even millions of species in a short space of time. Many biologists think that we are living through one of these waves today.

TRIED AND TESTED

The study of evolution dates back to the 19th century, with the work of English naturalist Charles Darwin. Darwin collected a mass of evidence showing that evolution occurs, and he identified the driving force behind it. During his lifetime, many people imagined that evolution followed a set path, steadily 'improving' living things in the same way that designers improve machines. But today, biologists take a rather different view. The reason for this is that, unlike a human designer, natural selection cannot plan ahead. Instead, it works like an impartial judge, testing every tiny variation, and rejecting any that do not have an immediate use. It cannot select anything that simply might prove useful in the future.

This way of selecting features means that complicated structures, such as eyes, legs or feathers, have to evolve through a succession of stages, and that each of these stages has to bring benefits of its own. Primitive feathers, for example, would have been useless for flight, so they must have served some other function when they first arose. Palaeontologists believe that they know what this function was – a discovery that has had a major impact on our understanding of dinosaurs as well as birds (page 132).

Another feature of evolution is that it can never start from scratch. Instead, natural selection works with living things as they currently exist, encouraging features that help them to make the most of their way of life. But no matter how much living things change on the outside, their bodies still contain the evidence of their long-distant evolutionary past. For palaeontologists, this evidence is a treasure-trove of information about how living things have evolved.

▽ *Elephants and their relatives arose from a single species, which lived over 40 million years ago. Fossils show that since that time at least 350 different species evolved. From left to right, this illustration shows* Phiomia, *which stood about 2.5m tall,* Gomphotherium, *which also had a short trunk and tusks, and* Deinotherium, *which had backward-curving tusks in its lower jaw.* Platybelodon *had lower tusks which worked like shovels, while the imperial mammoth,* Mammuthus imperator, *looked more like a modern elephant, with a long trunk and forward-curving tusks. These animals belonged to several different branches of the elephant line.*

Mammuthus imperator

Gomphotherium　　　　　Deinotherium　　　　　Platybelodon

EVIDENCE FROM THE PAST

BURIED IN SEDIMENT, TRAPPED IN AMBER
OR FROZEN IN ICE – THESE ARE JUST SOME
OF THE WAYS THAT PREHISTORIC ANIMALS
LEFT REMAINS THAT HAVE WITHSTOOD
THE TEST OF TIME.

Because most prehistoric animals are now extinct, our knowledge of them comes entirely from the remains they have left behind. With species that died out relatively recently – which in geological terms can mean thousands of years – these remains can include actual body parts, or even entire animals. But with species that lived much further back in time, no body parts are left. Instead, scientists study something else: remains that have literally turned into stone.

△ *This remarkable fossil shows a predatory* Coelophysis *with the remains of a young* Coelophysis *in its stomach. Rare finds like these give an insight into how prehistoric animals behaved.*

THE PAST PRESERVED

When an animal dies, its remains rarely stay in one piece for long. On land, scavengers soon home in on the corpse, tearing off flesh and bones. Insects lay their eggs in the remains, producing maggots that burrow through what is left. Anything left behind is broken down by bacteria, the most useful natural recyclers. Within days, or weeks if

FOSSIL EVIDENCE

This enormous egg – carefully pieced together from broken fragments – was laid by Aepyornis, *a giant flightless bird that lived in Madagascar until perhaps 500 years ago. Although* Aepyornis *is extinct, its eggs are still occasionally found on the island, usually when heavy rain reveals them by washing away the soil. The oldest specimens are fossilized, but this one consists of original shell.*

the weather is cold or dry, all that is left is a few scattered bones.

On rare occasions an animal's body is preserved. If the corpse is smothered by something that excludes air, such as volcanic ash or seabed sediment, scavengers and decomposing bacteria are not able to do their work. The corpse remains intact, and gradually disappears as further layers of sediment or ash build up above. The remains may then be fossilized (pages 18-19) – the ultimate form of preservation, because it can save the shape of living things for several billion years.

STICKY MOMENTS

For biologists interested in the Earth's past, fossils are by far the most useful kind of evidence. But prehistoric animals and plants can also be preserved in other ways. When a luckless insect or small animal encounters a blob of sticky resin oozing from a tree, it can become trapped and then enveloped, sealed inside a transparent tomb, which hardens as it dries. The animals's internal organs decompose, but its outer structure is preserved. Resin itself can fossilize, turning into a glassy substance called amber. Some beads of amber, and the animals locked up inside them, are over 50 million years old.

Resin is not a hazard for large animals, but sticky asphalt, a kind of tar, is. This natural substance seeps upwards to the surface of the ground, creating treacherous pools that can engulf an animal that ventures across it. The animal becomes impregnated with oily fluids from the tar, which make it very hard for decomposers to attack its remains. The flesh gradually breaks down, but the original unfossilized bones often remain. These relics have been found in several parts of the world, but the most famous is Rancho La Brea, in California. Here, an incredible variety of animals has been preserved from Ice Age times (page 212).

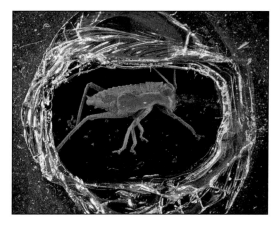

▷ *Trapped in amber, this grasshopper, found in Russia, is about 40 million years old.*

STOPPING THE CLOCK

Some kinds of preservation stop the clock for hundreds or even thousands of years. Mummification, used by the ancient Egyptians to preserve their dead, is one of these. When a corpse becomes mummified, it dries out completely, which protects it from bacterial attack. In nature, such remains are usually found in deserts and dry caves.

Being frozen is another way of putting decay on hold. In parts of the world where the ground is permanently frozen, such as northern Siberia, remains of Ice Age mammals are often preserved in this way.

▽ *A 10,000-year-old baby mammoth is lifted from frozen ground in northern Russia. The mammoth has been flattened by the weight of the ice above it, but it is completely preserved.*

HOW FOSSILS FORM

FOR A DEAD ANIMAL TO TURN INTO A FOSSIL,
CIRCUMSTANCES HAVE TO BE EXACTLY RIGHT.
MANY ANIMALS BEGIN TO FOSSILIZE, ONLY
TO DISAPPEAR WITHOUT TRACE.

The word 'fossil' originally meant any rock or mineral that was dug up out of the ground. Today, it means something much more precise – the remains of something that was once alive, which have been preserved in the Earth's crust. Unlike the original remains, fossils are tough, and they are also chemically stable, which means that they can survive for incredible lengths of time. Most fossils are at least 10,000 years old, but some date back to the very early days of life on Earth.

As well as preserving animals, fossils can also preserve traces that they leave behind. These traces include footprints – like these dinosaur prints from Utah – and also burrows, leftover food, 'stomach stones' or gastroliths, and also fossilized droppings, or coprolites. Trace fossils are interesting because they reveal details of animal behaviour, but matching them up with their makers is often a difficult task.

DEAD AND BURIED

The process of fossilization begins when something dies and is quickly covered up, for example by sediment, or by an avalanche of underwater mud. Sediment consists of very fine particles, which form a soft blanket over the remains. This blanket protects the remains from scavengers, and it also keeps oxygen out, making it hard for microbes to break down the remains in the normal way.

In many cases, this is where the story ends, because waves and currents often disturb remains in water, while wind and rain do the

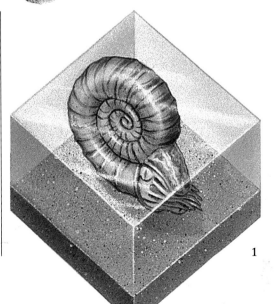

△ *Ammonites and their relatives often formed fossils, because they had hard shells, and because they lived in shallow seawater – an ideal environment for being buried after death. Like trilobites, their detailed anatomy changed as they evolved, and this allows them to be used as a fossil 'calendar' to determine the age of particular layers of rock.*

1

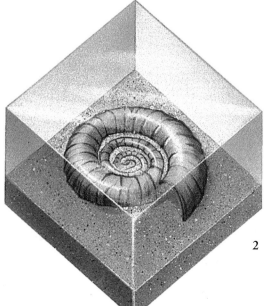

2

same on land. But if the dead animal lies undisturbed for long enough, more sediment builds up above it. This burial may take place at a rate of just a few millimetres a year, but as time goes by the stage is set for fossilization to begin.

TURNED TO STONE

Hidden away beneath the surface, the minerals that make up any hard body parts – such as bones and shells – often dissolve and recrystallize, becoming harder than before. Alternatively, underground water may seep through the body parts, dissolving their minerals and washing them away. New minerals are deposited, a process that is often described as 'turning to stone'. These changes occur very slowly, and the remains keep their original shape.

As sediment continues to pile up above, the remains become even more deeply buried. Time and increasing pressure do the rest, turning the remains into a fossil, and the sediment around it into solid rock.

BACK TO THE SURFACE

Even at this stage, things can go wrong. During the thousands or millions of years that it takes a fossil to form, the rock around it may change. The layers may buckle and bend, while extreme pressure may squash the fossil flat. Heat is another factor. If too much warmth reaches the rock from the crust below, the rock may partly melt, and any fossils that it contains will be destroyed. If a fossil manages to escape these hazards, it then has to resurface to be found. This occurs when sedimentary rock is eroded, usually by wind or rain. Then someone has to find the fossil before it falls away from the surrounding rock, breaks up, and finally disappears.

GAPS IN THE RECORD

Because fossilization is so chancy, the Earth's 'fossil record' gives a patchy view of prehistoric life. Some animals, such as trilobites and ammonites, fossilized in vast numbers because they had hard shells or body cases, and because they lived on the seabed. In the case of trilobites, these animals grew by shedding their skins. Each shed skin formed a perfect trilobite replica, which could also turn into a fossil.

But for some groups – even ones that had bones – fossilization was an uncommon event. This is particularly true of early primates, and other mammals that lived in trees. When they died, their bodies dropped to the ground, where scavenging animals fed on them, scattering the remains. Fossil-hunters occasionally discover solitary bones or teeth, but complete skeletons are very rare.

◁ *A fossilized* Archaeopteryx, *one of the earliest birds. Unusually for a fossil, this contains the outline of feathers. Soft body parts like these usually disappear during fossilization.*

▽ *The diagram at the bottom of these pages shows five typical steps in fossilization.*
1 *An ammonite sinks to the seabed, where it dies.*
2 *The ammonite's coiled shell rests on the seabed, where it is soon covered by fine particles of sediment drifting down from the water above.*
3 *During the process known as diagenesis, the shell's minerals are slowly altered and replaced.*
4 *Further layers of rock form above the fossil.*
5 *The rock is gradually eroded by wind and rain, exposing the fossil at the surface.*

3

4

5

STUDYING FOSSILS

WITHOUT FOSSILS, OUR KNOWLEDGE OF THE EARTH'S LIVING PAST WOULD STRETCH BACK ONLY A FEW THOUSAND YEARS. BUT WITH THEM, SCIENTISTS CAN INVESTIGATE THE ANIMALS THAT LIVED FAR BACK IN TIME.

Fossils are fascinating objects, which explains why many people enjoy collecting them. For palaeontologists – the scientists who study the Earth's living past – they are also a crucial source of information. They reveal when and how animals lived, what they ate and sometimes how they reproduced. They also show how different species were linked by evolution. Gathering this information starts with fossil-hunting, and it ends when a specimen is cleaned, studied and assembled, and ready to go on view.

FOSSIL-BEARING ROCKS

Fossil-finding is partly a matter of luck, and partly a matter of knowing where fossils are likely to be found. It is necessary to be able to recognize the three main types of rock, because two of them never contain fossils. The first fossil-free type, igneous rock, includes granite and basalt – rocks that are crystalline and also very hard. They develop from molten rock or magma, which obliterates any remains of living things. The second type, metamorphic rock, includes marble and slate. These rocks are ones that have been transformed by pressure or heat, which means that any fossils they may have contained will have been destroyed. The third category, sedimentary rock, includes limestone, sandstone and chalk. Sedimentary rocks are always laid down in layers – a key feature of all fossil-finding sites.

SEARCHING THE GROUND

Some of the world's most interesting fossils have been discovered in places where sedimentary rock is quarried or mined. Many fossils of flying reptiles have come from quarries in Germany, while some of the largest sauropod fossils have been discovered in quarries in the United States. Many other fossils are found by amateurs and professionals searching rocky outcrops where remains are brought to the surface by erosion. These outcrops include the dry, flat-topped hills in desert areas, and coastal cliffs were the rock is undermined by the sea. The softer the rock, the faster it erodes and the more quickly fossils come to the surface.

Sometimes fossils are intact when they are found, but with skeletons, wind or rain often separate the bones. Real skill is needed to work out how the bones are likely to have moved, and therefore where the rest of the skeleton is likely to be. This kind of hunt often leads up slopes of crumbling rock, until the 'parent material' is spotted high above.

△ *These sedimentary rocks at Ghost Ranch, New Mexico, are rich in dinosaur fossils. The red rock was laid down during the Triassic, when the Age of Reptiles began.*

▷ *Fossilized bones of an allosaur being removed at the Dinosaur National Monument, USA. Care is needed to prevent fossils breaking as they are extracted from the rock.*

UP AND AWAY

Once a fossil has been found, it is usually extracted so that it can be taken away and studied. For something as small as a trilobite, this can involve little more than a few taps with a hammer to free it from the surrounding matrix or bedrock. But when the fossil is a complete dinosaur skeleton, with individual bones that may be over 1m long, removing the fossil is a major operation that may take several years.

One of the difficulties with this kind of work is that fossilized bones often break up once that are exposed to rain and sunshine. To keep them intact, the bones are wrapped in jackets of quick-setting plaster before they are carried or winched away.

BACK IN THE LAB

Once a fossil has arrived in the lab, it often needs further work so that it can be fully revealed. Delicate specimens, such as insects or small fish, are cleaned using metal probes, brushes and machines that resemble dentists' drills. The specimen may also be dipped in a bath of acetic acid – the substance that gives vinegar its sharp smell. This loosens any surrounding rock, which eventually falls away. Fragile bones are hardened by treating them with a plastic, which holds any loose fragments in place.

When the fossil has been cleaned and treated, the process of studying it can begin. The tiniest irregularities or marks can reveal important details, so anything that looks unusual is given a closer look, sometimes with a microscope. This kind of work often resembles forensic science, and in some cases the examination turns up tooth marks or fractured bones, showing how the animal met its end.

Palaeontologists can also use medical scanners – a technique that allows them to look at the bony structures beneath the surface. This new way of studying fossils has been used with several kinds of dinosaur to investigate their brain size (page 129), and to try to work

out whether or not they were warm-blooded (page 148).

JOINING UP

Because museums have a limited amount of space, many fossils end up in store rooms, where they can be examined by experts carrying out research. The most important and impressive specimens – particularly of dinosaurs and prehistoric mammals – are reassembled to show what they would have looked like in real life. This process, called articulation, involves arranging the bones so that they are in the correct positions, and then supporting the entire skeleton so that it does not collapse. Articulation is a complex operation, and even the experts can make mistakes. In the nineteenth century, for example, the great American fossil-hunter Edward Drinker Cope put the skull of *Elasmosaurus* – a marine reptile – on the end of its tail!

△ *Before large bones can be removed, they have to be channelled out of the surrounding bedrock (top left). The bones are then covered with a pretective layer of plaster, before being raised with a pulley. Once in the laboratory (left), the plaster is removed. Here, the skull of a large allosaur is being examined.*

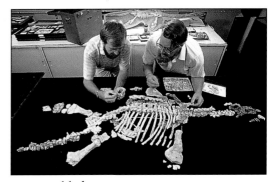

△ *Laid out on a laboratory bench, the fossilized remains of a plesiosaur are examined by two palaeontologists. The fossil was found near Coober Pedy, a mining town in Australia, and its pink colour comes from a form of silica found in this part of the world.*

▷ These six views of the Earth show how the continents have moved during the last 245 million years. This part of our planet's history has been dominated by the break-up of Pangaea, the supercontinent that existed when the Age of Reptiles began. Until about 100 million years ago, today's southern continents were joined to form a giant fragment of Pangaea called Gondwana, which slowly broke apart.

CONTINENTS ON THE MOVE

EVERY YEAR, SOME OF THE WORLD'S CONTINENTS DRIFT FURTHER APART, WHILE OTHERS CREEP CLOSER TOGETHER. THESE MOVEMENTS HAVE CHANGED THE FACE OF THE EARTH.

When continental drift was first suggested, nearly 100 years ago, most geologists found it impossible to believe. But today continental drift is an accepted scientific fact. It is not only continents that are on the move: Earth's entire outer crust is in motion, with new oceans opening up and forcing continents apart, and old oceans disappearing as continents collide. Because continents carry their wildlife with them, these changes have had a tremendous effect on animal evolution.

ONE WORLD
Today there are seven continents, scattered unevenly across the face of the globe. A journey from North America to Europe, or from Africa to Australia, involves crossing thousands of kilometres of open sea. But 245 million years ago, at the start of the Age of Reptiles, the world could hardly have looked more different. All the Earth's land was joined together to form a single supercontinent, called Pangaea, while the rest of the globe was covered by the vast Panthalassic Ocean. Theoretically, an animal could have walked across the world as long as it could negotiate the mountains and rivers in its way.

Continental drift started when dry land first formed, which was millions of years before Pangaea came into being. Little is known about the continents for most of that time, but it is clear that they also drifted, and that giant supercontinents formed several times. One of these ancient landmasses, called Pannotia, existed during the Vendian Period, about 650 million years ago. It broke apart after about 100 million years, creating the separate pieces from which Pangaea was made.

JOINING UP
Continents move at the rate of just a few centimetres each year, which adds up to only a tiny distance during an animal's lifetime. Even in the lifetime of an entire species, the positions of the continents barely change. But over millions of years, the movement starts to add up. It can split up some groups of animals as continents separate, and bring others together when they collide.

South America is a perfect example of how this can affect animal life. Until about three million years ago, it was an island – one that had been cut off from the rest of the world for nearly 100 million years. During this long period of isolation, it

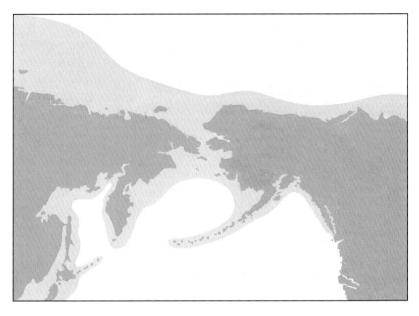

Continental drift also shapes the world's climate. It can do this by altering the path of ocean currents, which deliver warm water from the tropics to other parts of the world. Drifting continents also control the world's ice cover, because ice caps can only form over land. If there are no continents near the poles, the polar sea may freeze, but deep ice caps do not form.

For animals the earth's ice cover is important. The more ice there is in ice caps, the cooler and drier the world's climate becomes. At the same time, the world's sea levels fall, because so much of the world's water is in a frozen form. If the sea level falls far enough, it exposes parts of the seabed, and allows animals to travel between nearby continents without leaving dry land. This happened during the last Ice Age, when animals traveled from Asia to North America across the floor of the Bering Sea.

◁ *This map shows how low sea levels allowed animals (and people) to travel from Asia to North America toward the end of the last Ice Age. The dark brown areas show dry land as it exists today; the light brown areas show regions of the seabed that were dry land in Ice Age times.*

developed a wide range of unique animals, including some strange marsupials and the largest rodents that have ever lived. But when South America collided with North America, animals could move between the two continents, and many of South America's native mammals found themselves losing out in the struggle to survive. Three million years on, however, signs of South America's island past are not hard to find—its mammals and birds still include many families that do not exist anywhere else on Earth.

PARTING COMPANY

Further back in time continental drift had an even bigger impact on the way reptiles evolved. When the Age of Reptiles began, Pangaea still existed, so many families of reptiles were found over huge areas of the earth. But after Pangaea split up, some groups evolved in particular parts of the world. One example of these local reptiles was the ceratopsids—a group of armored dinosaurs that were restricted to North America. Another group was the segnosaurs —a little-known family whose remains have been found only in Asia and the Far East.

▷ Lystrosaurus *was a mammal-like reptile that lived in the Late Permian and Early Triassic Periods.*

▽ *Continental drift explains why the remains of some prehistoric land animals can be found in widely scattered regions of the world. The map below shows fossil finds of* Lystrosaurus, *which lived across much of Pangaea over 220 million years ago. After it became extinct its home was broken up by continental drift.*

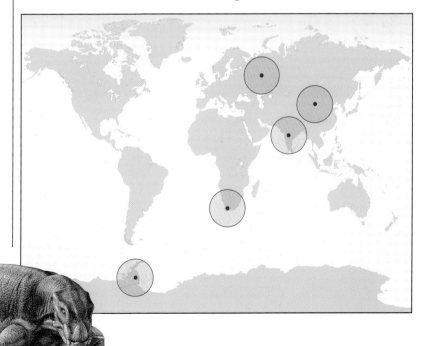

SETBACKS AND DISASTERS

THE FOSSIL RECORD SHOWS THAT LIFE ON EARTH IS A HAZARDOUS AND UNPREDICTABLE BUSINESS. ON SEVERAL OCCASIONS, HUGE NUMBERS OF SPECIES HAVE BEEN WIPED OUT IN RELATIVELY SHORT SPACES OF TIME.

Extinction is a natural feature of life on Earth, and it normally happens at a slow if rather unsteady rate. But from time to time, external events can trigger off extinctions on a truly colossal scale, and life can take several million years to recover. At least five mass extinctions have taken place in the distant past, with many smaller waves of extinction in between. Each one has rocked the living world, changing the course of animal evolution. The most famous of these extinctions wiped out the dinosaurs, but even greater catastrophes hit animal life further back in time.

TRIGGERING A CRASH

Mass extinctions are extremely rare and are spaced millions of years apart. Abrupt changes in the fossil record show that the last one occurred 66 million years ago, while the previous one happened over 140 million years before that. But although geologists can say when these catastrophes struck, deciding exactly what triggered them is a much more difficult matter.

In the case of the Cretaceous extinction, which swept away the dinosaurs, the most likely explanation is the sudden impact of a meteorite from space (page 204). Meteorite impacts happen all the time, but most of them involve small objects that either burn up in the Earth's atmosphere, or reach the ground but do little harm. The one that arrived 66 million years ago was a deadly exception: its explosive crash-landing obliterated huge areas of natural habitats, and brought the Age of Reptiles to an end.

WHEN LIFE GETS TOUGH

The Cretaceous extinction seems to have been exceptional, and no convincing evidence of giant meteorite strikes has been found for earlier mass extinctions.

Ordovician mass extinction 438 million years ago
Likely cause: climate change
50% of all species wiped out, mainly in the seas

Devonian mass extinction 360 million years ago
Likely cause: climate change
40% of all species wiped out

Permian mass extinction 245 million years ago
Likely causes: volcanic activity, climate change, formation of Pangaea
Over 70% of all species wiped out

Triassic mass extinction 208 million years ago
Likely cause: climatic change
45% of all species wiped out

Cretaceous mass extinction 66 million years ago
Likely causes: meteorite impact, volcanic eruptions
45% of all species wiped out

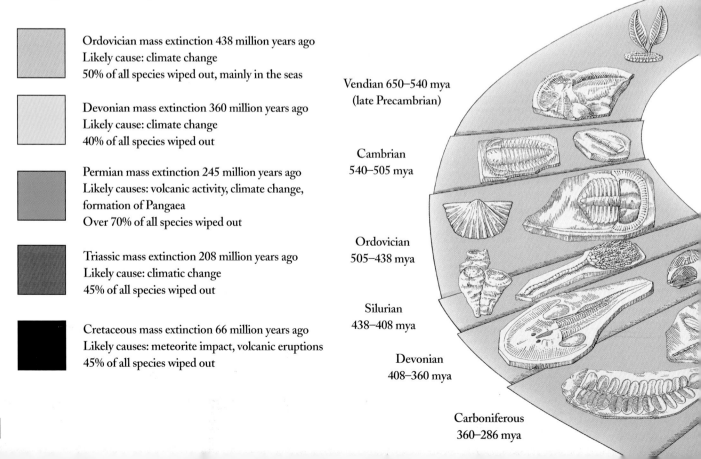

Vendian 650–540 mya
(late Precambrian)

Cambrian
540–505 mya

Ordovician
505–438 mya

Silurian
438–408 mya

Devonian
408–360 mya

Carboniferous
360–286 mya

Instead, most experts believe that these biological disasters were caused by natural processes taking place on Earth.

Volcanic eruptions have a lethal effect on almost all forms of life, and there is plenty of evidence from ancient lava flows that they were more common and more violent in the past. Changes in sea level have more subtle effects, but in the long term, they can be almost as deadly. When sea levels are high, the world's continental shelves are flooded, creating shallow seas that are rich habitats for marine life. When levels fall again, these shallow seas disappear, along with many of their animal inhabitants. Sea levels fell to record low levels 245 million years ago, and probably played a part in the mass extinction at the end of the Permian Period – the greatest setback for life ever known (page 56).

THE SIXTH EXTINCTION?
Climate change is a factor that we are all too familiar with today. In the past, the main danger to life was global cooling, rather than global warming, but any rapid change in weather patterns in either direction can interfere with plant life, making it harder for animals to find food. Today, there is a final factor to be added to the list: the spiralling rate with which humans use up resources and space. Many biologists think that this is now triggering a sixth mass extinction – one that is caused not by natural events, but by ourselves.

◁ *Immense lava flows, covering hundreds of thousands of square kilometres, are evidence of huge bursts of volcanic activity in prehistory.*

△ *Climate change, ice formation and changes in sea levels are connected factors that may have triggered off waves of extinctions.*

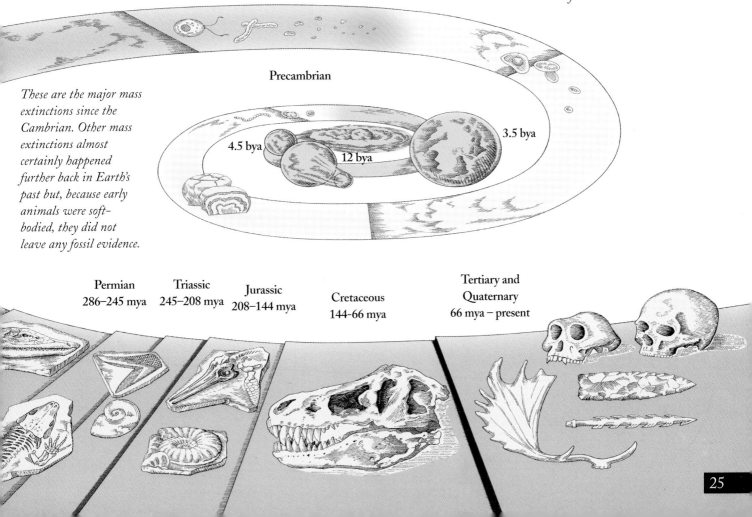

These are the major mass extinctions since the Cambrian. Other mass extinctions almost certainly happened further back in Earth's past but, because early animals were soft-bodied, they did not leave any fossil evidence.

Precambrian

4.5 bya

12 bya

3.5 bya

Permian
286–245 mya

Triassic
245–208 mya

Jurassic
208–144 mya

Cretaceous
144-66 mya

Tertiary and Quaternary
66 mya – present

DIVIDING UP TIME

One way to study the Earth's past is to split it into equal intervals – i.e. billions of years. But instead of doing this, geologists divide it into intervals that can be seen in layers of sedimentary rock. These layers have built up over millions of years, and they form a permanent record of the Earth's past, complete with fossils of plants and animals that were alive when the rock was formed. The boundaries between the layers mark times when conditions on the Earth changed rapidly. The changes altered the type of rock that was laid down, and they often made many existing forms of life extinct. The table below shows the names of these intervals, or layers, with the most recent times at the top, working backwards into the past. The largest intervals shown – eons – are divided into smaller ones called eras and periods. These, in turn, are often divided into epochs (only the most recent epochs are shown here). The dates shown for each time interval are approximate. MYA = million years ago and YA = years ago.

EON	ERA	PERIOD	EPOCH	DATES
PHANEROZOIC	CENOZOIC	QUATERNARY	Holocene	0–10,000 YA
			Pleistocene	10,000–1.6 MYA
		TERTIARY	Pliocene	1.6–5.3 MYA
			Miocene	5.3–23 MYA
			Oligocene	23–36 MYA
			Eocene	36–58 MYA
			Paleocene	58–66 MYA
	MESOZOIC	CRETACEOUS		66–144 MYA
		JURASSIC		144–208 MYA
		TRIASSIC		208–245 MYA
	PALEOZOIC	PERMIAN		245–286 MYA
		CARBONIFEROUS		286–360 MYA
		DEVONIAN		360–408 MYA
		SILURIAN		408–438 MYA
		ORDOVICIAN		438–505 MYA
		CAMBRIAN		505–540 MYA
PRECAMBRIAN	PROTEROZOIC	VENDIAN		540–650 MYA
		PRE-VENDIAN		650–2500 MYA
	ARCHAEAN			2500–3800 MYA
	HADEAN			3800–4600 MYA

THE AGE OF ANCIENT LIFE

Lasting over 350 million years, the Paleozoic Era – meaning 'ancient life' – was a momentous time in the animal world. It started in the Cambrian Period with a surge of evolution that has still not been fully explained. At this stage in Earth's history, animal life was confined to the seas, but as the era continued, some animals made the transition to dry land. By the late stages of the Paleozoic, reptiles and mammal-like animals appeared, but the era ended with the greatest mass extinction that the world has ever known.

THE CAMBRIAN PERIOD

BEGINNING ABOUT 540 MILLION YEARS AGO, THIS DISTANT PART OF THE EARTH'S PAST SAW THE APPEARANCE OF THE FIRST ANIMALS WITH HARD BODY PARTS, IN AN EXPLOSIVE BURST OF EVOLUTION.

Because the Cambrian Period was so far back in time, little is known about how the Earth looked. There was one major continent and several smaller ones, but for animal life, the habitable world lay in the sea. During Cambrian times, the climate was warm and sea levels rose, flooding large areas of low-lying land. These shallow seas created ideal conditions for new kinds of animal life, ones reinforced by shells, body cases or internal skeletons. These all fossilize easily, so unlike earlier soft-bodied animals, Cambrian animals left a vast store of remains.

▷ *The Cambrian Period was known as the Age of the Trilobites because these animals played such an important part in seabed life. Here, several different species of trilobite crawl over an ocean floor studded with vase-like archaeocyathan sponges, while jellyfish drift overhead. Most trilobites had well-developed eyes, but* Acadagnostus *(the small species in the foreground), was blind, and could roll up in a ball for self-defence.* Paradoxides *(the large trilobite in the centre), was usually 20cm, but could be 1m long.*

SHELLS AND SKELETONS

Fossils show that Cambrian animals evolved hard body parts relatively quickly, over a period of perhaps 20 million years. A question that puzzles biologists is why this happened, when animals had been soft-bodied for so long. One possibility concerns the Earth's atmosphere. Thanks to the work of cyanobacteria and algae (pages 10–11), the air's oxygen level had been rising steadily. By the time the Cambrian began, it may have been high enough for animals to lead more energy-intensive lives. Extra oxygen would have helped animals to 'burn' more food, giving them enough energy to build new body parts, such as shells and flexible cases.

WHY BE TOUGH?

Animals evolve new features only if they are useful, so these new body parts must have paid their way. For stationary animals, there were advantages to growing hard body parts. For example, sponge-like animals called archaeocyathans lived by filtering tiny particles of food from the Cambrian seas. They developed internal skeletons which enabled them to grow a few millimetres off the seabed. Although not a great height, it would have been better for collecting food.

For animals that moved about, a hard covering could be useful in different ways. For Cambrian molluscs, a shell, or exoskeleton, provided a mobile shelter that could be used in case of attack. It also acted as an anchor for the soft body parts to develop. For arthropods – which included trilobites and other animals with jointed limbs – hard parts played two separate roles. Their covering, a body case made of separate plates, provided protection, but because it could bend, it also helped them to move.

THE CAMBRIAN EXPLOSION

The Cambrian Period saw a huge expansion in animal life – the evolutionary equivalent of the Big Bang. These new animals included some that did not survive beyond the end of the Cambrian, such as animals that were first identified as fossils in the famous Burgess Shale (pages 32–35). The Cambrian Period also produced all the main animal groups that are alive today, including the chordates, the group to which we belong.

Known as the 'Cambrian explosion', this astonishing burst of evolution is difficult to explain. Nothing like it has happened since, so why did it take place? Scientists do not know, but many ideas have been put forward. One is that the explosion was not quite as explosive as it seems. According to this theory, many different kinds of animals may have existed before the start of the explosion, but if they were soft-bodied, they would have left few traces. Many scientists believe that this is true, but they also think that the Cambrian explosion was a real one, although not quite as abrupt as it first seems. It may have been triggered by changes in oxygen levels or in the layout of the seabed. Or life may have reached a critical point, triggering off a chain reaction in which many new body types were formed.

THE AGE OF ANCIENT LIFE

CAMBRIAN ANIMALS

Although Cambrian animals lived in the sea, few of them were creatures of open water. Instead, animal life hugged the seabed. Worms burrowed their way through the sediment, while snail-like molluscs crept across the surface, feeding on decaying remains. Trilobites also crawled across this surface layer, sometimes leaving telltale tracks that later become fossilized. The water itself was the territory of the fast movers of the Cambrian world: animals such as *Anomalocaris* (pages 32–33), and also – scientists have recently discovered – some of the earliest vertebrates.

△ *Brachiopods, or lampshells, became widespread in the Cambrian. These animals have shells like cockles and other bivalves, but they often grow on stalks.*

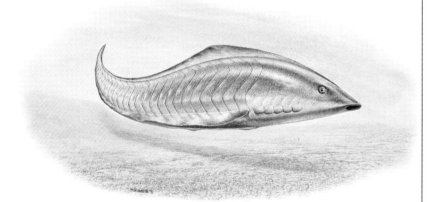

△ Myllokunmingia *sucked up food through its tiny jawless mouth. This 'proto-fish' had a skeleton of flexible cartilage.*

▷ *Some Cambrian molluscs, such as* Pleurotomaria *(centre) had spiral shells – a design that has lasted until the present day.*

▷ *This fossil-rich rock from Australia shows the remains of sponge-like archaeocyathans that date back 500 million years to Cambrian times.*

VERTEBRATES AND INVERTEBRATES
Biologists divide the animal world into two overall groups – the vertebrates and invertebrates. Vertebrates are animals that have backbones, while invertebrates are animals that do not. Today, vertebrates include all the largest and fastest animals, but invertebrates are far more varied, and much more common, making up about 97 per cent of all animal species on Earth.

Invertebrates were undoubtedly the first animals to evolve; fossils of Ediacaran invertebrates, for example, date back more than 50 million years before the Cambrian began (pages 12–13). During the Cambrian Period, a huge range of hard-bodied invertebrates appeared, including sponges and their relatives, arthropods, molluscs and lookalike animals called brachiopods. But the group the vertebrates belong to, the chordates, is more ancient than was thought.

The first chordates would have been soft-bodied, so have left very few remains, but when chordates began to develop hard body parts, made of cartilage and bone, the fossil record becomes more clear. In 1999, scientists in China announced that they had found two fossilized vertebrates in rocks 530 million years old – close to the time the Cambrian Period began. These two animals, named *Myllokunmingia* and *Haikouichthys*, are the world's oldest known fossil fish. Measuring less than 3cm long, they were a step along the evolutionary road that was to lead to amphibians and reptiles, including the giants of the dinosaur age.

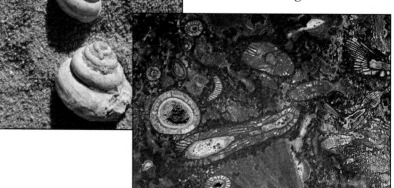

△ *This cross-section shows a reef from the early Cambrian, 535 million years ago. A variety of archaeocyathan sponges are growing on the reef's surface, while in crevices beneath, tracks reveal the presence of small animals hiding away for safety.*

1. SURFACE LAYER OF LIVING CYANOBACTERIA
2. BRANCHING ARCHAEOCYATHAN
3. RADIOCYATHAN
4. *CHANCELLORIA*
5. *OKULITCHICYATHUS*
6. ARTHROPOD TRACKS
7. CEMENTED REEF BASE

SPONGES ON A REEF

In Cambrian times, just as today, the shallow seabed was often carpeted with life, much of it fixed permanently in place. The most ancient of these seabed-dwellers were cyanobacteria – micro-organisms that first appeared over 3 billion years ago. Just like their distant ancestors, many Cambrian cyanobacteria collected calcium carbonate from the water and laid this hard mineral down around themselves. The result was a hard mat that built up to form a reef.

When cyanobacteria first evolved, animal life did not exist. But by Cambrian times, these crust-like reefs attracted animals that needed a safe anchorage so that they could collect their food. Foremost among them were archaeocyathans – sponge-like animals that grew into a wide variety of shapes, although few were more than 10cm high.

Like the cyanobacteria, archaeocyathans collected calcium carbonate from the water, and they used it to build up their mesh-like skeletons. Many looked like small vases, with a central hollow, while others resembled mushrooms, or a collection of branching twigs. Most of these animals lived on the surface of the reef, but some hid in crevices and cavities, sifting food that drifted down from above. As they grew upwards in the light and warmth, their dead remains became cemented together, steadily adding to the reef. Just like true sponges, archaeocyathans belonged to an unusual offshoot of the animal world. Instead of swallowing food through a mouth, as most animals do, they collected it by pumping water through tiny holes, or pores, in their bodies. As the water flowed through the pores, anything edible was filtered out and digested.

Archaeocyathans grew in warm, tropical waters, but unlike true sponges, their reign was relatively short. A few species survived into the closing stages of the Cambrian Period, but at that point, the entire group became extinct.

31

A SEABED GRAVEYARD

Rearing up over its prey, Anomalocaris – a giant shrimp-like predator from the Cambrian period – moves in to make a kill. Its intended victim, an animal called Marella, *speeds away by beating its slender legs. These two animals, like all the ones shown here, were found as fossils in the legendary Burgess Shale. See key on page 34.*

BURGESS SHALE

DISCOVERED IN 1909, IN CANADA'S ROCKY MOUNTAINS, THE BURGESS SHALE CONTAINS THOUSANDS OF FOSSILS, MANY SUPERBLY PRESERVED. TOGETHER, THEY PAINT A VIVID PICTURE OF LIFE IN THE CAMBRIAN SEAS.

The Burgess Shale was found by the American palaeontologist Charles D. Walcott, during a fossil-hunt in northwest Canada. The animals in the shale lived on or near the seabed, and were victims of underwater 'avalanches', which trapped them almost instantly in fine-grained mud. Because the mud was soft and contained very little oxygen, it preserved its victims remarkably well.

DOMINANT ARTHROPODS

The largest fossils in the Burgess Shale belong to arthropods – animals with a hard outer case that bends at flexible joints. Today, the most common arthropods include insects, spiders and crustaceans. In Cambrian times, these different groups did not yet exist. Instead, Cambrian arthropods included trilobites, and some remarkable animals found in the Burgess Shale.

The 'top predator' of the Burgess Shale was *Anomalocaris*, a name that means 'unusual shrimp'. The specimens in the Burgess Shale are up to 60cm long, while ones found more recently, from Cambrian rocks in China, are more than twice as big as this. *Anomalocaris* swam by rippling flaps along its sides, and it attacked its prey with a pair of fearsome mouthparts that looked like legs. Its mouth was disc-shaped, and had a ring of teeth that it used to crush hard-bodied prey. Other predatory arthropods included *Sanctacaris*, which looked like a smaller version of *Anomalocaris*, with a blunter head.

The most common Burgess Shale animal, called *Marella*, was another arthropod, but a much more delicate and graceful animal. It had long head spines sweeping backwards in elegant curves, and two pairs of 'feelers' or antennae. Rarely more than 2cm long, it had many pairs of legs, and probably fed by picking up small animals or dead remains on the surface of the seabed.

The Burgess Shale also includes many trilobites – a group of arthropods whose bodies were divided lengthways into three lobes. Trilobites went on to become some of the most successful invertebrates of the Paleozoic Era, and they were among the most important casualties during the mass extinction that brought it to a close.

SOFT-BODIED ANIMALS

The Burgess Shale also contains much rarer fossils, showing the complete outlines of soft-bodied animals. A typical example is *Ottoia*, a burrowing worm up to 15cm long. Its burrow was U-shaped, and it lurked inside, feeling for prey on the surface with a spike-tipped proboscis that could be extended like a trunk. When the trunk made contact with anything edible, it was swallowed whole. Fossils of *Ottoia* contain food remains – including chunks of other *Ottoia* worms, suggesting that the animal was cannibalistic.

The shale includes fossils of *Pikaia*, a soft-bodied animal with a reinforcing rod running down its body. This feature means that it was probably an early chordate – the group to which vertebrates also belong.

MYSTERY ANIMALS

Some Burgess Shale animals have no modern equivalent, leaving scientists guessing about how they were related to the rest of the animal world.

Animals such as *Hallucigenia*, *Opabinia* and *Wiwaxia* were very bizarre. The original fossils of *Hallucigenia* showed what seemed to be two rows of spiny legs, and a set of short tentacles emerging from the back. These were all attached to a short worm-like body without an obvious head. Working from these remains, *Hallucigenia* was reconstructed with the animal walking

on its spines and its tentacles waving above it. However, since then, further fossils have shown that researchers had mistakenly put the animal upside down. There are actually two sets of tentacles, and it is these that are *Hallucigenia*'s legs.

Opabinia looked like a shrimp, but had a bizarre claw-tipped snout, while *Wiwaxia* was like an armoured cushion that cruised across the seabed. Their ancestry remains a mystery, hidden in undiscovered fossils.

◁ *With its eccentric snout,* Opabinia *captures* Amwiskia. Opabinia *had five eyes, a body divided into segments and rows of swimming flaps, while* Amwiskia *had a flattened body and a horizontal tail.*

△ *When* Anomalocaris *died, its body often broke up. For many years, its mouth discs were thought to be the remains of jellyfish, and its forelimbs parts of a shrimp. Their true identity was established in 1985.*

◁ Sanctacaris *used its crushing mouthparts to attack animals on the seabed. Here, one pursues an animal called* Leanchoilia *(far left), while behind it, another attacks a* Wiwaxia.

ORDOVICIAN PERIOD

WHEN THE ORDOVICIAN PERIOD STARTED, 505 MILLION YEARS AGO, ANIMAL LIFE WAS FOUND ONLY IN THE SEA, BUT BY THE TIME IT ENDED, ANIMALS HAD TAKEN THEIR FIRST TENTATIVE STEPS ONTO THE LAND.

During the Ordovician Period, almost all the world's land was south of the equator. Africa lay over the South Pole, joined to South America, Antarctica and Australia, and together their land masses made up an ancient giant continent called Gondwana. Ordovician animals thrived in the shallow seas, but climate change eventually brought these good times to a close. Ancient scratch marks, created by glaciers, show that a large ice cap developed over Gondwana and, at the close of the Ordovician Period, conditions became so cold that over half of the world's animal species became extinct.

▷ *Nautiloids were the largest animals in the Ordovician seas. Forms with straight and coiled shells, like the ones shown here, hunted over an underwater landscape carpeted with algae, corals and crinoids – distant relatives of starfish which had feathery arms and slender stalks. Drifting or planktonic animals were common, but most animals still fed on or near the seabed. Here, a snail-like mollusc crawls across the reef in the foreground, flanked by brachiopods, which are filtering their food from the water.*

FILLING THE GAP

Like all major chapters in the Earth's history, the Ordovician started with animals recovering from a round of extinctions. Compared to the mass extinction that ended the Ordovician, these were small, but they particularly affected the trilobites, which had become the most important arthropods of the time. So the Ordovician Period opened with a large number of biological vacancies – ones that evolution soon started to fill.

One group of animals that moved into this gap were the nautiloids – molluscs related to today's pearly nautiluses, and more distantly to octopuses and squids. Unlike earlier molluscs, which lived on the seabed, nautiloids were able to swim. They could hover motionless above the seabed, watching for prey with well-developed eyes, or dart through the sea at speed by squirting a jet of water backwards from their body cavity.

This new way of life was made possible by the unusual design of nautiloid shells. They were conical or coiled, but instead of having a single internal chamber, like a snail's shell, they had a whole series of them, separated by thin partitions. The animal's body filled only the largest and most recent chamber, while the chambers behind it were hollow and filled with gas. A nautiloid could control the amount of gas in the chambers, allowing it to rise and fall like a submarine.

This new shell design was a sign of the times. Instead of hugging the seabed, more and more animals were starting to venture into open water above.

VACUUM-CLEANER FISH

Although fish-like animals have been found from the Cambrian Period, the Ordovician is the point when they become widespread as fossils. Compared to nautiloids, these early vertebrates were small animals, and their downward-pointing mouths suggest that they fed on the seabed. They did not have jaws, although they could probably have moved their 'lips'. At first, most of them were like living vacuum-cleaners, sucking up sediment and particles of food.

These fish – known as heterostracans – relied for survival on a bony shield that covered the front of their bodies. This reinforced plating became a common feature in early vertebrates, and it marked the start of an underwater arms race that was to continue for hundreds of millions of years.

REFUGE ON LAND

As the seas became more populated and more dangerous, some animals sought refuge in freshwater, and in the marshy shallows along the shore. Food grew here, in the form of simple mat-like plants, but air quickly dries out living cells, so for most soft-bodied animals, emerging out of damp mud and onto dry land would have been hazardous. Arthropods already had all-over body cases that would have helped to stop them drying out. There are no direct remains of these pioneering animals, but tracks in fossilized mud show that they were probably the first to emerge on land, 450 million years ago.

ORDOVICIAN ANIMALS

The Ordovician Period was a time when invertebrates were still the unchallenged rulers of the ocean floor. Like today's invertebrates, some were able to move about, but many others lived alone or in groups, anchored to the ocean floor. These anchored animals gathered food that drifted within reach, and did not need eyes or large brains. But for moving animals, life was more demanding and more dangerous. They relied on keen senses to find food, and quick reactions to avoid being attacked by other predators.

△ *Discovered in South Africa in the early 1990s,* Promissum *was a giant conodont measuring 40cm in length. Its bulbous eyes suggest that it was an active hunter.*

▽ *Early horseshoe crabs crawled across the seabed on five pairs of legs. Today there are four species of these 'living fossils' on the east coasts of North America and Asia.*

ARMOURED ARTHROPODS

When arthropods first appeared, in early Cambrian times, their bodies were small and their body cases – or exoskeletons – were paper-thin. But by the beginning of the Ordovician, several lines of arthropods had evolved their body cases into suits of armour to protect themselves from attack. One group of armoured arthropods, common in Ordovician times, were the horseshoe crabs.

Despite their name, these animals were not true crabs, but members of a line that later produced spiders and scorpions. The front of their body was protected by a domed shield, or carapace, which completely hid their mouth and legs. The back of the

△ Arandaspis *was a heterostracan, or armoured jawless fish. Like other early fish, it swam by flicking its tail, and did not have any fins.*

body was protected by a second, smaller shield, and ended in a long, spiny tail. This unusual design is clearly shown by fossils, but there is a much easier way of seeing how the horseshoe crab body worked, because these animals still survive today. They are not the same species that lived in Ordovician times, but amazingly, they have changed very little in over 400 million years.

Ordovician horseshoe crabs fed on small seabed animals, using pincer-tipped legs to pick up their food. Their pincers were hidden away underneath their head shields, which limited their size. Some close relatives of horseshoe crabs – eurypterids, or sea scorpions – carried their pincers out in the open. In the Ordovician Period, most sea scorpions were relatively small, but during the Silurian Period, which followed, they became the largest arthropods of the time.

MYSTERIOUS CONODONTS

For over a century, scientists collected and catalogued huge numbers of tiny tooth-like fossils which date back to the Ordovician and sometimes beyond. Known as conodonts, because they are often cone-shaped, these

2

6

5

1

3

4

△ This view of an Ordovician reef is based on Newfoundland fossils almost 500 million years old. Two nautiloids scan the seabed, while trilobites and gastropods (snail-like molluscs) creep over the surface below them. Clusters of crinoids, bend over by the current, filter out small particles of food.

1. **STRAIGHT-SHELLED NAUTILOID**
2. **COILED NAUTILOID**
3. **TRILOBITE**
4. **GASTROPOD**
5. **CORAL**
6. **CRINOID**

objects clearly belonged to animals because their shapes evolved as time went by. These shapes are so characteristic that geologists could often estimate the age of rocks simply by looking at the conodonts that they contain. Despite years of searching, the animals that grew these miniature teeth were never found.

A breakthrough came in 1993, when fossils were discovered in Scotland of complete conodont animals with their 'teeth'. Further fossils have been found in North America and South Africa, including one species – *Promissum* – which dates back to Ordovician times. The mystery animals turned out to be creatures with slender, snake-like bodies and well-developed eyes. Some fossils show traces of V-shaped muscle blocks and a notochord – features that are found in vertebrates and their relatives.

Many scientists think that conodonts were vertebrates, which would make them some of the earliest to have evolved. But, unlike

the main vertebrate line which went on to produce four-legged animals, the conodonts did not last. By the end of the Triassic, when the first dinosaurs appeared, conodont teeth vanish from the fossil record, showing that this group of animals had become extinct.

PLANT LOOKALIKES
During the Ordovician, a rare event occurred: a completely new group of animals appeared – one of the very few to appear after the Cambrian explosion (page 28). Known as bryozoans, these were tiny invertebrates protected by box-like skeletons. They grew side by side in colonies, forming shapes that often looked like plants. Bryozoans proved to be a very successful addition to the animal world, and are still widespread today.

The Ordovician seabed was also home to a collection of much larger plant-like animals, the crinoids, or sea lilies. Belonging to the same group of animals as starfish and sea urchins, they had a long stalk made of chalky discs, and a crown of brittle arms that gathered in food. Later, some crinoids broke free from this static existence, and took up a free-ranging life in the sea. Today, both kinds of crinoids still exist.

THE SILURIAN PERIOD

DURING THE SILURIAN PERIOD, ANIMAL LIFE RECOVERED IN THE SEAS, AS THE EARTH'S CLIMATE BECAME WARMER AND MORE STABLE. AT THE SAME TIME, ANIMALS MANAGED TO STRENGTHEN THEIR HOLD ON LAND.

When the Silurian Period started, 438 million years ago, animal life was emerging from the worst catastrophe so far. During the Silurian, conditions improved: the climate warmed and sea levels rose, creating shallow seas that triggered a surge in animal evolution. On land, important changes were also underway. The first true plants appeared, creating ankle-high 'jungles' that grew on marshy ground. By the time the Silurian ended, after only 30 million years, land-based animals were widespread, although few were more than a few centimetres long.

▷ *Crawling over the sea bed, a giant eurypterid – sea scorpion – catches a meal. These huge arthropods probably lived by hunting and also by scavenging dead remains. Like most modern arthropods, their eyes were compound – they were divided into many compartments. Eurypterids would probably have been fairly poor at registering detail, but very good at spotting movement.*

ARMOURED PREDATORS

In Silurian times, the largest sea animals were giant eurypterids, or sea scorpions – relatives of horseshoe crabs (page 38). One species, called *Pterygotus rhenanius*, was nearly 3m long, making it a deadly threat to other animals as it roamed the sea floor. Like other eurypterids, it had an armour-plated body, which could bend at flexible joints. Four pairs of its legs were used for walking, while the fifth pair – at the rear – were flattened and worked like oars. Slung underneath its head was a pair of powerful pincers, while the head itself was equipped with a pair of saucer-sized eyes. As the sea scorpion lumbered over the seabed, animals would have panicked, but their escape would have been cut short by a lunge of its claws.

Eurypterids lived in brackish water as well as the sea. The Silurian Period marked the heyday of eurypterids as the top predators in water, because fish were also increasing in size. Eventually, fish would become a threat to the eurypterids, but during the Silurian, things were still the other way around.

WEIGHTY MATTERS

While sea scorpions hunted in the shallows, other arthropods were evolving on land. These included primitive centipedes and also arachnids – the ancestors of spiders and their relatives. These land-based arthropods went on to become extremely successful, but none of them ever rivalled eurypterids in size. Without water to buoy it up, a giant armour-plated body is so heavy that it is almost impossible to move. This factor explains why today's land-based arthropods, such as insects and spiders, are still relatively small, while aquatic species, such as lobsters, can grow to a much larger size.

LIFE AFLOAT

At the other extreme in size, the Silurian seas teemed with planktonic animals – ones that were small and light enough to drift in open water. These included the developing young, or larvae, of molluscs and trilobites, and also a group of remarkable invertebrates called graptolites. Graptolites appeared in the Cambrian and flourished for 200 million years. Then the entire group became extinct.

Individual graptolites were rarely more than a few millimetres long, but they lived in colonies or groups that could be 20cm or more in length. Each member of the colony produced a hard, protective cup, built out of a similar material to the one found in mammals' hooves and claws, and the cups were joined together to form a colony. The shape of the colonies varied enormously; some looked like leaves or small bunches of twigs, while others resembled tuning forks, wheels or even spiders' webs.

Fossil graptolites are extremely common, but scientists once had difficulty deciding what they were. Some were thought to be fossilized plants, or even naturally occurring crystals that had grown through sedimentary rock. It is now thought that graptolites were hemichordates – distant relatives of obscure worm-like animals that still exist today.

THE AGE OF ANCIENT LIFE

SILURIAN ANIMALS

Despite the lead taken by small arthropods, the vast majority of Silurian animals lived in freshwater or in the sea. Underwater life was still dominated by animals without backbones, but among vertebrates, some momentous changes were underway. One of these was the evolution of the first fish with true jaws. In time, jaws turned out to be a decisive invention, allowing vertebrates to become the most widespread large animals on Earth. But during the Silurian, that still lay in the future, as jawed and jawless fishes experimented with different ways of life.

▷ Jamoytius *belonged to a group of fish called anaspids, which had over a dozen gill openings, arranged like port holes in the side of a ship. It was about 30cm long, and had three long fins – one on its back and two on its sides, as well as a fin on its tail.*

▽ *For early fish, sea scorpions like this* Pterygotus *were a major hazard. But as fish evolved, many of them became faster and more manoeuverable, moving away from the seabed and the dangers that it held.*

JAWED FISH

When the Silurian Period opened, the only fish in existence were ones that did not have jaws. To us, a jawless mouth may sound like a contradiction in terms, but the numerous fossils of jawless fish suggest that it worked perfectly well. However, jawless fish had limited options when it came to taking in food. One feeding method was to use the mouth like a scoop to dig up sediment – a technique that was probably used by *Jamoytius*, a common species of the time. Alternatively, the mouth could be used like a sucker, attaching the fish to its food. This feeding method is used by lampreys – parasitic animals that are among the few jawless fish that still survive today.

In the early Silurian, a group of fish called acanthodians, or spiny sharks, came up with a radical alternative to both these ways of feeding. A part of their skeleton – the struts that supported its first pair of gills –

gradually turned into a set of jaws. Unlike fish with jawless mouths, these fish could use their jaws as weapons to attack their prey. They could also bite off pieces of food, instead of having to swallow prey whole.

THE ACANTHODIANS

Despite their name, spiny sharks were not true sharks, because these did not evolve until Devonian times. However, they did have bony spines that supported their fins. One common late Silurian, called *Climatius*, was about the size of a typical goldfish, but some later forms grew to over 2m long. Their skeletons were made of cartilage, rather than bone, and they had strongly upturned tails. Unlike true sharks, acanthodians had large eyes and short snouts, suggesting that smell played little part in finding prey. Their teeth were small, and although they were constantly replaced, they often grew only in the lower jaw. But they did have another 'first' – a flap, called an operculum, that covered their gills. This could be used like a pump, allowing these fish to breathe without having to swim. For a while, spiny sharks were the world's only vertebrates that had jaws, but this unique status was not to last. Once the Silurian came to an end, new groups of jawed fish appeared, and by the early stages of the Permian Period, these original trailblazers became extinct.

CORAL REEFS

Until Silurian times, algae and sponges had been common inhabitants of reefs, but corals were rarer animals. During the Silurian, things changed: corals became widespread, and the first coral reefs began to form. The corals that we know today had yet to evolve, but Silurian corals were like them in many ways. Some species were solitary, meaning that individuals lived on their own, but the reef-building species formed large colonies, with hard cases or cups firmly cemented together. As young coral colonies developed, the older ones beneath them died, forming

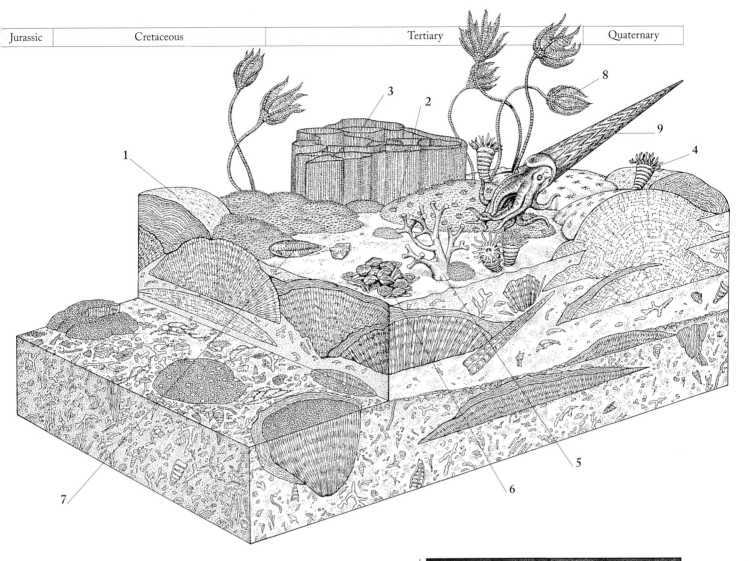

Labels for diagram:

1. TABULATE CORAL
2. TABULATE CORAL
3. TABULATE CORAL
4. SOLITARY RUGOSE CORAL
5. BRYOZOAN
6. BRACHIOPOD
7. TRILOBITE
8. CRINOID
9. NAUTILOID

△ *This view of a Silurian reef is based on fossils found in England about 430 million years old. It contains tabulate and rugose corals – two groups that became extinct at the end of the Paleozoic Era. Silurian reefs gave safe anchorage for other invertebrates, such as brachiopods, bryozoans and crinoids.*

layers of hard remains. These became glued together by dissolved minerals, turning them into deposits of solid rock.

The way that colonies grew gave each kind a distinctive shape. Some had branches that divided repeatedly, making them look like a set of antlers. These branching colonies often grew quickly, but because they were brittle, could only survive where there was no danger of being broken up by the waves. Others grew more slowly, and had rounded or flattened shapes. These types were much better at surviving in rough water, and they often grew on the outer edges of reefs, where breakers rolled in from the open sea.

Modern reef-building corals generally need light to thrive, because they contain microscopic algae that live as on-board partners, using sunlight to make food. Early corals, on the other hand, survived entirely by catching tiny animals, which they trapped with tentacles that carried stinging cells. It was a highly effective system, and can still be seen in corals and jellyfish today.

△ *Crinoids became increasingly successful during the Paleozoic. Their chalky stalks usually fell apart after they died, but the main part of the body with its feeding arms was often preserved in fossils (above).*

43

THE DEVONIAN PERIOD

OFTEN KNOWN AS THE AGE OF FISHES, THE DEVONIAN PERIOD WAS A TIME WHEN ANIMALS WITH BACKBONES BEGAN THEIR SUPREMACY OF LIFE IN THE SEA, AND MADE THEIR FIRST MOVES ONTO LAND.

The Devonian Period began about 408 million years ago, at a time when major changes were taking place in the way the world looked. The giant continent of Gondwana still lay near the South Pole, but it was moving northwards, while parts of Europe and North America, together with Greenland, were joined to form a single continent that straddled the equator. The climate was warm, and on land, the simple, low-growing plants of Silurian times gradually gave way to ones that were much better at surviving out of water. By the time the Devonian Period ended, the first forests had formed.

▷ *The giant placoderm* Dunkleosteus *closes in on a young* Cladoselache, *a species of primitive shark.* Dunkleosteus *had a set of tooth plates that lasted for life, while* Cladoselache, *like today's sharks, had dozens of triangular teeth that grew from the inside edge of its jaws, on a non-stop production line. Both of these early fish swam by waving their tails; their other fins were stiff, and acted as stabilizers to keep them on course.*

JAWS REVISITED

Evolution has often 'invented' the same adaptation in animal life several times. This is what seems to have happened during the Devonian Period, with a group of fish called the placoderms. Placoderms had powerful jaws – blade-like plates that made effective teeth. But as placoderms were not direct descendants of the first jawed fish (page 42), most experts think that they must have evolved jaws themselves. As well as jaws, these fish had two hard shields – one that covered the head, and one on the front part of the trunk. The shields were connected by a pair of hinges, allowing the front of the head to lift when the fish bit into its prey.

Some placoderms lived on the seabed, where they fed on molluscs and other hard-bodied animals, but towards the late Devonian, others became hunters that lived in open water. Here, they became some of the largest predators in the history of animal life so far. One of them, called *Dunkleosteus*, was nearly 4m long, with mouth plates that could slice other fish in two.

FISH BRANCH OUT

During the Devonian, placoderms shared the seas with several other groups of fish. They included jawless species with bizarrely shaped armoured bodies (page 46), as well as non-armoured fish, which looked much more like the fish we know today. These non-armoured species were of two kinds: some had skeletons made of cartilage, while others had ones made of bone.

The cartilaginous fish were the ancestors of today's sharks and rays. Their bodies were covered in small, rough scales known as denticles, and in their mouths, specially enlarged denticles formed a never-ending supply of sharp teeth. Even from their early days, many of these fish had the familiar shark-like shape, and by the late Devonian, one species, called *Cladoselache*, was already 2m long. The bony fish were generally small, and were covered in scales that became thinner and lighter as time went by. These fish developed gas-filled swimbladders that controlled their buoyancy, and mobile fins that made them highly manoeuvrable.

One group of bony fish, called the lobe-fins, had fins with a fleshy base containing muscles and bones. These interest scientists greatly because they were the animals from which four-legged vertebrates evolved. Not all lobe-fins left the water: several species, including the lungfishes and the coelacanths, still live in freshwater or the sea to this day.

LIFE ON LAND

Despite many years of research, experts do not yet know which of the lobe-finned fish gave rise to primitive amphibians – the first vertebrates to live partly on land. But by the time the Devonian ended, the transition had been made. When the first amphibians appeared, they would have seemed slow and awkward compared to other land creatures, but it was a move that would change the whole course of animal life.

DEVONIAN ANIMALS

During the Devonian, invertebrate life continued to evolve, although not at the hectic pace that marked the Silurian. Spiral-shelled ammonoids developed from nautiloids, creating a group of molluscs often superbly preserved as fossils. Trilobites and sea scorpions were on the wane, although when the Devonian ended, both groups still managed to survive for a further 100 million years. But for animal life as a whole, the key developments during the Silurian occurred among vertebrates – particularly those that pioneered the difficult move onto land.

▽ *This trio of jawless fish from Devonian times show different forms of armour protection.* Drepanaspis *(top) and* Cephalaspis *(left) were both bottom-dwellers, with flattened undersides and tails that were triangular in cross-section.* Pteraspis *(right) was more streamlined, and was built for life in open water.*

FISH THAT 'WALKED'

One of the striking features of the Devonian period is the number of fish that had heavily armoured heads. Armoured fish are rare today, but during the Devonian, a wide variety of them lived on the seabed, and in rivers and lakes. Most of them were bottom-dwellers, because their armour – while useful against predators – made swimming in open water hard work.

Among the placoderms (page 44), species that are common as fossils include *Bothriolepis*, which had a semicircular head shield and narrow pectoral (front) fins. It may have used the fins for balancing on the bottom, or perhaps for 'walking' along riverbeds. Another species, called *Pterichthyodes*, looked like a fish that had swum into a bony box, leaving only its tail outside. It too had elongated pectoral fins, which may have enabled it to crawl across the mud in lakes. *Groenlandaspis*, a finger-sized species that lived in freshwater, was extrememly widespread. Fossils of this little fish have been found not only in Greenland, but also as far away as Australia and Antarctica.

THE END OF ARMOUR

Jawless fish also specialized in armour protection in Devonian times. One group, known as the osteostracans, are known for their flattened and horseshoe-shaped heads, which are often well preserved in fossils. One typical species, a freshwater fish called *Cephalaspis*, had a head shield that ended in two backward-pointing 'horns'. The head shield was made of a single piece of bone, which meant that it probably could not grow once it had been fully formed. As a result, the shield probably developed when the fish reached adult size. Like its relatives, *Cephalaspis* had another unusual feature – patches of sensory nerves on the sides and top of the shield. These probably helped it to navigate or find food, perhaps by sensing vibrations or weak electrical fields.

Armoured jawless fish also included species such as *Drepanaspis*, with a shield that was almost round, and *Pteraspis*, an open-water species that had a sharply pointed snout. For tens of millions of years, these armoured animals were very successful, but as other fish began to evolve alongside them, speed and manoeuvrability eventually proved to be more useful in the struggle for survival.

BREATHING AIR

In early Devonian times, tropical lakes and rivers became the home of the world's first

DEVONIAN ANIMALS

lungfish – fish that had gills, but which could breathe air when the water's oxygen supply was low. This was particularly useful in warm, stagnant water, where other fish ran the risk of suffocation. One of the earliest of lungfish, called *Dipterus*, is known from fossils discovered in Europe and North America. It was about 50cm long, with a cylindrical body and sharply upturned tail.

FINS AND LIMBS

Lungfish belonged to the group known as the lobe-fins (page 44), which had bones and muscles in their fins, making them similar to limbs. This combination of lungs and limb-like fins made some biologists believe they were ancestors of amphibians, and therefore of all four-legged vertebrates. But a closer look at lungfish shows that they probably did not make the move onto land.

Today, a different group of lobe-fins are thought to be the most likely candidates for this important position in the vertebrate world's family tree. Known as rhipidistians, they included species such as *Eusthenopteron*, a blunt-headed fish 1.2m long, with fin bones arranged very much like those in an amphibian's legs. *Eusthenopteron* also had a brain-case like the ones found in early amphibians, providing further evidence that it, or one of its relatives, produced animals that made the move onto land.

THE FIRST AMPHIBIANS

While Devonian fish left many fossils, Devonian amphibians are extremely rare. Fossils of the two best-known examples – *Ichthyostega* and *Acanthostega* – were both found in Greenland. They had long fish-like bodies, four legs, but webbed fish-like tails. Despite their fishy origins, these animals had many adaptations for life on land. They breathed partly through lungs and partly through their skin, and their skeletons were strengthened to support the extra weight they had to bear out of water. Reconstructions of *Ichthyostega* and *Acanthostega* often show these two animals hunting on land, with their bodies half-crawling and half-slithering across marshy Devonian landscapes. But recent studies of their fossils show that their legs may have had difficulty supporting their weight, making some scientists doubt if they were as agile on land as was once assumed. Instead of being land animals that sometimes took to the water, the real situation may have been the other way around. For *Ichthyostega* and *Acanthostega*, water would have been a place to feed and breed, while land would have made a useful refuge from the predatory fish that shared their freshwater home.

◁ *With a body up to 60cm long, including its webbed tail,* Acanthostega *had webbed feet with eight fingers and toes. Apart from this, it looked much like some salamanders alive today. However, it had many fish-like features, including a streamlined head, and a system of sensors, called a lateral line, which today's fish use to detect waterborne vibrations.*

▽ *Grasping a centipede firmly between its jaws,* Ichthyostega *prepares to swallow its prey. In theory, at 1m long, it would have been able to tackle many land animals of its time. However, whether it could actually hunt like this is a matter of debate – some experts think it made slow progress out of water.*

THE CARBONIFEROUS PERIOD

A TIME OF IMPORTANT DEVELOPMENTS FOR LIFE ON LAND, THE CARBONIFEROUS SAW THE GROWTH OF VAST LOWLAND FORESTS, THE EVOLUTION OF BOTH THE FIRST REPTILES AND THE FIRST ANIMALS THAT COULD FLY.

The Carboniferous Period began 360 million years ago, after a mass extinction – thought to have been triggered by a cooling climate – that killed up to 70 per cent of marine animals. In the western hemisphere, land stretched almost from pole to pole, while in the east, most of the world was covered by a Pacific-sized ocean. During the Carboniferous, rising sea levels, together with a generally warm and humid climate, created perfect conditions for forests of giant clubmosses and ferns, growing on swampy, low-lying ground. The remains of these forests eventually turned into seams of coal, giving the Carboniferous its name.

▷ Hylonomus, *one of the world's earliest known reptiles, was about 20cm long. It was fully at home on land. Its remains were discovered inside fossilized tree-stumps, together with those of other Carboniferous animals. It seems likely that* Hylonomus *fell into the tree-stumps while hunting, and was unable to get out.*

ADAPTING TO LIFE ON LAND

At the beginning of the Carboniferous, early amphibians were still tied to a water-based way of life. Like today's frogs and toads, they laid their eggs in ponds and streams, and their young went through an aquatic tadpole stage, initially breathing through feathery gills. Even as adults, they had to stay close to water, because their skins were thin, and they had to keep moist.

In the Carboniferous, extensive swamps meant that animals like these were rarely short of somewhere to breed. But water-based life had its dangers. Fish ate a large proportion of amphibian tadpoles as well as the adults themselves. Amphibians also faced great competition for food – not only from fish and water scorpions, but also from each other. These were just some of the reasons why nature favoured amphibians that were better at coping with life on dry land.

BECOMING WATERPROOF

For water-based animals with thin skins, the greatest danger on land was drying out. The problem began to diminish when some amphibians developed thicker skin that was protected by scales. This kind of skin acted like a waterproof jacket, keeping most of the body's moisture inside. More importantly, they evolved a new kind of egg – one that was surrounded by a tough membrane called an amnion, which was itself enclosed in a porous shell. The membrane and shell let oxygen in so that the developing embryo could breathe, but they let very little water escape into the air outside. This 'amniotic' egg was an immense leap forward, because it allowed vertebrates to breed away from water. Instead of hatching into swimming tadpoles, their young hatched out as miniature versions of their parents, fully fitted out for life on land.

FROM AMPHIBIAN TO REPTILE

In the hunt for the first reptiles, scientists have examined a wide range of fossils to find the earliest ones that fall on the reptile side of the amphibian–reptile divide. Skin and eggs are often missing from the fossil record, but another sign of reptile status is a ribcage that can expand. Unlike amphibians, which gulp air when they breathe, reptiles use their ribcage to suck air into their lungs.

At present, the earliest animals that seem to meet all these criteria are *Palaeothyris* and *Hylonomus*, two lizard-like creatures that have been found in present-day Nova Scotia. They were slim and agile, and had well-developed legs without any webbing on their feet and a cylindrical rather than a flattened tail. *Palaeothyris* and *Hylonomus* lived in the swampy surroundings of Carboniferous forests, but as reptiles evolved, they moved further and further away from damp surroundings. Eventually – well before the age of the dinosaurs – they would spread to the driest places on Earth.

CARBONIFEROUS ANIMALS

On land, invertebrates still made up the vast majority of animal species during the Carboniferous, but their place at life's top table was no longer secure. Four-legged vertebrates, or tetrapods, were evolving fast, and by the late Carboniferous, they became the largest predators of their day. Meanwhile, in the freshwater and the seas, there was growing success for the cartilaginous and bony fish, mirrored by a steady decline in fish without jaws. During this period in the Earth's history, crinoids – sea-lilies – continued to thrive, and in some places they formed great underwater 'forests' that carpeted the ocean floor.

△ *With its webbed tail and small, widely spaced legs,* Eogyrinus *was well-equipped for hunting in shallow water, but not suited to life on land. Other amphibians of the Carboniferous – particularly the smaller species – spent much of their adult life out of water, just like most amphibians do today.*

EARLY TETRAPODS

In the Carboniferous, many of the largest hunters lived like today's crocodiles and alligators, attacking their prey in lakes and shallows, but sometimes hauling up on dry land. One of the largest was *Eogyrinus*, which measured over 4m from the end of its snout to the tip of its webbed tail. *Eogyrinus* was an amphibian, and it belonged to a group called the anthracosaurs – a name that means 'coal lizards' – which survived until the Permian Period and then became extinct. Anthracosaurs are thought to be the group from which the reptiles evolved.

Another anthracosaur, *Seymouria*, was better adapted to life on the land, with stronger legs than *Eogyrinus* and no webbing on its tail. Although it looked like a reptile as an adult, fossils of its young show signs of a lateral line – the sensory system used during their life in water. Because it grew up in the water, *Seymouria*, fails the 'reptile test'.

AMPHIBIAN ARRAY

Several different groups, all now extinct, shared the Carboniferous lakes and swamps with their anthracosaur relatives. Among them were amphibians called temnospondyls, a group of species that are the probable ancestors of frogs and toads. One of the largest was an animal called *Eryops*, which looked like a small frog-eyed crocodile, supported by stubby legs. *Eryops* was about 2m long and, like all amphibians, had thin scale-less skin. It also had bony plates along its back, which may have protected it when it hauled itself out of the shallows. Although *Eryops* was large, it was not the biggest of its group. One species, called *Mastodonsaurus*, had a skull over 1m long – large enough to make it a threat to many of the other amphibians around it.

Over the years, palaeontologists have found many fossilized tadpoles of *Eryops* and its relatives. Today, they are recognized for what they are, but earlier they were thought to be separate species.

REPTILES AND THEIR SKULLS

The earliest reptiles evolved in the late Carboniferous, and included *Palaeothyris* and *Hylonomus* (page 48). Despite their place at the foot of the reptile family tree, these two animals look very like lizards, and could easily be mistaken for them if they lived today. However, internally, they had several features that made them quite distinct. One of the most important was that their skulls had no openings apart from the ones that housed their nostrils and eyes. Reptiles that are built in this way are called anapsids which literally means 'without arches'. Anapsids inherited this kind of skull from their amphibian ancestors, and only turtles and tortoises have this kind of skull today. Other reptiles went on to develop extra openings, which saved weight and provided anchorage for their jaw muscles. Synapsids evolved one pair of extra openings, positioned behind the eyes, while diapsids evolved two.

▽ Meganeuropsis *was a giant dragonfly that flew over swamps. Like modern dragonflies, its two pairs of wings could beat in opposite directions, enabling it to hover like a helicopter as it watched for prey.*

These 'fossae' are of great interest because they help in piecing together the path of evolution. Synapsids include animals that went on to produce mammals, while diapsids include the ruling reptiles or archosaurs – the group to which all dinosaurs belonged.

TAKING TO THE AIR

For anyone averse to 'creepy-crawlies', the Carboniferous landscape would have to be a nightmare. Scorpions up to 75cm long crawled over the ground in search of prey, while giant cockroaches and millipedes vied for rotting plant remains. Centipedes preyed with poison fangs on other land animals after dark. In the air, primitive dragonflies swooped on airborne insects over pools and among trees, flying on rustling wings that could be over 60cm from tip to tip. Insects were the first animals to fly, and in Carboniferous times they had their air to themselves. However, as yet, scientists have found few clues to how and when the first winged species

evolved. According to one theory, insect wings may have developed from the flattened pads that some fossil species have attached to their body segments. Initially, these pads may have been used for temperature regulation, or perhaps in courtship displays, but if they became large enough, they could have been used for gliding. To become true wings, they would have then had to develop hinges at the point where they meet the body. Their owners would have had to develop flight muscles by modifying existing muscles inside the middle part of the body or thorax. As this happened, they would have changed from gliders to the first true aviators.

Because winged insects are well developed by the Carboniferous period, it is likely that they first appeared in the Devonian, but so far no fossils have been discovered that date this far back in time.

▽ *Terrestrial scorpions evolved from ancestors that lived in water. Aquatic scorpions breathed through gills, but land-dwelling forms developed 'book lungs' inside their bodies. In a book lung, air flows past thin flaps that are stacked like pages of a book.*

THE PERMIAN PERIOD

THE PERMIAN PERIOD WAS THE FINAL STAGE IN THE PALEOZOIC ERA. IT IS KNOWN CHIEFLY FOR THE DRAMATIC WAY THAT IT ENDED – WITH THE LARGEST MASS EXTINCTION IN THE HISTORY OF LIFE ON EARTH.

By the beginning of the Permian, 286 million years ago, the Earth's land masses had converged to form a single supercontinent called Pangaea. Because Pangaea was so vast, climatic conditions on land varied enormously. Over the South Pole, an ice cap remained from Carboniferous times, but across the tropics and much of the north, Pangaea was a place of baking heat and little rain. In these arid conditions, the moisture-loving trees of Carboniferous times went into retreat, to be replaced by conifers and other seed-forming plants that were better at coping with drought.

▷ *Basking in the early morning sunshine, pelycosaurs soak up its warmth through their vertical 'sails'. Both the species shown here –* Dimetrodon *(foreground) and* Edaphosaurus *(background) – lived in the early Permian, and grew to a length of about 3m.* Dimetrodon *was a predator, armed with stabbing teeth, while* Edaphosaurus *was a herbivore. In both species, the sail was kept permanently upright by struts of bone.*

WATER AND WARMTH

Evolution cannot plan ahead, so it could not prepare animals for the changed conditions of Permian times. But reptiles turned out to be quite well-suited to the drier climate that developed when the Permian began. They spread across the supercontinent, to habitats where amphibians could not survive. As they evolved, they became better at economizing with water until they could live in desert conditions, like many reptiles do today.

Reptiles also had to deal with the large temperature changes that often occur on land. In water and wetlands, where the first four-legged vertebrates evolved, temperature changes were gradual, and the highest were rarely very high. But in Pangaea's interior, it could be close to freezing at dawn, and over 40°C by the middle of the day. Because reptiles were (and still are) ectothermic, or cold-blooded, their body temperatures rose and fell with the temperature of their surroundings. They would be almost immobilized by the cold at dawn, but by noon, they could be at risk of overheating.

AN INSIDE SOLUTION

Early reptiles would have dealt with this problem in the same way that reptiles do now: by basking in the sunshine when they were cold, or by hiding in the shade when they were too hot. In time, some reptiles – most notably the pelycosaurs – developed tall 'sails' that probably acted as heat exchangers, helping them to warm up and make an earlier start to the day. But later in the Permian, descendants of the pelycosaurs called therapsids evolved a very different answer to the problem of temperature control. Instead of depending on the sun's warmth, they started to conserve the heat that their own bodies generated by breaking down food. In other words, they became endothermic, or warm-blooded. To keep in heat, they used something quite new – fur.

WARM-BLOODED VERTEBRATES

Fur rarely shows up in fossils, and there is no direct evidence that furred therapsids actually existed during the Permian Period, or at any later time. However, several pieces of evidence suggest that it is very likely. One is that therapsids evolved adaptations that improved their breathing rate and oxygen supply – something that is essential in animals that 'burn' lots of food. Another is that some therapsids lived in the south of Pangaea, where winter conditions would have been severe. This is an unlikely habitat for a cold-blooded reptile, but for one that could keep itself warm by 'burning' food, life would have been much easier.

Therapsids were the animals that went on to give rise to the mammals, but they were not mammals themselves. Even though Permian forms probably had fur, they were unlike mammals as we know them today. But being warm-blooded was a key innovation – one that would eventually enable four-legged vertebrates to conquer every habitat of Earth, including high mountains and polar ice.

◁ *Cacops was an armoured amphibian that lived in the Permian. About 40cm long, it was well-adapted to life on land, but probably laid its eggs in water.*

PERMIAN ANIMALS

D uring the Permian, therapsids – or mammal-like reptiles – became an increasingly important part of life on land. Although they never reached the gigantic sizes of reptiles in the Mesozoic Era, they were the dinosaurs of their day. Soon after they first appeared, they evolved into a variety of hunters and plant-eaters, reaching sizes of up to 5m long and weights of over 1 tonne. In the Permian, four-legged vertebrates also included a wide variety of amphibians, pelycosaurs, as well as the archosaurs, the group of animals to which the dinosaurs belonged.

▽ Anteosaurus *launches an attack on* Moschops, *in a region of Gondwana that is now South Africa's Karoo Basin.*

THERAPSIDS OF THE KAROO
Much of our knowledge of Permian therapsids comes from fossils found in central and European Russia, and in the Karoo, a region of South

Africa. The Karoo fossils often consist of complete skeletons, allowing animals to be reconstructed down to the smallest details.

One of the largest plant-eaters from the Karoo was *Moschops*, an animal that grew to about 4m in length. It had a much shorter tail than most of the earliest reptiles, and the typical barrel-shaped body of a large plant-eater, supported by sturdy legs. *Moschops* also had a remarkably thick skull. Some palaeontologists think that this would have been used in head-butting contests, although others have suggested that this bony growth might have been the result of disease. Despite its size, *Moschops* did not lead an entirely tranquil life, because the Karoo was home to some formidable flesh-eating therapsids, including *Anteosaurus*, which rivalled *Moschops* for size. In general build, the two animals were similar, but while *Moschops* had chisel-like teeth, *Anteosaurus* had extra-long stabbing teeth near the front of its jaws – the sign of an animal with a carnivorous way of life.

RUSSIAN THERAPSIDS
Russian therapsids included some decidedly strange-looking animals. One of the oddest was *Estemmenosuchus*, a name that means

◁ *While a herd of* Estemmenosuchus *wander down to a lake to drink, a solitary* Eotitanosuchus *watches them from the opposite shore, sizing up the possibility of making a kill. In the generally dry conditions of Permian times, oases like these would have made good hunting grounds.*

▽ *Watched by* Varanosaurus, *two* Caseas *lie on a sandy bank, soaking up the sunshine. Casea's sprawling gait meant that it rested with its body on the ground – unlike many plant-eaters of later times, which spent most of their time on all fours.*

'crowned crocodile'. With its bulky body and short tail, *Estemmenosuchus* bore very little resemblance to a crocodile, but it did have a crown of four horn-like outgrowths – two projecting from the sides of its face, and two from the top of its head. These outgrowths could have been used for defence, but as they were short and blunt, a more likely explanation is that they were used to show an animal's status during courtship displays. The 'horns' would have been largest in adult animals, particularly mature males.

Scientists disagree as to whether *Estemmenosuchus* was carnivorous, but another large therapsid from late Permian Russia, called *Eotitanosuchus*, certainly was. It had sabre-like canine teeth, set in a skull that had narrow and powerful jaws.

PERMIAN PELYCOSAURS

Although pelycosaurs gave rise to the therapsids, they continued to flourish alongside them during Permian times. The best-known examples are the sail-backed species (page 53), but the pelycosaur group also included animals that looked much more like some reptiles that exist today. One carnivorous species, called *Varanosaurus*, has been given its name because of its resemblance to today's monitor lizards, and like them could be over 1.5m long. Another species, called *Casea*, was a plant-eater, and a member of the last family of pelycosaurs to

appear. It had a fat, sprawling body like that of a modern iguana, with a small head and a slender tail. Its dentition was highly unusual, with peg-like teeth in the upper jaw, but no teeth in its lower jaw – exactly the reverse of the arrangement in many large plant-eaters today. This curious feature must have been an asset rather than a handicap, because *Casea*'s descendants became abundant, and survived almost to the time when the Permian Period came to its calamitous close.

THE AGE OF ANCIENT LIFE

END OF AN ERA

About 245 million years ago, the Permian Period came to an end in the greatest mass extinction since animal life began. Its effects were worst in the oceans, where about 96 per cent of all marine species died out, while on land the figure was about 75 per cent. The victims of this great calamity included trilobites, Paleozoic corals and a host of other invertebrates, as well as the pelycosaurs, which in Permian times had been some of the most successful reptiles on land. By clearing away so many living species, this immense upheaval had a profound effect on the future course of animal evolution.

▷ *Some scientists believe that the existence of a single supercontinent, Pangaea, triggered environmental changes that devastated life at the end of the Permian.*

▷ *After existing for over 260 million years, and surviving two mass extinctions, trilobites finally became extinct.*

▽ *Volcanic gases from eruptions may have trapped incoming heat and made temperatures spiral upwards.*

MISSING EVIDENCE

Many theories have been put forward to explain the Permian mass extinction, but there are three or four main suspects, or several of them acting together. The first of these – and the most quick-acting – is an impact by an asteroid, or some other object from space. If this was large enough, it would have created a devastating shock wave that spread around the world, mirroring the event believed to have wiped out the dinosaurs (page 204). Chemical evidence has recently given weight to this idea, but it is still thought that the extinction was caused by natural changes on Earth.

A HOME-GROWN DISASTER

One leading 'Earth-centred' theory is that a massive wave of volcanic eruptions blasted billions of tonnes of ash into the sky. If the eruptions continued over a long period, the ash clouds would have cut off much of the sunlight on which plant life depends. Without plants on land and microscopic algae in the sea, most animals would soon have perished. Signs of immense eruption have been found in Siberia.

Another possiblity is that falling sea levels in the late Permian obliterated the shallow inshore waters on which much of marine life depended. As Pangaea had a relatively short coastline, this would have left corals and other invertebrates with a rapidly shrinking habitat. However, the decimation of land life is harder to explain, which is why falling sea levels may have been an additional factor in the mass extinction, rather than its chief cause.

Many scientists think that the fourth suspect – climate change – might have dealt a deadly blow. There is evidence that the climate warmed and then suddenly cooled as the Permian drew to a close, which would have made life difficult for animals on land and in the sea. With falling sea levels and volcanic eruptions thrown into the equation, the result might have been the cataclysm that the fossil record shows.

THE AGE OF REPTILES

The Mesozoic Era – between 245 and 66 million years ago – was the time when reptiles became the unchallenged rulers of life on Earth. The dinosaurs became the largest plant-eaters and predators to exist on land, while other groups of reptiles successfully conquered the seas and took to the skies. Divided into three periods – the Triassic, Jurassic and Cretaceous – the Mesozoic saw immense changes in the face of the Earth. Sea levels rose and fell, and Pangaea, the giant supercontinent, slowly broke up. The Mesozoic Era ended with the most famous of all mass extinctions.

THE TRIASSIC PERIOD

AT THE BEGINNING OF THE TRIASSIC PERIOD, ANIMAL LIFE WAS EMERGING FROM THE AFTERMATH OF THE PERMIAN MASS EXTINCTION. BY THE TIME THE TRIASSIC ENDED, THE FIRST DINOSAURS HAD APPEARED.

The Triassic Period gets its name from the Latin word for 'three', because it was first identified from three layers of rock found in Germany. At the start of the Triassic, about 245 million years ago, most of the world's land was still locked together in the supercontinent Pangaea, but as the Triassic came to an end, Pangaea began to break apart. Until this happened, land filled much of the western hemisphere, and sea levels were at record lows. Across most of Pangaea, the climate was warm and dry, but it cooled as the northern and southern continents began to move apart.

▷ *In the heart of Pangaea, moisture-loving plants create a splash of greenery in an arid landscape. In Triassic times, these plants included tree-ferns and horsetails, and also conifers, which often grew on drier ground. These ribbons of green were vital for plant-eating reptiles – and for the animals that stalked them as food.*

THERAPSIDS IN DECLINE

The Triassic world was not unlike Earth in Permian times. Instead of being kept separate by the sea, land animals could roam all over, and fossils of the same species are found in places far apart. The therapsids, which had evolved during the Permian, made full use of this freedom to spread. Fossils of one plant-eating species – a barrel-shaped animal called *Lystrosaurus* (page 61) – have been found in places as far apart as Europe and Antarctica, providing evidence that these continents were once joined.

However, for therapsids as a whole, the Triassic period brought difficult times. Although they dominated life on land during the Permian, they failed to maintain their position after the great extinction that brought the Permian to a close. A group of reptiles, the archosaurs, went through a rapid burst of evolution, consigning the therapsids to a dwindling share of the stage. During their decline, the therapsids gave rise to the earliest mammals, but these remained small and unobtrusive. They stayed that way for millions of years, until the Age of Reptiles came to its violent end.

THE RULING REPTILES

The first archosaurs – or 'ruling reptiles' – appeared just before the beginning of the Triassic, from long-bodied animals that looked like crocodiles, but which were often adapted for life on land. Unlike earlier reptiles, their hind legs were usually longer than their front legs, and they evolved specialized ankles that allowed them to walk with a more upright posture, instead of sprawling with their legs out to the side.

Early offshoots of the archosaur line included *Tanystropheus* (page 60), a fish-eater with a bizarrely long neck, and *Scaphonyx* (page 63), a 'beaked lizard' or rhynchosaur. By the late Triassic, archosaurs themselves went on to become a much more diverse collection of animals. Among them were a host of new reptile groups, including the pterosaurs or flying reptiles, the dinosaurs, and the crocodilians – the only one of these groups that has survived to the present day.

In Triassic times, most archosaurs were predators, and they included some fearsome animals such as *Saurosuchus* (page 63). Although *Saurosuchus* was not a dinosaur, its impressive size provided a hint of what the future held. By comparison, the earliest dinosaurs themselves were sometimes surprisingly small – *Eoraptor* (pages 86–87), for example, which dates back to the late Triassic, was just 1m long.

MARINE GIANTS

In Triassic times, reptiles included nothosaurs – lizard-like animals that probably spent much of their time on the shore – and pistosaurs, which had paddles rather than claws. One group of reptiles, the ichthyosaurs, had become as well-adapted for ocean life as whales and dolphins are today. *Shonisaurus* (page 193), a late Triassic species, was the largest reptile afloat, weighing perhaps as much as 20 tonnes.

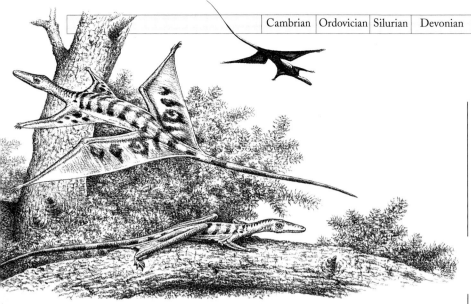

◁ Sharovipteryx *was one of the first vertebrates to take to the air, gliding from tree to tree. It had large rear wings, and possibly a smaller front pair to steer.*

This bizarre reptile may have fished from rocks. It belonged to a group of reptiles called prolacertiforms, which died out when the Triassic came to an end.

MAXIMUM LENGTH	3m
TIME	Mid Triassic
FOSSIL FINDS	Europe (Germany), Asia (Israel)

PROTEROSUCHUS

This animal is the earliest archosaur for which complete fossilized skeletons have been found. Like today's crocodiles, it had sprawling legs, and it probably spent much of its time in water, catching fish and other animals with its powerful jaws. It had sharp, conical teeth, and there were secondary teeth in the roof of its mouth – a feature shared by other early archosaurs, but lost as they evolved.

MAXIMUM LENGTH	2m
TIME	Early Triassic
FOSSIL FINDS	Africa (South Africa), Asia (China)

TRIASSIC ANIMALS

During the Triassic Period, reptiles strengthened their hold on life on land. Dinosaurs appeared in the late Triassic, and until then, an array of different reptiles competed for supremacy. Many were carnivores – hunting smaller reptiles and fish – while others had teeth or sharp-edged jaws that had evolved for cropping plants. With the rise of the archosaurs, these forerunners of today's mammals found themselves increasingly threatened.

▷ *Like other early archosaurs,* Proterosuchus *probably lowered its underside onto the ground when resting, raising it to move.*

▽ Tanystropheus *may have used its extraordinary neck to catch fish without having to enter the water.*

TANYSTROPHEUS

Tanystropheus was one of the most remarkable vertebrates of all time. Its head was small, but its slender neck was longer than the rest of its body. The front and rear of its body look so dissimilar that when the first fragmentary fossils were found, they were thought to belong to two quite different animals. *Tanystropheus*' neck had only 13 vertebrae in some species, and as few as 9 in others – which would have limited its ability to bend.

SHAROVIPTERYX

Discovered in the early 1970s, this extraordinary animal is one of the earliest known gliding reptiles, and also one of the strangest. Attached to its hind legs, and perhaps its front legs as well, were flaps of elastic skin, which could be stretched out to form wings. Its main wings were positioned at the rear of its body, so its tail would have been crucial for staying balanced in mid-air.

MAXIMUM LENGTH	19cm
TIME	Late Triassic
FOSSIL FINDS	Asia (Russia)

ERYTHROSUCHUS

Meaning 'red crocodile', *Erythrosuchus* was a close relative of *Proterosuchus*, but better adapted to hunting prey on land. One of the largest land-based predators of the early Triassic, it weighed half a tonne and its head was about 1m long. *Erythrosuchus* would have fed mainly on plant-eaters, including therapsids such as *Lystrosaurus*, grasping and killing them with its large, backward-curving teeth.

MAXIMUM LENGTH	5m
TIME	Early Triassic
FOSSIL FINDS	Africa (South Africa)

TICINOSUCHUS

Fossils of this archosaur show an animal that was well-equipped for running down fast-moving prey. Although its body was crocodile-like, it had legs that were upright instead of sprawling, and feet with fully developed ankles and heels. This foot anatomy was important because, by lifting its heels, it could push down its feet, giving the leverage needed to run.

MAXIMUM LENGTH	3m
TIME	Mid Triassic
FOSSIL FINDS	Europe (Switzerland)

LYSTROSAURUS

Unlike the other animals on these two pages, *Lystrosaurus* belonged to a group of plant-eating therapsids called dicynodonts, which evolved in the late Permian period, becoming extinct at the end of the Triassic. It had only two teeth which grew in its upper jaw. It cut through its food with a sharp-edged beak, in much the same way that tortoises do today.

MAXIMUM LENGTH	1m
TIME	Early Triassic
FOSSIL FINDS	Africa (South Africa), Asia (India, China, Russia), Antarctica

◁ Ticinosuchus' *upright stance was similar to that of later dinosaurs.*

▽ *As well as moving its lower jaw up and down,* Lystrosaurus *could slide it backwards to slice through giant horsetails.*

THE AGE OF REPTILES

◁ Longisquama *may have used its scales to glide through forests, folding them back when it had landed. Only one fossil of this animal has been found.*

LONGISQUAMA

Ever since its fossilized remains were found in 1969, debate has raged over this small and enigmatic reptile. *Longisquama* had a lizard-like body, with two rows of what look like feathers fastened to its back. If they are true feathers – as some experts believe – it suggests that this animal is a direct ancestor of birds (page 132), and may have been able to fly. However, most palaeontologists are not convinced. They believe that the feathers are actually long scales, which may have been used by the animal to regulate its temperature, or as display during courtship. *Longisquama*'s mouth was lined with small, sharp teeth, suggesting that it might have fed on insects.

MAXIMUM LENGTH 15cm
TIME Late Triassic
FOSSIL FINDS Asia (Turkestan)

▽ *Lightly built, fast on its feet, and armed with sharp, backward-curving teeth,* Euparkeria *was well equipped for hunting and killing. The bony plates running down its back protected it from larger predators, although its first defence would have been to run away on its back legs.*

STAGONOLEPIS

With its short legs and long, scaly body, *Stagonolepis* looked like an early crocodile, as did many other early archosaurs. But instead of having long jaws that match a predatory life, it had short ones shaped for feeding on plants. Its teeth were peg-like and were positioned at the back of its mouth. The end of its snout was shaped like a trowel, which suggests that it may have rooted for food on or beneath the ground. *Stagonolepis* was slow-moving, but had armoured scales that would have helped to protect it from attack.

MAXIMUM LENGTH 3m
TIME Late Triassic
FOSSIL FINDS Europe (Scotland)

EUPARKERIA

Like *Stagonolepis*, this slender-bodied archosaur also bore some resemblance to a small-scale crocodile, with viciously toothed jaws, a series of bony scales along its back and a long, powerful tail. But its legs were quite unlike a crocodile's, partly because they were more upright, but also because the hind legs were significantly larger than the front pair. This difference makes it very likely that *Euparkeria* could run on two legs – either to escape danger, or to catch its prey. This way of moving was rare in early reptiles, but became widespread when dinosaurs evolved.

MAXIMUM LENGTH 60cm
TIME Late Triassic
FOSSIL FINDS Africa (South Africa)

LAGOSUCHUS

The remains of four skeletons – missing only parts of the skull – show that *Lagosuchus* was a slender, long-legged and long-tailed archosaur, which could probably raise itself up on its back legs to run. Its elongated shin bones, combined with its light build, mean that it would have been an effective sprinter, enabling it to catch insects and small reptiles. Its feet were also shaped for speed. They had long metatarsals (bones that form part of the sole in human feet), and these were carried off the ground, helping to increase the length of the stride.

MAXIMUM LENGTH 40cm

TIME Mid Triassic

FOSSIL FINDS South America (Argentina)

SCAPHONYX

Scaphonyx was a typical rhynchosaur – a plant-eating relative of the archosaurs with a barrel-shaped body, a narrow 'beak' equipped with tusks, and highly unusual teeth. The teeth on each side of the upper jaws formed a flat plate with a central groove, and the teeth in the lower jaw were pointed and pressed into the groove when the mouth was closed. Most palaeontologists think that rhynchosaurs used these strange teeth to feed on plants, chopping them up with a scissor-like action, and perhaps digging up roots with their tusks. Rhynchosaur fossils have been found on every continent except Australia, and their numbers suggest they were as common as grazing mammals today.

MAXIMUM LENGTH 2m

TIME Mid Triassic

FOSSIL FINDS South America (Brazil)

△ Lagosuchus *had elongated feet, with only the toes touching the ground. This anatomy became common in carnivorous dinosaurs, as well as many mammals.*

▷ Scaphonyx *and its relatives were the Triassic equivalent of pigs – stoutly built animals that rooted around for vegetable matter. For* Saurosuchus*, these stocky plant-eaters would have been ideal and tasty prey.*

SAUROSUCHUS

Weighing up to 2 tonnes, this archosaur was one of the largest land-based predators in late Triassic times. Its head alone was up to 1m long, and armed with teeth like a crocodile's to tear chunks of flesh from its prey. Although not a dinosaur, *Saurosuchus* showed some striking similarities to tyrannosaurs and other hunters, particularly in the shape of its jaws and teeth and in the way its legs were arranged – almost vertically beneath its body. Unlike a tyrannosaur, it moved mainly on all fours, but it is likely that it could run on its back legs alone to launch an attack. *Saurosuchus* belonged to a group of archosaurs called rauisuchids, which also included *Ticinosuchus* (page 61). These animals were an early example of the

increasing size in reptiles – which gathered momentum as the Triassic Period neared its end.

MAXIMUM LENGTH 7m

TIME Late Triassic

FOSSIL FINDS South America (Argentina)

EARLY DINOSAURS

THE FIRST DINOSAURS EVOLVED IN THE LATE TRIASSIC – OVER 15 MILLION YEARS AFTER THE AGE OF REPTILES BEGAN. RARE AT FIRST, THEY BECAME THE LEADING LAND ANIMALS BY THE TIME THE JURASSIC PERIOD BEGAN.

Studies of dinosaur anatomy show that they all share several key features, which means that they must have evolved from a single shared ancestor. That ancestor was almost certainly a thecodont, or primitive archosaur, and gave rise to a new line of reptiles that often walked on two legs. How and when the ornithischians and saurischians split is not yet known, but the result was a range of reptiles that developed major differences in body shape and ways of life.

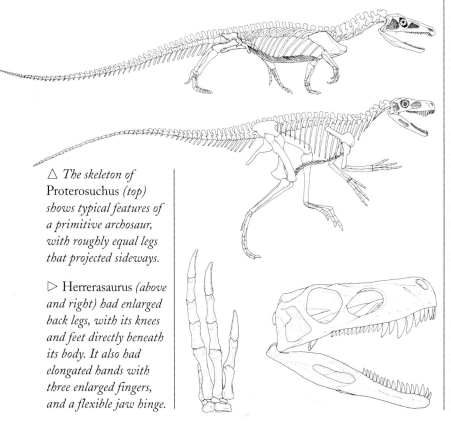

△ *The skeleton of* Proterosuchus *(top) shows typical features of a primitive archosaur, with roughly equal legs that projected sideways.*

▷ Herrerasaurus *(above and right) had enlarged back legs, with its knees and feet directly beneath its body. It also had elongated hands with three enlarged fingers, and a flexible jaw hinge.*

FOSSIL EVIDENCE

Early dinosaurs walked with just three of their toes in contact with the ground, rather than four or five. As a result, three-toed footprints are strong evidence of dinosaurs on the move. One or two specimens have been dated back to the early Triassic, but most palaeontologists are unconvinced. The earliest reliable dinosaur footprints date back to the late Triassic – the time Herrerasaurus *and* Eoraptor *were alive.*

EARLY DAYS

Proterosuchus (page 60) looked much more like a crocodile than a dinosaur – but in fact, both crocodiles and dinosaurs evolved from animals like this. While crocodiles kept *Proterosuchus'* sprawling four-legged gait, the dinosaurs developed differently. Their back legs became larger than their front legs, and the femur, or thighbone, evolved a sharp bend near the point where it joined the rest of the body. Also, the head of the femur developed a ball-like shape, fitting into a socket in the hip. These changes added up to one thing – a new group of carnivorous reptiles that could stand upright on their back legs, instead of moving on legs that sprawled outwards to their sides.

Dinosaurs had several features that help separate them from other reptiles. Among these were a reduced number of bones in the fourth finger (if present), and hip sockets that had a central hole or 'window'. By contrast, typical hip sockets – including human ones – are closed, like a cup.

WORLDWIDE HUNT

Where these animals first appeared is still not clear, partly because most of the world's land was joined together in Triassic times. But Argentina's 'wild west' has produced a clutch of fossils that include some of the earliest dinosaurs on record. Fragments of one, *Herrerasaurus*, were found in the late 1950s, followed by a partial skeleton in 1988 that showed *Herrerasaurus* was a bipedal carnivore up to 6m long, with long jaws and backward-curving teeth. It resembled a theropod (page 113), with long-fingered hands for grasping prey.

In 1991, the same part of the world produced fossils of *Eoraptor*, or 'dawn thief', a bipedal hunter just 1m long. *Eoraptor* lived about 228 million years ago, and was less specialized than *Herrerasaurus*, making it even closer to the original 'proto-dinosaur'. But in 1999, palaeontologists working in Madagascar found jawbones of two even earlier dinosaurs, provisionally dated at more than 230 million years old. The bones showed that these dinosaurs were not carnivores, but plant-eaters called prosauropods, which some thought had evolved from meat-eating ancestors.

CHANGING TIMES

The existence of plant-eating dinosaurs so long ago shows that dinosaurs were already diversifying as the mid-Triassic ended, and the late Triassic began. Many existing animal groups, such as the mammal-like reptiles or therapsids, either declined or disappeared. Dinosaurs may have triggered this change by out-competing existing animals, but another possibility is that the world's climate might have abruptly altered, triggering off a wave of extinctions and clearing the way for dinosaurs to expand.

◁ *Herrerasaurus may have been an early theropod – a group that included all the predatory dinosaurs. The bipedal posture was effective for hunting, and in the Cretaceous, theropods included the largest carnivores ever.*

▽ *Known from many well-preserved fossils, Plateosaurus was a plant-eating prosauropod that lived in the late Triassic. Compared to the small prosauropods recently found in Madagascar, it was a large animal, about 7m long. Prosauropods looked similar to sauropods (page 71), but had feet with long toes.*

THE JURASSIC PERIOD

FAMOUS FOR ITS DINOSAURS, THE JURASSIC PERIOD WAS AN EVENTFUL TIME FOR REPTILIAN LIFE AS A WHOLE. FOR THE FIRST TIME, REPTILES DOMINATED LIFE ON LAND, IN THE SEA AND IN THE AIR.

Named after a chain of mountains in Europe, the Jurassic started about 208 million years ago. Compared to the Triassic Period, it was a time of great changes in the Earth's crust, as the great supercontinent of Pangaea began to break up. The climate became wetter and warmer, and sea levels rose, flooding large areas of low-lying land. For animal life, these changes created new opportunities. On land, a moister climate meant that plant food was easier to find, while in the sea, warm shallows created perfect conditions for coral reefs.

▷ *Average temperatures were warm in the Jurassic, with little or no ice at the poles. This scene shows a typical landscape from the time, dominated by forests of conifers, with scattered cycads and tree-ferns. The cycads probably used dinosaurs to scatter their seeds, just like some plants use mammals today.*

A PARTING OF THE WAYS

With the break-up of Pangaea, the continents began their long journey into the positions that they are in today. The Atlantic Ocean started to form, and North and South America split apart. These changes had an important effect on land animals, because it meant that they could no longer mix freely. Instead, each continent began to develop its own characteristic wildlife – a feature that became more pronounced the longer they remained apart. The separation can often be seen by where fossils are found. For example, giant sauropods lived in both North and South America during the Jurassic, but each continent had its own particular 'brands' – none is found in both.

DINOSAURS IN THE ASCENDANT

When the Jurassic Period began, dinosaurs had established themselves as the prominent animals on land. They had already split into several lines, and most of these were set to continue for nearly 150 million years, until the Age of Reptiles abruptly came to an end. However, there were some casualties along the way. Among the sauropods, for example, the cetiosaur family died out at the end of the Jurassic, and several other dinosaur families disappeared.

The warm and humid conditions that lasted for most of the Jurassic were ideal for large plant-eaters to evolve, because there was a vast supply of food. And as plant-eaters increased in size, so did the animals that preyed upon them. From relatively modest beginnings, predatory dinosaurs evolved into giants such as *Megalosaurus*, which was up to 9m long. Outwardly, *Megalosaurus* was simliar to the better – known tyrannosaurs, but it evolved millions of years before they appeared.

These huge predators had no natural enemies, but not all dinosaurs were built on a giant scale. *Compsognathus*, which lived in the late Jurassic, was also a hunter, but it weighed only about 3kg.

LIFE IN THE SEA AND AIR

During the Jurassic, several new families of marine reptiles appeared. Among them were the long-necked plesiosaurs and elasmosaurs, and also the pliosaurs, which included some of the largest predators to live in the seas. Marine life was particularly rich in the Jurassic, because sea levels were generally higher than they are today. Sunlit shallows rich in sediment teemed with molluscs and other small animals.

In the air, even greater changes were underway. The first flying reptiles, or pterosaurs, had evolved in the late Triassic, and during the Jurassic they took command of the skies on their leathery wings. But from a branch of the dinosaur world – the theropods – a completely new group of flying animals came into being. Instead of flying on wings of skin, they used feathers (page 133), and they rapidly diversified as the Jurassic came to its end. We know them as birds – the only dinosaurs that are still alive today.

THE CRETACEOUS PERIOD

A TIME OF DRAMATIC SHIFTS IN THE WORLD'S CONTINENTS, TOGETHER WITH RECORD SEA LEVELS, THE CRETACEOUS PERIOD SAW AN EXPLOSIVE GROWTH IN LIFE – ONE THAT CAME TO A CATACLYSMIC END.

The Cretaceous Period began 144 million years ago, when the supercontinent of Pangaea had broken up. Two major fragments – Laurasia in the north, and Gondwana in the south – began cracking up in turn to form the continents that exist today. These continental movements produced major changes in the Earth's climate, and sea levels up to 200m higher than they are now. Microscopic life abounded in the seas, and tiny shells built up in vast banks on the sea floor, eventually turning into chalk. Known in Latin as *creta*, chalk gave the Cretaceous its name.

▷ *With volcanoes erupting in the distance, late Cretaceous plants bloom to attract pollinating insects. Volcanic activity was a feature of the Cretaceous Period, and average temperatures were much higher than they are today. Sub-tropical landscapes – like the one shown here - extended as far north as modern-day New York.*

LIFE ON LAND
Unlike the Triassic or Jurassic periods, the Cretaceous was similar in some ways to the world we know today. Flowering plants probably evolved in the late Jurassic or early Cretaceous, but it was during the Cretaceous that they really began to make their mark. These plants included the first broad-leaved trees, which slowly ousted conifers in many parts of the world. As flowering plants evolved, so did pollinating insects such as bees. It was the start of a phenomenally successful partnership, which continues to the present day.

The Cretaceous landscape was also home to mammals, which had clung on to life throughout Jurassic times. Like their Jurassic forebears, they were still small, and they avoided head-to-head competition with reptiles by foraging for food at night. They included primitive marsupials, which raised their young in a pouch, as well as some pocket-sized placentals – species that grew their young inside their bodies, as most mammals do today. There were birds, but much more evident were pterosaurs – a sign that the reign of reptiles was still at its height. The Cretaceous also produced the largest, fastest and most intelligent dinosaurs that the world had yet seen.

LATE ARRIVALS
By the beginning of the Cretaceous, dinosaurs already had a history dating back more than 80 million years. During this long finale of the reptile age, several new groups of dinosaurs came into being, while others rapidly expanded. They included the armoured dinosaurs, the duck-billed dinosaurs or hadrosaurs, and the titanosaurs – a group of southern sauropods which may have included the heaviest dinosaurs. Apart from these plant-eaters, the late Cretaceous also saw the arrival of the tyrannosaurs, a family that included the largest land predators ever to have stalked the Earth.

In the seas, reptiles still held sway. They included plesiosaurs and ichthyosaurs, which had existed throughout the Jurassic, and a new group – the mosasaurs – giant marine lizards that became the dominant sea-going reptiles as the Cretaceous neared its end. Turtles were common, having changed little in over 200 million years. These shared the seas with fish, known as teleosts, which had thinner and lighter scales than earlier fish, making them faster and more manoeuvrable.

END OF THE CRETACEOUS
If the Cretaceous world had continued, reptiles might still be Earth's dominant animals and mammals might have died out. But 66 million years ago, something happened that devastated life on land and in the sea, sweeping aside all of the dinosaurs, and many other reptiles as well. Most experts now believe that this catastrophe was caused by an impact from outer space (page 204), but other factors – such as volcanic eruptions – may have already set the process in motion. In any event, with this multiple catastrophe the Mesozoic Era ended, and the great Age of Reptiles was over.

THE AGE OF REPTILES

DINOSAUR GROUPS

Early in their evolution, dinosaurs split into two groups: the ornithischians, or bird-hipped dinosaurs, and the saurischians, or lizard-hipped dinosaurs. As well as a different hip anatomy, these two groups developed other distinctive features, and different ways of life. The ornithischians were plant-eaters, and walked either on four legs or on two. The saurischians included the plant-eating sauropods, which walked on all fours, and all the predatory dinosaurs or theropods, which were almost entirely bipedal. Birds are actually descended from lizard-hipped dinosaurs, and they are the only members of the two groups alive today.

Bird-hipped dinosaur (ornithischian)

Lizard-hipped dinosaur (saurischian)

△ *In bird-hipped dinosaurs, two hip bones – the ischium and pubis – pointed backwards, and were close together. In lizard-hipped dinosaurs, the two bones pointed in different directions.*

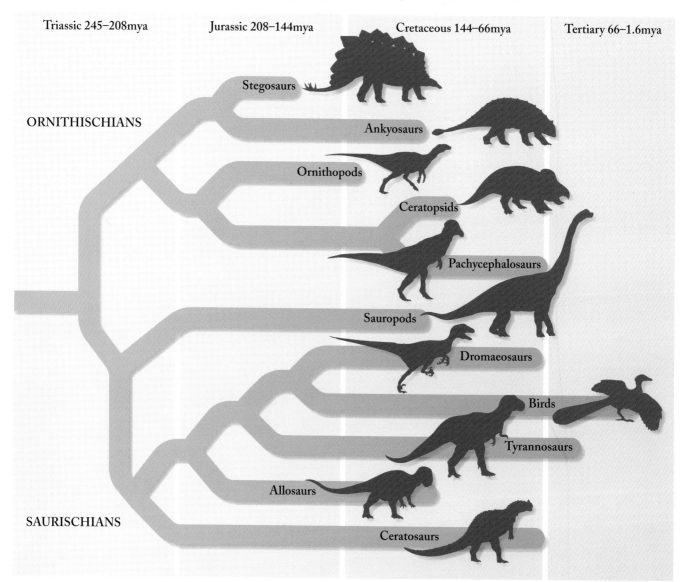

Triassic 245–208mya   Jurassic 208–144mya   Cretaceous 144–66mya   Tertiary 66–1.6mya

ORNITHISCHIANS

Stegosaurs
Ankyosaurs
Ornithopods
Ceratopsids
Pachycephalosaurs
Sauropods
Dromaeosaurs
Birds
Tyrannosaurs
Allosaurs

SAURISCHIANS

Ceratosaurs

PLANT-EATING GIANTS

With their gigantic necks and barrel-shaped bodies, the sauropods were the unrivalled giants of the dinosaur world. These slow-moving plant-eaters evolved during the Jurassic Period, and over the next 50 million years, they developed into the largest land animals the world has ever seen. Some of them tipped the scales at over 80 tonnes – close to the limit for any animal that moves on legs. There were several families of sauropods, including cetiosaurs, brachiosaurs, diplodocids and titanosaurs, and they processed almost unbelievable amounts of plant food.

GIANTS AMONG GIANTS

A carnosaur, Ceratosaurus (page 117), lurks menacingly on a hillside overlooking a herd of Apatosaurus (page 80) as the gentle diplodocids munch their way through a forest. Diplodocids probably used their long, whip-like tails and their massive forelimbs to defend themselves against attack from such predatory carnosaurs.

PLANT-EATING GIANTS

CETIOSAURS

Cetiosaurs were among the first sauropods, dating back to the early Jurassic, and they were also the first to be discovered. Their huge bodies were supported by four pillar-like legs, and they had quite small heads, but extremely long necks and tails. They browsed on trees and low-growing plants, swallowing their food whole because, like most plant-eating dinosaurs, they were not able to chew. The cetiosaur family share a key characteristic – vertebrae that were almost solid. This feature is a primitive one, and as sauropods evolved, their backbones become increasingly hollowed out as a way of saving weight.

OMEISAURUS
Identified in 1939, this Chinese cetiosaur was named after the mountain where its fossils were found. Fragments of most parts of its skeleton have been discovered, giving us quite a good picture of what it looked like. *Omeisaurus* had a long neck and small, wedge-shaped head, and a slightly forward-sloping gait, with its hips higher than its shoulders. Its tail was relatively short – although still huge by today's standards –

and it may have had a clubbed tip, though this may not have been a feature of all species. Like all sauropods, *Omeisaurus* did not simply trail its tail on the ground. Instead, it probably held its tail almost horizontally when on the move, using it as a counterweight, or even as a weapon.

MAXIMUM LENGTH 15–20m
TIME Late Jurassic
FOSSIL FINDS Asia (China)

CETIOSAURUS
The first fossils of *Cetiosaurus* were found in the early 1800s, several decades before the existence of dinosaurs became known. Its name, which means 'whale lizard' was given to it in 1841 – one of many examples of dinosaur remains being confused with those of other animals. It was originally thought to be some kind of giant marine reptile, until it was finally recognized as a dinosaur in 1869. *Cetiosaurus* was a massive animal, weighing up to 27 tonnes. It had a relatively short neck and tail, but its legs were impressive: its thigh bones were nearly 2m long. Its front and back legs appear to have been roughly the same length, which means that its back would have been almost level. This sets it apart from many later sauropods, which had front and back legs of quite different lengths. No traces of a skull have been found, so scientists do not know how it fed, but its teeth probably worked like a rake, enabling it to strip leaves from trees and other plants.

MAXIMUM LENGTH 18m
TIME Mid to late Jurassic
FOSSIL FINDS Europe (England), Africa (Morocco)

◁ Omeisaurus *was almost certainly a herd-forming animal. Despite its size, it was vulnerable to predators and needed the protection that came with living in groups.*

CETIOSAURS

◁ For many years, Cetiosaurus *was the largest land animal known to science. Since then, many other sauropod fossils have been discovered. They show that, despite its great size,* Cetiosaurus *was actually a middleweight member of the sauropod group.*

BARAPASAURUS

This animal is the oldest sauropod so far discovered. Its exact classification is uncertain, but it was a massively built animal, equal to *Cetiosaurus* in size and weight, or possibly even heavier. Six partial skeletons of *Barapasaurus* have been uncovered, and a host of much more incomplete remains, but so far none of them includes skulls or feet. However, palaeontologists have found fossilized teeth, spoon-shaped with serrated edges and ideal for tearing off leaves. *Barapasaurus* shows that sauropods were already very large animals near the beginning of the Jurassic. Some scientists classify this animal in a separate family of very primitive sauropods, called the vulcanodontids. The founder member of this family, called *Vulcanodon*, was found in Africa.

MAXIMUM LENGTH 18m
TIME Early Jurassic
FOSSIL FINDS Asia (India)

SHUNOSAURUS

Compared to some cetiosaurs, this Chinese dinosaur is a recent discovery, with the first fossil find dating back to 1977. Measuring just 10m long, it was almost petite by sauropod standards, and probably weighed no more than a fully grown female elephant. Apart from its small size, its most interesting feature is the tip of its tail. This ended in a bony club, which would have made a very effective weapon. A similar defence system appeared later in a different group of plant-eaters – the ankylosaurs (page 164). Over 20 discoveries of almost complete *Shunosaurus* skeletons have been found, giving an unusually good picture of what this animal looked like. Compared to most sauropods, its nostrils were positioned low down on its muzzle, and it had relatively small teeth with elongated crowns.

MAXIMUM LENGTH 10m
TIME Mid Jurassic
FOSSIL FINDS Asia (China)

HAPLOCANTHOSAURUS

Haplocanthosaurus is the most primitive sauropod that has been discovered in North America with the first known fossils being unearthed about a century ago. It had a long neck and tail, and showed similarities to the brachiosaurs (page 76) and the diplodocids (page 80). Establishing its exact place in classification is not easy because, as with many other cetiosaurs, no skull remains have been found. In evolutionary terms, *Haplocanthosaurus* seems to have been something of a throwback. It lived towards the end of the Jurassic period – a time when most other cetiosaurs had died out – and has been described as a 'living fossil' of its time.

MAXIMUM LENGTH 22m
TIME Late Jurassic
FOSSIL FINDS North America

▽ Barapasaurus *is the earliest known sauropod. Its weight may have been as much as 30 tonnes.*

△ By flicking its tail like a whip, Shunosaurus *would have been able to inflict a deadly blow with its tail club. The spikes in the club were extensions of the bones inside its tail.*

PLANT-EATING GIANTS

BRACHIOSAURS AND CAMARASAURS

The brachiosaurs were spectacularly long-necked sauropods, while the camarasaurs were smaller with shorter necks and tails. Although both groups were plant-eaters, differences in their body shape and in the design of their teeth mean that they were unlikely to have eaten the same food. Brachiosaurs had remarkably long front legs, and their teeth were shaped like chisels. Camarasaurs looked more like other sauropods, but they had forward-pointing teeth set in an unusual bulldog-like snout.

◁ Brachiosaurus *was the dinosaur equivalent of the giraffe, but on a hugely bigger scale. Its blood pressure was exceptionally high – an adaptation that ensured oxygen reached its brain.*

▽ Brachiosaurus' *neck had a framework of 14 hollow but extremely strong vertebrae. Like the jib of a crane, it raised its head high into the treetops.*

BRACHIOSAURUS

As well as being one of the heaviest dinosaurs, with a weight of up to 80 tonnes, *Brachiosaurus* is the largest species to have had its skeleton assembled in a museum (page 161). Its front legs were much longer than its hind legs, and this – together with its long neck – allowed it to reach up to 16m, which is more than two-and-a-half times as high as a giraffe. Its head was relatively small, with large upward-facing nostrils that opened in a dome on its crown. At one time, palaeontologists thought that *Brachiosaurus*' nostrils showed that it fed in lakes. However, this is unlikely to be true, because its lungs would have collapsed if they were more than a few metres underwater. Despite its huge size,

BRACHIOSAURS AND CAMARASAURS

Brachiosaurus may not have been the largest member of its family. In 1994, an American team unearthed fossils of a bigger animal, *Sauroposeidon*, which stood over 18m tall.

MAXIMUM LENGTH 26m

TIME Mid to late Jurassic

FOSSIL FINDS North America, Africa, Europe (Portugal)

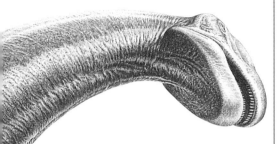

CAMARASAURUS

Weighing about 20 tonnes, *Camarasaurus* was much more compact than *Brachiosaurus*. Many fossils of this dinosaur have been found, including several complete skeletons – which for a sauropod, makes this species almost unique. *Camarasaurus* would have probably lived in herds for protection, although like *Brachiosaurus*, it could have lashed out at its enemies with extra-long claws on its thumbs. *Camarasaurus* had large nostrils, and may have had a keen sense of smell. The size of its nostrils, and its box-like head, have led some scientists to suggest that it had an elephant-like trunk. However, trunks are made entirely from soft tissue, which very rarely shows up in fossils. As a result, this intriguing idea – which has been suggested for other sauropods – is very difficult to prove.

MAXIMUM LENGTH 18m

TIME Late Jurassic

FOSSIL FINDS North America (USA), Europe (Portugal)

OPISTHOCOELICAUDIA

The only known skeleton of this sauropod was found in 1965, minus its head and neck. As a result, its exact appearance is still a matter of guesswork, and so is its place in the sauropod world. It had one highly distinctive feature: tail vertebrae that were hollowed out behind, rather than in front, which is the more normal pattern for sauropods. This arrangement would have made its tail unusually strong, allowing *Opisthocoelicaudia* to rear up on its hind legs, using its tail as a prop.

MAXIMUM LENGTH 12m

TIME Late Cretaceous

FOSSIL FINDS Central Asia

EUHELOPUS

Smaller than *Camarasaurus*, but similar in overall shape, *Euhelopus* would never have crossed paths with its American relative, since it lived in the Far East. Its neck was much longer, and its head was also longer and more pointed, although still with a steeply sloping front. *Euhelopus* had up to 19 neck vertebrae, unlike *Camarasaurus*, which had 12 – one reason why it is sometimes classified in a separate family.

MAXIMUM LENGTH 15m

TIME Late Jurassic

FOSSIL FINDS Asia (China)

▽ Camarasaurus *(top) means 'chambered lizard'. It gets its name from the hollow chambers in its vertebrae, which kept it light for its size. Its neck was relatively short.*

▽ Opisthocoelicaudia *(middle) may have been a camarasaur, but some palaeontologists think it is more likely to have been a titanosaur (page 88).*

▽ Euhelopus *(bottom) probably weighed 15–20 tonnes. It had teeth all around its jaws; many other sauropods had them only at the front.*

FEEDING ON PLANTS

ALTHOUGH THE EARLIEST DINOSAURS WERE
HUNTERS, PLANT-EATING SPECIES STEADILY
OUTNUMBERED THEM AS THE AGE OF
REPTILES WORE ON. MANY COULD NOT CHEW
– THEY SWALLOWED THEIR FOOD WHOLE.

When the first plant-eating dinosaurs evolved, in the late Triassic, there were no flowering plants, so there was no grass. Instead of grazing, like many of today's hoofed mammals, early plant-eating dinosaurs fed on coniferous trees, and other plants with tough foliage and tall trunks or stems. The same was true for most of the Jurassic period, but during the Cretaceous, flowering plants became widespread. They created a carpet of succulent, low-growing foliage, which made it easier to feed at or near ground level.

These fossilized stones are gastroliths or 'stomach stones', from a plant-eating dinosaur find. Dinosaurs swallowed these to help them grind up their food – an important digestive aid for animals often lacking chewing teeth. The food would travel through the digestive system, but the stones, being heavier, stayed behind. Crocodiles, ostriches and some other birds do the same thing today.

▷ *Ferns, cycads and horsetails (left to right), were important foods for dinosaurs in the Jurassic.*

▽ *Magnolias were among the first flowering plants. Compared to other prehistoric plants, their leaves were juicy and nutritious.*

A CHANGING MENU

Plant-eating dinosaurs evolved in step with the vegetation around them. During the Triassic and Jurassic, most had long necks, to enable them to browse high off the ground. They may also have used their necks like horizontal booms, so that they could crop wide areas of shorter plants, but many palaeontologists doubt that this was common, as there was probably not enough of this vegetation to make low-level feeding worthwhile. With the evolution of flowering plants, this began to change. For the first time, there was plenty of plant food close to the ground, and because flowering plants tended to be faster-growing, they recovered quickly after being eaten. This new food supply was quite different to the plant cover of the past, and it probably explains why smaller ornithopods (pages 91–112) and armoured dinosaurs (151–168) became so widespread in Cretaceous times.

HOW SAUROPODS FED

Plant-eating mammals have two main types of teeth. The incisors, at the front of the jaw, bite off the food, while the molars, near the back, chew it up. By comparison, sauropods – by far the largest plant-eating dinosaurs – had a much simpler arrangement. Their teeth formed a matching set, usually in the front of the jaw, and they could collect food, but they could not chew it. A sauropod would swallow food whole, and it was ground up in its stomach. The plant pulp was then broken down by microbes living in

▷ Apatosaurus' *muscular stomach worked like a cement mixer, churning up leaves, branches and even tough cones, and breaking them into small, easily digested pieces with the help of stomach stones.*

the animal's stomach. Once the microbes had done their work, the dinosaur could absorb the nutrients released.

CHEWING TEETH

Ornithopods had a more mammal-like way of eating. Many gathered their food using a toothless 'beak' that formed the front of the jaw. They would then move the food to the back of their mouths, where it was sliced or ground up by a battery of specialized teeth. By the time the food arrived in the stomach, it was ready-prepared for microbes to break down. Some bird-hipped dinosaurs had just a handful of teeth, but hadrosaurs (pages 104–7) often had hundreds.

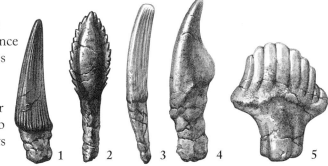

△ *Plant–eaters' teeth were usually peg-like, although some were flat. They all had an endless supply of teeth throughout their lives. From right to left, these teeth belonged to* Heterodontosaurus (1), Plateosaurus (2), Diplodocus (3), Apatosaurus (4) *and* Stegosaurus (5).

▽ *A fully grown* Apatosaurus *probably ate under half a tonne of food a day – less that one-fiftieth of its body weight. It could survive on this meagre diet because it was cold-blooded. Today's warm-blooded plant-eaters need a much higher food intake.*

PLANT-EATING DINOSAURS

DIPLODOCIDS

The diplodocids include the longest dinosaurs that are known from complete skeletons. *Diplodocus*, the best-known species, was up to 27m long, but the partial remains of *Seismosaurus* (page 83) suggest that some diplodocids were even longer than this. If so, they may well have been the longest vertebrates ever to have existed on Earth. Diplodocids were built like living suspension bridges, will pillar-like legs, and extraordinarily long necks, and even longer narrow-tipped tails. Despite their great length, they were not as heavy as many other sauropods, because their skeletons were shaped to save weight. They had elongated heads, large nostrils located on top near their eyes and unusually small, rod-like teeth.

DIPLODOCUS

Diplodocus means 'double beam' – a name that describes this dinosaur's tail. Beneath each of its tail vertebra was a length of bone, and these ran forwards and backwards, strengthening the tail and protecting the blood vessels inside it. It could lash out with the tip of its tail if it came under attack. *Diplodocus'* remarkable length has led to many questions about how it moved and fed. Some scientists believe that it would have moved with its head held almost horizontally in front, and its tail in a similar position at the rear. It is also likely that it could raise itself on its hind legs, and lift its head high up into the trees to feed.

Diplodocus

Like its relatives, *Diplodocus* had teeth only in the front of its mouth.

MAXIMUM LENGTH	27m
TIME	Late Jurassic
FOSSIL FINDS	North America (western USA)

Apatosaurus

▷ *The first fossil of* Apatosaurus – *minus the skull – was found in 1877, but the first complete skeleton of this dinosaur was not assembled until 1975.*

▷ Diplodocus *had slender teeth that worked like a comb, gathering in the soft parts of plants. It may have fed on low-growing vegetation as well as trees.*

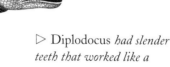

Dicraeosaurus

▷ Dicraeosaurus *was smaller than most diplodocids, and probably fed on low-growing plants. Unlike its later relatives, it did not have a whip-like tip to its tail.*

▽ Mamenchisaurus' *neck accounted for half the entire length of its body. It had 19 neck vertebrae and they were 'stretched' to give the neck its length.*

Mamenchisaurus

▷ Barosaurus' *thigh bone measured up to 2.5m – longer than an adult man. Its back legs and tail may have acted like a tripod, allowing it to reach high into the trees.*

Barosaurus

APATOSAURUS

Once also known as *Brontosaurus*, *Apatosaurus* was slightly smaller than *Diplodocus* but, at 30 tonnes, much more heavily built. As with *Diplodocus*, uncertainty surrounds exactly how it lived. For many years, scientists have assumed that it could rear up on its hind legs to feed, using its tail as a prop. But some recent research suggests that its neck might have been surprisingly inflexible, so that when it was on all fours, it could raise its head no more than 5m above the ground. *Apatosaurus* probably defended itself by using its tail, and the sharp toe claw on each of its front feet. *Apatosaurus* bones have been found with *Allosaurus* teeth marks, but it is not possible to tell whether these giant plant-eaters had been attacked while alive, or scavenged when already dead.

MAXIMUM LENGTH 25m

TIME Late Jurassic

FOSSIL FINDS North America (western USA)

DICRAEOSAURUS

Dicraeosaurus was a relatively compact diplodocid, and one of the earliest members of the family. Compared to later forms, it had a short neck and tail, and a comparatively large head. Its vertebrae also show some peculiarities, with unusual Y-shaped spines running along the length of the backbone, and into the neck. These may

have channelled supporting ligaments, and would have formed a clearly visible ridge along its spine.

MAXIMUM LENGTH 14m

TIME Late Jurassic

FOSSIL FINDS Africa (Tanzania)

MAMENCHISAURUS

Until the discovery of *Sauroposeidon* in 1994 (page 82) *Mamenchisaurus* held the record for neck length for a dinosaur – an astounding 14m. This crane-like neck may have been used horizontally as much as vertically, allowing *Mamenchisaurus* to reach out for plants growing on marshy ground, or in dense thickets, while the rest of its body was safely outside. When this dinosaur was on the move, it probably held its head directly in front of its body, so that its neck was roughly level. Its neck vertebrae were unusually light and thin, with interconnecting rod-like ribs for strength. Its neck was not very flexible, and bent mainly at the head and shoulders, rather than in between. Some palaeontologists think that *Mamenchisaurus* is so unusual that it should be classified in a family of its own.

MAXIMUM LENGTH 25m

TIME Late Jurassic

FOSSIL FINDS Asia (China)

BAROSAURUS

Barosaurus, which means 'heavy lizard', was a huge diplodocid, weighing perhaps as much as 40 tonnes. Similar in form and structure to *Diplodocus*, but with particularly elongated neck vertebrae, it would have used size as its main defence. Like some of its relatives, *Barosaurus*' centre of gravity was far back down its body – a feature that would have helped it if it reared up on its back legs to feed from trees. Judging from fossil finds in Africa and America, this dinosaur was one of the most widespread members of the diplodocid family.

MAXIMUM LENGTH 27m

TIME Late Jurassic

FOSSIL FINDS North America (western USA), Africa (Tanzania)

PLANT-EATING GIANTS

▷ *Giant sauropods like* Supersaurus *(on the left) had very similar body structures, albeit on a giantic scale. The exact size and weight of these enormous plant-eaters is uncertain, because no complete fossils have yet been found. Other contenders for the title of biggest dinosaur ever include* Argentinosaurus *(page 88) and a colossal brachiosaur called* Sauroposeidon, *whose remains were found in the grounds of a prison in Oklahoma, USA, in 1994.*

AMARGASAURUS

An almost complete skeleton of *Amargasaurus* was discovered in Argentinian Patagonia in 1984. It revealed that this diplodocid had a highly unusual row of vertebral spines, up to 65cm long, running along the back of its neck. These may have formed a spiky mane, or they may have been covered in skin, creating a structure like a double sail. Whichever form they took, they were a remarkable feature, and may have played a part in the animal's social life, or they may have been used in defence – a valuable plus for an animal that was under half the length of many of its larger cousins. *Amargasaurus* also had a slender whip-like tail, and blunt teeth, shaped for stripping foliage from branches. Like other sauropods, it probably swallowed stones or gastroliths (page 78) to help it break down its food. With it spiny vertebrae, *Amargasaurus* is similar to *Dicraeosaurus* (page 81), and some palaeontologists classify these two dinosaurs in a family of their own.

MAXIMUM LENGTH 12m

TIME Early Cretaceous

FOSSIL FINDS South America (Argentina)

SUPERSAURUS

A giant among giants, *Supersaurus* has the distinction of being one of the largest land animals ever to have walked the Earth. The first fossils were discovered in 1972, in the Dry Mesa Quarry, Colorado – a site that has produced some of the world's most spectacular sauropod finds. The *Supersaurus* remains were far from complete, but they included shoulder blades 2.4m long and nearly 1m wide – enough for two people to lie on, with plenty of legroom to spare. From remains like these, palaeontologists estimate that *Supersaurus* might have weighed as much as 50 tonnes, and with its head held high, would have towered 15m above the ground – higher than the average house. *Supersaurus'* tremendous weight was supported by four pillar-shaped legs, the hind legs being longer than the front ones. Like other diplodocids, it had elephant-like feet with five toes, and a large claw on each front 'thumb'. The claws may have been used as defensive weapons, although its huge tail would have been a more substantial deterrent. Analysis of its fossilized tracks show that it moved slowly – as would be expected for an animal of its size.

MAXIMUM LENGTH	42m
TIME	Late Jurassic
FOSSIL FINDS	North America (Colorado)

ULTRASAUROS

There are doubts about whether *Ultrasauros* is truly a separate species of dinosaur, or whether its remains are actually a mixture from two other dinosaurs – *Supersaurus* and *Brachiosaurus*. The first of these remains, which were found in 1979, came from the same quarry that produced *Supersaurus*, and they include bones that show *Ultrasauros* would have stood about 8m tall at the shoulder, over four times the height of an average man.

Ultrasauros gets its unusual spelling because scientific names can never be used twice for different animals. It was originally called *Ultrasaurus*, but had to be renamed because the name *Ultrasaurus* had already been used two years earlier, for a smaller sauropod found in South Korea.

MAXIMUM LENGTH	30m
TIME	Late Jurassic
FOSSIL FINDS	North America (Colorado)

SEISMOSAURUS

Known from remains discovered in 1979, *Seismosaurus* – meaning 'earthquake lizard' – was built on a massive scale. Some estimates put its total length at up to 50m, although 40m is probably more likely. However, with a weight of perhaps 30 tonnes, or more than double that according to some calculations, it would have more than lived up to its name. Like other diplodocids, it had extra bones beneath its spine to help support its neck and tail. Its tail had the 'standard' diplodocid whip-like tip, but it also seems to have had a kink – a feature that has not yet been explained. By comparison to the rest of its body, its head was tiny – a characteristic feature of sauropods as a whole. Stomach stones, or gastroliths, have been found among *Seismosaurus'* fossilized remains, indicating that it lived on a diet of tough plants that needed to be ground down before they could be digested. The only known fossil of this dinosaur has still not been fully excavated, because it lies deeply buried in sandstone. The latest technology – including ground-penetrating radar – has been used to pinpoint the fossilized bones that still remain hidden beneath the surface.

MAXIMUM LENGTH	up to 50m
TIME	Late Jurassic
FOSSIL FINDS	North America (New Mexico)

◁ *This reconstruction of* Ultrasauros *(centre) is very much an artist's impression, because only partial remains of this animal have been found, and they may not even belong to the same animal. If* Ultrasauros *really did exist, its weight might have been well over 50 tonnes.*

◁ *The only known remains of* Seismosaurus *(on the right) were found when two hikers literally stumbled on the tip of its fossilized tail. When palaeontologists began to excavate the remains, they turned out to be among the largest so far discovered. The fossils show that* Seismosaurus *was a typical diplodocid, but one built on an extra-large scale.*

A QUESTION OF SIZE

How heavy were the largest dinosaurs, and why did they grow to such enormous sizes? Questions like these are easy to ask but, palaeontologists have discovered, not so easy to answer.

Sauropod dinosaurs were without doubt the largest land animals that have ever lived on Earth, weighing perhaps 15 times as much as any four-legged animal alive today. For biologists, and for engineers, these giant plant-eaters exert a powerful fascination, because they probably reached the physical proportions that limit animal size. Enormous dimensions must have brought advantages, or these giants would not have evolved, but they would also have created a range of practical problems – ones that evolution had to overcome.

Why be big?

There are several reasons why 'gigantism' may have evolved in plant-eating dinosaurs. One is that plant digestion works best on a large scale. Like today's plant-eaters, sauropods relied on microbes to break down their food, and the microbes released heat as they worked. This heat helped to speed up the process of digestion, and the bigger the dinosaur's stomach, the more heat it would have generated. In relative terms, giant dinosaurs needed less food for each tonne of body weight, as they used proportionately less in moving about and staying alive.

Being gigantic is also a useful defence against predators, once an animal has safely come through its early years and reached adult size. This explains why many kinds of

△ *American scientist Robert Bakker stands behind an* Apatosaurus *femur. Sauropod femurs are the largest single dinosaur bones.*

These sauropod bones are part of an immense collection at Dinosaur National Monument, on the border of Colorado and Utah in the USA. Giant leg bones, like the ones shown in the foreground, have been used to estimate the weight of the heaviest dinosaurs, including plant-eaters and their predators. These estimates are made by measuring the bones' cross-sectional area at their narrowest point.

plant-eaters, from horses to elephants, have grown larger during their evolutionary history. Unfortunately (from a plant-eater's point of view), predators can also increase in size. During the dinosaur age, the trend towards increasing size in plant-eaters was mirrored by a similar trend in carnivores. This meant natural selection favoured even larger plant-eaters, and the process went on.

Reaching the top

The bigger-is-better trend could not continue indefinitely, because the problems of being gigantic eventually started to outweigh the benefits. One of these problems was the difficulty of pumping blood to a head that towered many metres above the ground. *Brachiosaurus* and other long-necked sauropods would have needed powerful hearts, even if they did have tiny brains. Animals like these would also have faced increasing difficulties mating and laying eggs – a major consideration, because producing plenty of young is the key to evolutionary success. But from an engineering standpoint, a more fundamental problem concerned their weight: as they evolved larger and larger bodies, this climbed at a prodigious rate.

To visualize how this happened, imagine three 'dinosaurs' shaped like cubes, with sides 1m, 5m and 10m long. The second dinosaur is only five times as long as the first, but its weight is 125 times as great (the result of multiplying 5x5x5). The third dinosaur is 10 times as long, which means that it weighs a thousand times as much as the first. Once sauropods reached lengths of about 20m, each additional metre meant a jump in weight of over a tonne – a tremendous burden that still had to be supported by just four legs.

The strength of a leg depends on its cross-sectional area, rather than its volume. This means that if an animal gets larger while keeping the same overall shape, its weight outstrips its strength, so its legs are put under greater and greater stress. Sauropods coped with this by modifying their leg bones, and by keeping bending to a minimum, but in the end it would have been weight, rather than anything else, that brought their growth to a halt.

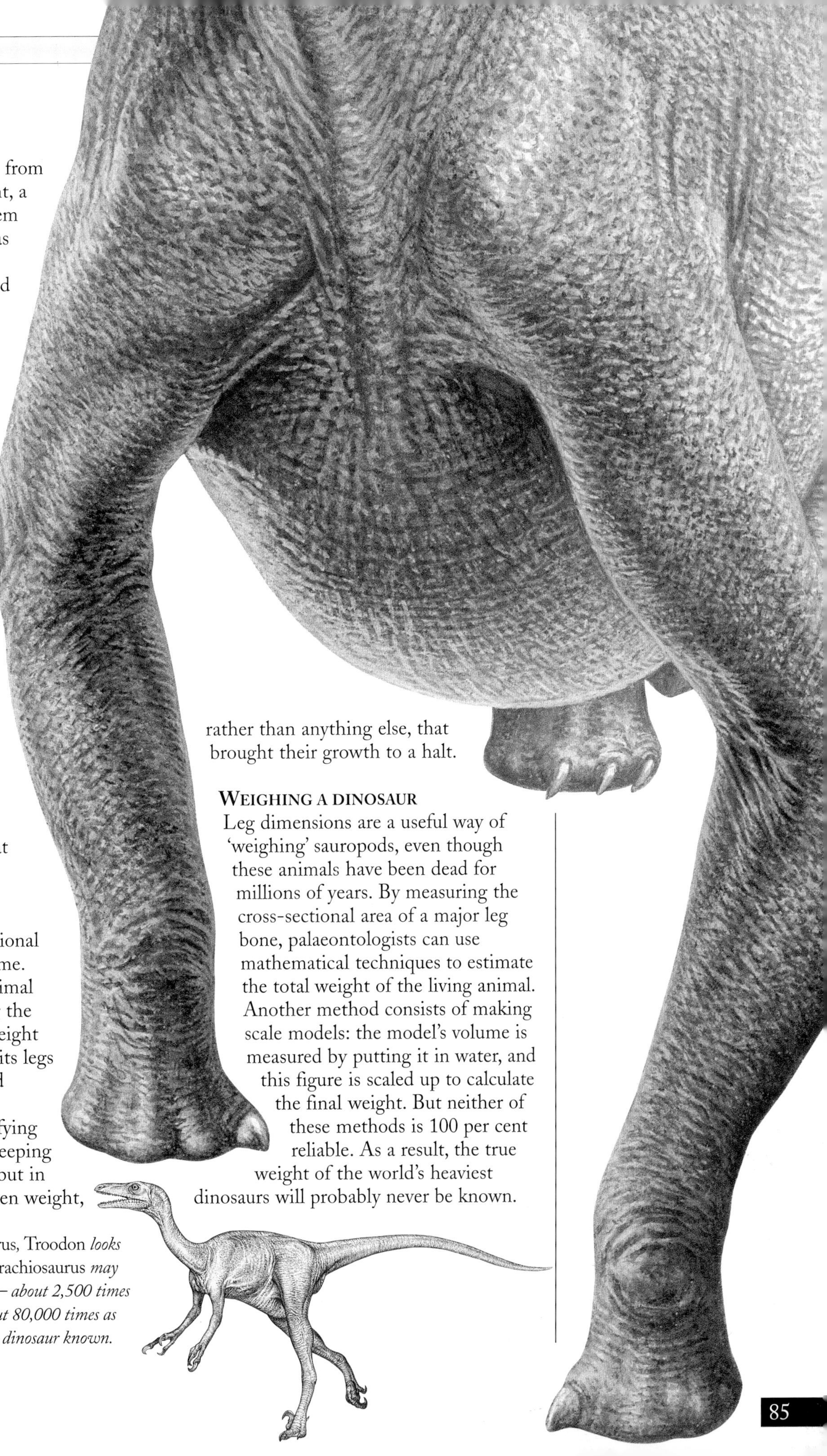

WEIGHING A DINOSAUR
Leg dimensions are a useful way of 'weighing' sauropods, even though these animals have been dead for millions of years. By measuring the cross-sectional area of a major leg bone, palaeontologists can use mathematical techniques to estimate the total weight of the living animal. Another method consists of making scale models: the model's volume is measured by putting it in water, and this figure is scaled up to calculate the final weight. But neither of these methods is 100 per cent reliable. As a result, the true weight of the world's heaviest dinosaurs will probably never be known.

▷ Seen next to a Brachiosaurus, Troodon *looks in danger of being squashed.* Brachiosaurus *may have weighed up to 80 tonnes – about 2,500 times as much as* Troodon, *and about 80,000 times as much as* Saltopus, *the smallest dinosaur known.*

FOSSIL-HUNTING IN SOUTH AMERICA

SOUTH AMERICA HAS PRODUCED SOME OF THE EARLIEST FOSSIL DINOSAURS, AND ALSO THE LARGEST, AS WELL AS SOME REMARKABLE EXTINCT MAMMALS AND BIRDS FROM MORE RECENT TIMES.

The geological history of South America makes it a fascinating place. Until the middle of the Mesozoic Era, it was part of the great southern continent, Gondwana, which means that it shared many of the dinosaur families found in today's Africa and India. After the dinosaurs died out, South America became an island, before joining with North America in more recent times.

▽ *Rodolfo Coria – the scientist who unearthed* Argentiosaurus *– rests on one of the dinosaur's enormous spinal vertebrae.*

IN PATAGONIA

Over 150 years ago, the renowned English biologist Charles Darwin visited South America during his round-the-world voyage on HMS *Beagle*. As ship's naturalist, he found fossils of extinct mammals such as the giant ground sloth *Megatherium* – an animal almost as large as an elephant – which was buried in gravel near the shore. The first fossil *Megatherium* had been seen by European scientists 50 years before, but for Darwin the process of uncovering its remains was momentous. It helped him to appreciate the fact that extinction was a natural process – something that contributed to his theory of evolution.

Palaeontologists still comb the bleak Patagonian coastline

This fossilized skull, found in Ischigualasto National Park, Argentina, belonged to one of the earliest known dinosaurs, Eoraptor, a bipedal hunter just 1m long. Although it lived over 200 million years ago, several almost complete skeletons have been found. In outward appearance, this small reptile was remarkably similar to some predatory dinosaurs that lived 100 million years later.

today, collecting fossils from the crumbling sedimentary rocks. But some of the most important discoveries have been found much further inland, along the foothills that separate Argentina from neighbouring Chile. This is South America's dinosaur country – a dry and dramatic part of the world where much older rocks bring a wealth of remains to the surface.

THE HUNT FOR EARLY DINOSAURS

From the late 1950s onwards, the moon-like surroundings of Argentina's Ischigualasto National Park have been the scene of some major dinosaur discoveries. In 1958, a local farmer found the first fragments of a small meat-eating animal which lived during the late Triassic, making it the earliest dinosaur then known. Named *Herrerasaurus*, it threw new light on how dinosaurs might have originated from carnivorous reptiles (page 64). In 1988, American palaeontologist Paul Sereno found further remains – a complete *Herrerasaurus* skull and several partial skeletons. In 1991, he identified the remains of an even older animal, called *Eoraptor*, which provided clues as to how dinosaurs might have evolved.

As South America was part of Gondwana at the time when these animals were alive, it is unlikely that they lived only in this part of the world. But bare ground makes fossil-hunting easier, which is why Ischigualasto is one of South America's foremost fossil-hunting sites.

SOUTHERN GIANTS

South America is well-known as a source of fossil sauropods – particularly titanosaurs, which were widespread in the southern continents. The list of species discovered in Argentina reads almost like a road map, because many of them, such as *Saltasaurus* and *Neuquensaurus*, take their names from the provinces where their fossil remains were found. But pride of place among these giants goes to *Argentinosaurus*, an animal named by two leading palaeontologists, José F. Bonaparte and Rodolfo Coria, in 1993. *Argentinosaurus* may prove to be the world's largest dinosaur, although in North America, there are also several contenders.

Rodolfo Coria also identified a giant predator, *Giganotosaurus*, whose remains were spotted in 1994 by an amateur fossil-hunter in the foothills of the Andes. Weighing up to 8 tonnes, this tyrannosaur lookalike might have been the world's largest carnivorous dinosaur. Like *Argentinosaurus*, it lived throughout the late Cretaceous, until the Age of Reptiles came to an end. So the world's largest plant-eater and meat-eater may have lived at the same time, and also in the same place – a double first!

FLYING GIANTS

In Argentina, palaeontologists have also found the remains of some enormous birds. Some of these were flightless, but one, *Argentavis magnificens*, may well have been the largest ever to have existed. Discovered in 1979, in the dusty pampas west of Buenos Aires, this animal had a wingspan of about 7.5m, which is more than twice the size of the largest flying birds today. *Argentavis* lived about 6 million years ago, and it belonged to a group of vulture-like birds called the teratorns, which later became extinct. It probably hunted living prey, using its large hooked beak to make its kills. So did the phorusrhacoids or 'terror birds' – a line of flightless South American predators that stood up to 3m high. Fossils suggest that these fearsome animals ran down their prey, before using their beaks to rip it apart. Remains of over two dozen species have been found but, as with the teratorns, the entire group eventually disappeared.

◁ *In the far west of Argentina, the stark landscape of Ischigualasto National Park, with its strangely sculpted cliffs and plateaux, is a magnet for palaeontologists. Conditions can be tough: in summer the heat is stifling and the layers of pale clay-like rock give off an intense glare in the bright sunshine.*

△ *A team of excavators including Rodolfo Coria (centre) works at the Plaza Huincul site in Argentina, uncovering the enormous fossil bones of* Argentinosaurus huinculensis.

◁ *Unlike earlier reptiles,* Eoraptor *had fused vertebrae in its hip region. This gave it the extra structural strength needed to maintain an upright posture, with just two legs in contact with the ground.*

PLANT-EATING GIANTS

TITANOSAURS

Titanosaurs were the last sauropods to evolve, appearing in the late Jurassic and surviving some 80 million years until the end of the Cretaceous. They were found across most of the world, but they were most widespread in the ancient southern continent of Gondwana. South America – which formed part of Gondwana – is where most of their remains have been discovered. They bore some resemblance to diplodocids, but were unique among sauropods in having bony armour, which consisted of hard plates scattered over their backs. Their other claim to fame is that a few grew to a truly incredible size. Remains of one as yet unclassified sauropod were found in southern Patagonia in 1999. The fossils included two vertebrae measuring 1.2m in height, and a thighbone 1.8m long!

▽ *A titan among titans,* Argentinosaurus *may have been the largest dinosaur ever to have walked the Earth – albeit at a slow pace. As an adult, this gigantic animal would probably have been immune from attack by most predators, but its young would still have been vulnerable. Here, an adult is shown without armour-plating: whether it had plates is not known.*

ARGENTINOSAURUS
Argentina has produced some exciting fossil finds in recent years, and many palaeontologists believe that this species – named in 1993 – may turn out to be the largest dinosaur ever, although not the longest. So far, only a few vertebrae and limb bones have been found, but they are built on an awe-inspiring scale. The biggest of the vertebrae measures 1.5m in height, with a load-bearing centre the size of a small tree. Scaling up from remains like these, experts estimate that the complete animal may have weighed in the range of 80 to 100 tonnes. Like other titanosaurs, *Argentinosaurus* had some unusual anotomical features not found in other sauropods. It had an extra vertebra in its sacrum – the part of the backbone that joins on to the pelvic girdle. If it was like its relatives, its tail vertebrae would have been linked together with ball-and-socket joints. No traces of armour-plating have actually been found, but as these plates are often scattered after death, it is still possible that *Argentinosaurus* shared this common family feature. With so little fossil evidence, it is hard to say how this immense animal lived, although given its size, it would probably have needed to eat several tonnes of food a day.

MAXIMUM LENGTH 30m
TIME Late Cretaceous
FOSSIL FINDS South America (Argentina)

ANTARCTOSAURUS
Despite its name, remains of this dinosaur have not been found in the Antarctic, but they have been discovered in South America and India, which once formed part of the great southern continent, Gondwana. None of these fossils is complete, but – unusually for a titanosaur – they include parts of the skull. From these finds, *Antarctosaurus* seems to have been one of the biggest and most widespread dinosaurs in the southern hemisphere. It had a square-ended lower jaw and small teeth, but so far no traces of armour-plating have been unearthed. In South America, fossilized eggs have been found which are likely to have belonged either to this species, or to other members of the titanosaur family. About the size of a small melon, some of them contain the fossilized embryos complete with impressions of skin.

MAXIMUM LENGTH 18m
TIME Late Cretaceous
FOSSIL FINDS South America (Argentina, Uruguay, Chile, Brazil), Asia (India)

△ *When an adult,* Antarctosaurus *probably weighed more than 35 tonnes. Like several of its relatives, it is believed to have had a covering of bony plates, or osteoderms.*

SALTASAURUS

Saltasaurus was officially named in 1980, after a province in Argentina where it was found. Compared to *Argentinosaurus*, it was a relatively small animal, with a back not much higher than an elephant's, although with a much longer and heavier body overall. Several fossilized skeletons have been found, with thousands of small bony plates lying around them, leading palaeontologists to conclude that these plates would have covered their skin like armour. Some of the plates are no larger than peas, and are attached to small relics of skin. Others are about the size of a human hand, and may have had a defensive spike. This discovery solved a long-running puzzle, because scattered plates have been uncovered before *Saltasaurus* fossils were found. Some scientists thought they belonged to nodosaurs (page 164), a group of unrelated dinosaurs that used armour for protection. *Saltasaurus* had robust limbs and a flexible tail, which may have helped it to sit upright to feed. Remains of *Antarctosaurus* and *Argyrosaurus* have been found close to *Saltasaurus* fossils, raising the possibility that they too would have had armour-plated skin.

MAXIMUM LENGTH	12m
TIME	Late Cretaceous
FOSSIL FINDS	South America (Argentina, Uruguay)

△ Saltasaurus *(centre right), with its bony body armour which would have protected it from predators, was a compact and stocky titanosaur with a small head and blunt teeth.*

NEUQUENSAURUS

Named after a town in Patagonia, this dinosaur closely resembled *Saltasaurus*, with a relatively small body covered in bony plates. The evidence for this comes from several fossil finds, including vertebrae, limb bones and plates that were found in 1997. The similarities between the two dinosaurs seem to be very strong, and it is possible that future finds may show that they were actually the same dinosaur.

MAXIMUM LENGTH	15m
TIME	Late Cretaceous
FOSSIL FINDS	South America (Argentina)

ARGYROSAURUS

The first remains of *Argyrosaurus* were discovered in the late 1800s. Its name means 'silver lizard' – a reference to Argentina, or the land of silver, which is where its fossils have been found. A massive animal, weighing as much as 80 tonnes, *Argyrosaurus* is known from only a few body parts, including the legs and some vertebrae. Palaeontologists are not all agreed about where this animal fits into the titanosaur family – some think that the fossils may actually belong to *Antarctosaurus*.

MAXIMUM LENGTH	18m
TIME	Late Cretaceous
FOSSIL FINDS	South America (Argentina)

HYPSELOSAURUS

Hypselosaurus was a relatively compact European titanosaur, first identified from fossils in southern France nearly 150 years ago. The fossils were missing their skulls, but alongside them were several dozen football-sized eggs. These eggs were almost certainly laid by female *Hypselosaurus* and, at about 30cm long, they are some of the largest dinosaur eggs currently known. Sauropods probably squatted down when they were ready to lay, but they may also have had an egg-laying tube that allowed the eggs to slide gently down to the ground.

MAXIMUM LENGTH	12m
TIME	Late Cretaceous
FOSSIL FINDS	Europe (France, Spain)

PLANT-EATING GIANTS

MALAWISAURUS

Originally known as *Gigantosaurus* – a name easily confused with *Giganotosaurus* (page 143), a meat-eating allosaur – *Malawisaurus* is the oldest-known titanosaur from Africa, dating back to over 100 million years ago. Relatively small by titanosaur standards, it may have been armour-plated, but fossilized plates have yet to be found. However, some *Malawisaurus* fossils do include parts of the animal's skull – a rare situation for a titanosaur, and for sauropods as a whole. Recently, titanosaur remains have also been found in nearby Madagascar. By a stroke of luck, these remains also include parts of the skull.

MAXIMUM LENGTH 10m

TIME Early Cretaceous

FOSSIL FINDS Africa (Malawi)

TITANOSAURUS

The most widespread member of its family, *Titanosaurus* was first discovered in 1877 in India. The original fossil consisted of a broken thighbone and some tail vertebrae, but since then further finds have been made in many places around the world, including Madagascar. The Indian find was particularly important, because it was the first major dinosaur discovery in what was once part of Gondwana, although continental drift was not known about at the time. Some palaeontologists think that *Titanosaurus* had armour-plating, but the evidence is uncertain.

MAXIMUM LENGTH 20m

TIME Late Cretaceous

FOSSIL FINDS South America (Argentina), Europe (France), Asia (India), Africa (Madagascar)

ALAMOSAURUS

Alamosaurus is the only titanosaur that has been found in North America. It was also one of the very last sauropods, surviving right until the end of the Cretaceous Period when it – and all other dinosaurs – died out. Found in the western USA, its remains are more complete than those of most of its relatives although, as usual, they are missing the skull. *Alamosaurus* weighed about 30 tonnes, and had a long whip-ended tail. Unlike many other titanosaurs, it seems to have had no body armour. Even when it was alive, *Alamosaurus* would have looked like a relic from the past, because by the late Cretaceous Period, sauropods were no longer the dominant plant-eaters, and had dwindled to a fraction of the importance they had had in Jurassic times. *Alamosaurus'* status as North America's sole titanosaur is probably explained by geological changes. For millions of years, North and South America were separated by sea, but during the late Cretaceous, temporary land-bridges linked the two continents. *Alamosaurus* – or its ancestors – took this opportunity to head north, but its history was cut short when the Age of Dinosaurs came to an end.

MAXIMUM LENGTH 21m

TIME Late Cretaceous

FOSSIL FINDS North America (Montana, New Mexico, Texas, Utah)

▽ Alamosaurus *lived in North America in the dying days of the dinosaurs. It was named after the Ojo Alamo trading post in New Mexico, where one set of its remains was found.*

ORNITHOPODS

The ornithopods were a group of ornithischian or 'bird-hipped' plant-eaters that first appeared early in the Jurassic, about 200 million years ago. They included the iguanodonts – some of the first dinosaurs to be discovered – as well as the hadrosaurs, a remarkable family of reptiles often adorned with bizarre crests. Together with the fabrosaurs, heterodontosaurs and hypsilophodonts, these animals included some of the most successful and numerous plant-eaters during the Cretaceous. Ornithopods never equalled sauropods in size, but they were abundant when sauropods themselves were in decline.

DANGER ON THE HORIZON

Making their daily visit to a sandy riverbed, a mixed group of hadrosaurs – including mothers with their young – pause to drink and rest in the morning sunshine. But this tranquil scene is not destined to last. A tyrannosaur has appeared on a distant sandbank, and some of the adult hadrosaurs are already getting ready to run. The hadrosaurs could call to each other using their hollow crests to warn of the impending danger. See key on page 94.

LIFE IN A GROUP

FOR PLANT-EATING DINOSAURS, HERDING TOGETHER WAS A VITAL SURVIVAL TECHNIQUE IN A WORLD FULL OF DANGEROUS PREDATORS.

Millions of years after the dinosaurs died out, there is still plenty of evidence showing that some of them lived in herds. This evidence includes fossilized 'mass graves', where entire herds were overtaken by disasters such as sand storms, as well as communal nesting sites, and sets of tracks left by herds on the move.

HERD SIZES

How big were dinosaur herds? Fossilized bones and tracks provide the best clues, but they have to be interpreted with care. Animals can be at the same place at the same time without forming a herd. This often happens at waterholes, when animals that normally live on their own gather to drink. Collections of bones can also be misleading, because they may belong to animals that died weeks or even years apart. This can happen when they fall victim to the same hazard – a slippery slope – or when hunters use a favourite spot for attacking their prey.

Palaeontologists have examined many sets of fossils, and come up with a variety of figures for different species. There are records of iguanodonts travelling in groups of four or five, while hadrosaurs such as *Maiasaura* seem to have lived in herds of several hundred, scattered over a wide area.

DINOSAUR SOCIAL LIFE

Herd-forming species almost certainly showed complex forms of behaviour. As in today's herding mammals, animals of different ages and sexes would have had a different status, and often a different position in the herd. Some fossilized tracks back up this idea, because the smallest prints – belonging to young animals – are often found in the centre, while those left by the largest adults are at the front, and around the sides. This would have protected the

young, and enabled the adults to form a barrier if a predator did try to attack.

JOINING AND LEAVING

Because animals grow up and die, the make-up of a herd changes all the time. But herds can change in other ways. In many of today's herding animals, such as elephants, males leave the herd once they can look after themselves, and live in 'bachelor herds' for several years. The strongest adult males then head herds of their own, which include several females and young. It is likely that some dinosaurs had similar social systems. During their time in bachelor herds, the males would have engaged in mock fights with their rivals. This kind of fighting is unlikely to have caused permanent injuries, but it would have sorted out the strongest and fittest males, allowing them to father the most young.

INDIVIDUAL RECOGNITION

Dinosaur fossils often show variations between members of the same species. The most obvious differences are between males and females, but there are also differences between one individual and another. These small variations may have worked like identity badges, helping herd members to identify each other. Because dinosaurs were often long-lived, older animals could have decades of experience in recognizing the other members of their herd. Each animal would have known where it fitted in the herd's 'pecking order', and where its place was if the herd came under attack.

▽ *Threatened by a pair of tyrannosaurs, adult* Centrosaurus *form a defensive ring around their young. In this kind of emergency, the young animals would have instinctively rushed for the middle of the ring, while the adults turned their horns on the aggressors. The disadvantage of the ring defence was that the entire herd was effectively trapped – until the predators either abandoned their attack or made a kill.*

ORNITHOPODS

HYPSILOPHODONTS

The hypsilophodonts were the dinosaur world's equivalent of horses and antelopes, living in large herds, and feeding on low-growing plants. Like other ornithopods, they had a short, beak-like muzzle, muscular cheeks and well-developed chewing teeth. Their cheeks were an important step forward, because they helped them to hold their food in place to chew. Hypsilophodonts were fairly small animals, but during their 100-million-year history they became widespread, and were eventually found on almost every continent, including Australia.

▽ Hypsilophodon *(left) gets its name from its tall, ridged cheek teeth. The upper and lower sets met to form a perfect grinding surface, and they were self-sharpening – features that were shared by all members of the family.* Dryosaurus *(right) used its beak to tear up mouthfuls of vegetation. While it was chewing, it would probably have raised its head so that it could watch for danger – a kind of behaviour seen in most of today's plant-eaters that live in open habitats.*

DRYOSAURUS

Dryosaurus was a medium-sized member of the family, and one of the earliest to evolve. Its body was supported by a pair of sturdy legs, with a stiff, heavy tail acting as a counterbalance for its head and neck, and its large plant-eater's stomach. Its muzzle ended in a hard-edged beak which could tear off plants close to the ground. Like other ornithopods, it had few defences, and it is likely to have been an effective middle-distance runner. Unusually for a hypsilophodont, its feet had only three toes.

MAXIMUM LENGTH	4m
TIME	Late Jurassic
FOSSIL FINDS	Africa (Tanzania), North America (Colorado, Wyoming)

HYPSILOPHODON

Standing less that 1m tall, with a head no larger than a human hand, *Hypsilophodon* is known from some superbly preserved fossils. They include a group of about two dozen animals, discovered on the Isle of Wight, which may have been members of a small herd trapped by a rising tide. These fossils show that it had five-fingered hands and four-toed feet, and perhaps a double row of bony plates running down its back. During the 19th century, when *Hypsilophodon* was first discovered, British zoologist Thomas Huxley suggested it was shaped for climbing and might have lived in trees like today's tree kangaroo. Palaeontologists now think that it is likely to have lived on the ground.

MAXIMUM LENGTH	2.3m
TIME	Early Cretaceous
FOSSIL FINDS	Europe (UK, Spain, Portugal), North America (South Dakota)

HYPSILOPHODONTS

LEAELLYNASAURA

Studies of this Australian hypsilophodont have provided support for the idea that some dinosaurs were warm-blooded (page 148). Its fossilized remains were found at a site on the coast of South Australia, known as Dinosaur Cove, which was well within the Antarctic Circle when *Leaellynasaura* was alive. Although the climate was significantly

FULGUROTHERIUM

This dinosaur was named after Lightning Ridge in New South Wales, a well-known opal mining area and dinosaur fossil site, where very incomplete remains – a skull, femur and teeth – were found in 1932.

MAXIMUM LENGTH	2m
TIME	Early Cretaceous
FOSSIL FINDS	Australia (New South Wales)

△ *Weighing as little as 10 kilos,* Leaellynasaura *(left) was about the size of an ostrich. If it was warm-blooded it may have had feather-like insulation. It lived in herds, feeding on cycads, ferns and conifers.* Fulgurotherium *(right) also lived during the Cretaceous, when Australia was one of the coldest parts of the southern continent, Gondwana.*

warmer then, life this far south would still have been a challenge – particularly in winter, when daylight and food were in short supply. If *Laeallynasaura* was warm-blooded rather than cold-blooded, it could have remained active all year round.

There is no physical evidence for this, but *Leaellynasaura* did have enlarged eye sockets and a large brain, which mean that it would have been good at finding its way in the dim winter light. *Leallynasaura* was discovered in 1989, and named after the daughter of the two palaeontologists who found it.

MAXIMUM LENGTH	3m
TIME	Mid Cretaceous
FOSSIL FINDS	Australia (Victoria)

TENONTOSAURUS

Tenontosaurus was exceptionally large for a hypsilophodont, and this, with details of its skull anatomy, make some palaeontologists think that it may have been an iguanodont. However, its teeth are of the typical hypsilophodont type – an important pointer, because it is rare for identical tooth types to evolve twice. Like other ornithopods, *Tenontosaurus* probably dropped onto all fours when feeding, but as it weighed over 1 tonne, it may have rested like this as well.

MAXIMUM LENGTH	7m
TIME	Early Cretaceous
FOSSIL FINDS	North America (Arizona, Montana, Oklahoma, Texas)

Cambrian	Ordovician	Silurian	Devonian	Carboniferous	Permian	Triassic

ORNITHOPODS

FABROSAURS

Small and lightly built, the fabrosaurs were the reptilian equivalent of hares or small deer, using their narrow mouths to pick out nutritious vegetation on or close to the ground. They walked and ran on their back legs alone, using their long tails for balance. Most of them were less than 2m long and, unlike many other plant-eaters, they may have foraged alone. Fabrosaurs were among the earliest ornithopods to evolve. Some palaeontologists actually consider them to be a parallel group, because they did not have the features shared by ornithopods as a whole.

▽ *Although not tough enough to deter large predators,* Scutellosaurus' *body armour would have made it a tricky target for a hunter nearer its own size. Body armour was an unusual feature in dinosaurs this small.*

▽ *From the neck down,* Lesothosaurus *looked similar to some of the smaller theropods, but its shorter jaws showed that it was a plant-eater, not a hunter.*

LESOTHOSAURUS

Only a handful of *Lesothosaurus* fossils are known, but one set is very interesting, because it shows a pair of animals huddled together, possibly in a burrow underground. *Lesothosaurus* lived in a hot, dry habitat, and the likeliest explanation for this huddle is that the two animals were aestivating – a summer equivalent of hibernation. By becoming dormant, they would have saved energy at a time of year when plant food was difficult to find. Physically, *Lesothosaurus* looked like some small predatory dinosaurs, but its pointed teeth were shaped for dealing with plants. It had long leg bones, and its defence against predators would have been to run away.

MAXIMUM LENGTH	1m
TIME	Early Jurassic
FOSSIL FINDS	Africa (Lesotho)

▷ Echindon *is sometimes classified as a heterodontosaur, as it shared their pattern of varied teeth. As a small plant-eater, it could not precess large quantities of food, and it probably survived by being selective about what it ate. Its narrow snout was ideal for this way of life.*

SCUTELLOSAURUS

This fabrosaur's name means 'little shield lizard'. It is the only fabrosaur known to have had body armour, consisting of small bony plates down its neck and back. This coat of armour brought practical problems – chiefly extra weight. *Scutellosaurus* may have spent some of its time on all fours, to spread the load. However, even with its armour, it probably weighed only about 10kg.

MAXIMUM LENGTH	1.2m
TIME	Early Jurassic
FOSSIL FINDS	North America (Arizona)

ECHINDON

Echinodon was a tiny plant-eater, weighing not much more than a large pet cat. It had a small head and narrow snout, with two types of teeth. It probably nipped off nutritious new plant growth, leaving tougher leaves for other animals.

MAXIMUM LENGTH	60cm
TIME	Late Jurassic
FOSSIL FINDS	Europe (England)

HETERODONTOSAURS

Dinosaurs sometimes had lots of teeth, but as a rule, each kind of dinosaur had only a single type. Heterdontosaurs were quite different, because they had teeth that were specially shaped for carrying out different tasks. This kind of specialized dentition is common in mammals, including humans, but in reptiles it was – and still is – highly unusual. Heterodontosaurs walked on their hind legs, and they relied on speed to escape from their enemies.

HETERODONTOSAURUS

When *Heterodontosaurus* was discovered, in the 1960s, it quickly became clear that it was an early ornithopod, but one with some remarkable features. It had three types of teeth: sharp cutting teeth at the front of its upper jaw, which bit down onto a toothless lower beak, and cheek teeth, which ground up its food. It also had two pairs of extra-long teeth, or tusks, that resembled a mammal's stabbing canines – strange for an animal that clearly fed on plants. The most widely accepted explanation is that *Heterodontosaurus* used the tusks for fighting rivals. A very similar animal, called *Abrictosaurus*, did not have tusks, and many experts think this is actually a female *Heterodontosaurus* that has been classified by mistake. When adult, *Heterodontosaurus* stood about 50cm high, and probably weighed less than 20kg.

MAXIMUM LENGTH 1.2m

TIME Early Jurassic

FOSSIL FINDS Africa (South Africa)

LYCORHINUS

Like *Heterodontosaurus*, this small plant-eater also lived in southern Africa, but so far only its lower jaw has been discovered. It was thought to belong to a mammal, because it had specialized teeth, including two tusks. However, a closer look showed that the animal's lower jaw was made of several bones rather than one – a sign that it was actually a reptile. Judging from its jaw, *Lycorhinus* was similar in size to *Heterodontosaurus*, and would also have been a browser feeding on low-growing plants.

MAXIMUM LENGTH 1.2m

TIME Early Jurassic

FOSSIL FINDS Africa (South Africa)

PISANOSAURUS

Uncertainty surrounds this small South American plant-eater, which was discovered in the 1960s. From its fragmentary remains, some palaeontologists have concluded that it was an ornithopod, perhaps belonging to the heterodontosaur line. If true, this would make it one of the earliest ornithischians or bird-hipped dinosaurs (page 70). If they were heterodontosaurs, this family provides the evidence that Africa and South America were joined together in Triassic times.

MAXIMUM LENGTH 1m

TIME Late Triassic

FOSSIL FINDS South America (Argentina)

△ *The name* Heterodontosaurus *means 'different teeth'. The animal in this reconstruction has large canines, which may have been a feature found only in males. The front of the lower jaw was toothless, while the upper jaw had teeth, an interesting reversal of the situation in many of today's grazing mammals.*

◁ Pisanosaurus *was discovered in the same rock formation as* Herrerasaurus *and* Eoraptor, *two other very early dinosaurs from South America. However, unlike these animals, it was a plant-eater, although it still retained the primitive feature of walking on two legs.*

ORNITHOPODS

IGUANODONTS

Iguanodonts were among the first dinosaurs to be discovered and identified, nearly 200 years ago. They were probably descended from the hypsilophodonts, but they got their name because their teeth resembled those of present-day iguanas. Iguanodonts were large, relatively slow-moving plant-eaters. Their back legs were larger than their front legs, and they could probably move on either four legs or two. Most species had sharply pointed 'thumbs'.

▷ *Iguanodonts may have used their spike-like thumbs as defensive weapons. Here, an* Iguanodon *fends off a predatory theropod.*

▽ *Many iguanodonts had dextrous front feet, with four fingers, as well as a sharp thumb. The three middle claws had hoof-like claws. The fourth was much smaller and could fold across the palm. It allowed them to pick up food.*

IGUANODON
Easily the biggest member of its family, *Iguanodon* stood three times the height of a man, and weighed 4.5 tonnes. It is one of the most famous dinosaurs, since it was discovered in 1822, by Mary Mantell, when dinosaurs were still unknown to science. The English geologist who described it – Mary's husband, Gideon Mantell – realized that it was a giant reptile, but mistakenly thought that its thumb spikes were horns. *Iguanodon* was a highly successful plant-eater with a long skull, beak-like jaws and rows of grinding cheek-teeth that help to distinguish ornithopods from other herbivorous dinosaurs. It lived on all the continents except Antarctica. In some fossil sites – for example in Belgium – the remains of many iguanodons have been found side by side, suggesting that they lived in herds.

MAXIMUM LENGTH	9m
TIME	Early Cretaceous
FOSSIL FINDS	Europe, North Africa, Asia (Mongolia), North America

CALLOVOSAURUS
Little is known about *Callovosaurus*, because the only fossil remains are of a single thigh bone, which was discovered in England. However, the rocks surrounding this fossil show that this is the earliest iguanodont that has been found so far. It was probably similar in general appearance to *Camptosaurus*, although little more than half its length.

MAXIMUM LENGTH	3.5m
TIME	Mid Jurassic
FOSSIL FINDS	Europe (England)

CAMPTOSAURUS
Another early iguanodont, *Camptosaurus* was common in North America and Europe about 150 million years ago, where it almost certainly lived in herds. It was a heavy-boned creature, weighing over one tonne, with much shorter arms than legs, and a long skull that ended in a toothless beak. Its teeth were at the rear of its mouth – the ideal place for producing the force needed to crush plant food. While earlier plant-eaters had to pause to breathe, *Camptosaurus* had a long bony palate attached to the roof of its mouth, allowing it to breathe and eat simultaneously. Unlike *Iguanodon*, its wrists were not well-developed, which suggests that it walked on its back legs, rather than on all fours.

MAXIMUM LENGTH	7m
TIME	Late Jurassic
FOSSIL FINDS	Western North America, Europe (England, Portugal)

VECTISAURUS
Vectisaurus – named after the Latin word for the Isle of Wight, UK – was a very close relative of *Iguanodon*, and lived at the same time. It differed only in its smaller size, and in having a spiny ridge running along its

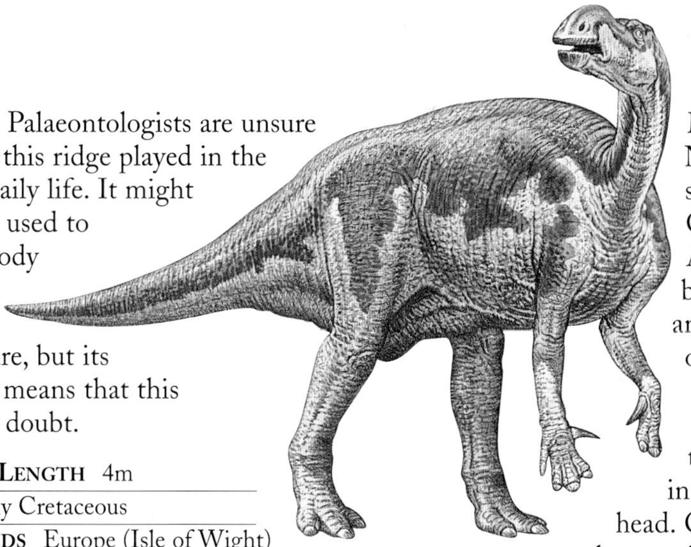

backbone. Palaeontologists are unsure what part this ridge played in the animal's daily life. It might have been used to regulate body temperature, but its small size means that this is open to doubt.

MAXIMUM LENGTH 4m
TIME Early Cretaceous
FOSSIL FINDS Europe (Isle of Wight)

OURANOSAURUS

Like *Vectisaurus*, this animal also had a spiny ridge along its back, but it was much more pronounced, forming a fan-shaped structure up to 50cm high. The ridge ran from the shoulders and extended halfway down the tail. *Ouranosaurus* also had an unusual head for an iguanodont, with a flat top, a raised bony brow above the eyes, and a sloping snout leading to a wide beak-like mouth.

MAXIMUM LENGTH 7m
TIME Early Cretaceous
FOSSIL FINDS West Africa

MUTTABURRASAURUS

Named after a small town in Queensland, Australia, *Muttaburrasaurus* is believed to have been another close relative of *Iguanodon*. It was similar, although smaller, with some tell-tale differences in the structure of its head. One of these was a characteristic bony lump on its nose, which may have been used in courtship displays. Another was a pair of unusually large nostrils, suggesting that it needed a good sense of smell to find food. *Muttaburrasaurus* also had teeth shaped for cutting rather than grinding, which may mean that it was at least partly carnivorous. Like most other iguanodonts, it had large spike-like thumbs.

MAXIMUM LENGTH 7m
TIME Early Cretaceous
FOSSIL FINDS Australia

◁ *The first remains of* Muttaburrasaurus *were discovered in 1963. This iguanodont lived at a time when Australia was slowly separating from other southern continents, carrying dinosaurs and other animals with it. The dinosaurs of Australia are still poorly known.*

▽ Ouranosaurus *herds once roamed what is now West Africa, feeding on plants in the hot and sometimes swampy landscape. The fan-shaped skin on their backs may have helped with heat regulation. By turning the fan to face the sun, they could have absorbed heat.*

COLOURS AND CAMOUFLAGE

AT ONE TIME, DINOSAURS WERE THOUGHT OF AS BEING UNIFORMLY DRAB AND GREY. BY CONTRAST, TODAY'S EXPERTS BELIEVE THAT THE DINOSAUR WORLD MAY HAVE BEEN A SURPRISINGLY COLOURFUL PLACE.

Fossils reveal a great deal about the internal structure of dinosaurs, but they very rarely include any signs of their skin. This is because, like most other soft parts of the body, skin usually breaks down before fossils are formed. Occasionally, some traces of the skin texture are left, and these show that dinosaurs were often covered with pebble-like nodules, or sometimes lizard-like scales. But so far, no clear evidence of skin pigments has been found. Without these, palaeontologists have to rely on studies of living animals to picture what dinosaurs may have looked like.

HIDING AWAY
The colours and patterns of dinosaurs almost certainly depended on how they lived. Giant plant-eaters, such as the brachiosaurs and titanosaurs, had relatively few enemies when they were fully grown, so they had very little need to hide away. Added to this, their huge size means that they would have been almost impossible to conceal. As a result, they probably had plain but muted colours – the sort of colour schemes that all dinosaurs were once thought to have, and the ones that elephants and rhinos have today.

But with smaller plant-eaters, such as hadrosaurs, the situation was quite different. These animals had many enemies, and one of their best defences – apart from running away – was to avoid being seen. Over a long period of time, evolution may well have given them camouflage as a form of self-protection. To see what they might have looked like, biologists turn to reptiles that live today. Plant-eating reptiles are now quite rare, and most of them – such as iguanas – are brown or green.

CHANGING COLOUR
Some of today's reptiles, most famously the chameleons, can change their colour to improve their background. It is quite likely that some dinosaurs were also able to do this, because the few fossils that have been found show that their skin seems to have the same structure. But chameleons do not switch colour only to hide – they also do it to show their mood. Unlike camouflage colours, these mood-indicating colours are often vivid, with contrasting streaks and stripes. As a form of communication, they are difficult to miss.

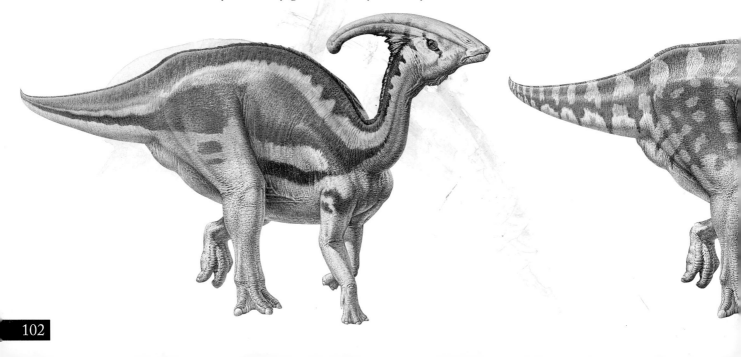

FLUSHES AND BLUSHES

The variations in skin colours would have been produced by pigment-containing cells close to the surface of the skin. By altering the distribution of pigment in each cell, different colour schemes could be produced. But there is another way that dinosaurs might have coloured up – by altering the flow of blood. Many experts believed this could have happened in stegosaurs (pages 158–159), which had rows of bony plates extending down their backs. There are signs that these plates had a rich blood supply flowing through them and through a surface layer of skin. Stegosaurs may have used the plates to warm up or cool down, 'blushing' as they increased their supply of blood.

These blushes might have had a double function, by acting as a form of communication between the dinosaurs as well. It is not hard to imagine one blushing male *Stegosaurus* squaring up to another, as the two prepare to fight.

SEX DIFFERENCES

In living reptiles, males and females often look similar, but the same is not true of many birds. As dinosaur were the ancestors of birds, it is possible that they too showed marked colour differences between the two sexes. In some species – for example the bone-headed dinosaurs (pages 166–167) – males and females differed in size, so they may have differed in colour as well.

FOSSIL EVIDENCE

This remarkable fossil from Wyoming, USA, shows the knobbly skin of Edmontosaurus, a duck-billed dinosaur. The fossil was formed from a mummified corpse. The process of mummification turns the skin hard, so that it fossilizes along with the animal's bones. Traces of skin texture are sometimes preserved in dinosaurs that died on damp mud. The mud makes a 'mould' of the skin, and this is preserved when the mud is fossilized.

▽ *These three reconstructions show imaginary colour schemes for* Parasaurolophus, *a duck-billed dinosaur. Even though it grew to 10m long,* Parasaurolophus *would have made a tempting target for tyrannosaurs, and camouflage would have been a useful first step towards avoiding attack. The green and brown pigments shown here are typical of ones found in living reptiles.*

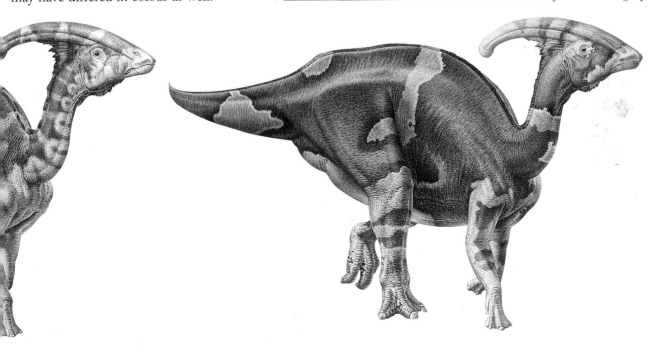

HADROSAURS

Hadrosaurs are often known as duck-billed dinosaurs because they had flattened beak-like snouts. Some also sported hollow crests, which had a variety of eccentric shapes. These crests contained nasal tubes, and it is possible that they enabled hadrosaurs to make loud calls (page 112). Hadrosaurs were herd-forming vegetarians, feeding on four legs, but able to run away on two. They were one of the last and most successful of the dinosaur families, originating in Asia, and spreading to North America and Europe.

MAIASAURA

Many of the dinosaurs left few traces to show how they lived and bred, but with *Maiasaura*, the evidence is astounding. Palaeontologists have discovered this hadrosaur's nests and eggs, and animals at almost every age, from hatchlings to adults. The females built nest mounds out of mud, and they may have covered their eggs with soil to keep them warm, and hidden from hungry eyes.

After the young hatched, it is likely that the females cared for them until they were capable of fending for themselves. Fossils also show that *Maiasaura* lived in herds – possibly thousands strong. *Maiasaura* had only a modest crest, but when fully grown, it weighed up to four tonnes. Fossilized droppings indicate that it fed on tough, woody plants.

MAXIMUM LENGTH 9m
TIME Late Cretaceous
FOSSIL FINDS North America

BACTROSAURUS

Bactrosaurus was probably one of the earliest hadrosaurs to evolve, with fewer teeth in its cheeks than later species. It was also one of the smallest, although still a substantial animal. It had a flat, uncrested head, and high spines on its vertebrae, producing a ridge down its back. Unlike larger hadrosaurs, it always walked on its hind legs.

MAXIMUM LENGTH 6m
TIME Late Cretaceous
FOSSIL FINDS Asia (Mongolia, China)

HADROSAURUS

Hadrosaurus, which means 'big lizard', was the first dinosaur to be discovered in the USA, in 1858. The partial remains – which were missing the skull – were enough to show that this massive plant-eater could stand on two legs. Since then, many more fossils have been found, revealing that *Hadrosaurus* had a duck-billed head with a raised lump on its snout, but not a crest, like some other members of its family. It also had a battery of grinding teeth at the back of its jaws. These were continuously replaced as they wore down, unlike the teeth of today's plant-eating mammals, which have to last for life. *Hadrosaurus* fed on a tough diet of leaves, branches and seeds.

MAXIMUM LENGTH 10m
TIME Late Cretaceous
FOSSIL FINDS North America (New Jersey, Montana, New Mexico, and Alberta in Canada)

◁ *Standing by her nest mound, a female* Maiasaura *tends her newly hatched young.* Maiasaura *nests were up to 2m across, and held up to two dozen grapefruit-sized eggs.*

HADROSAURS

TSINTAOSAURUS

This Chinese hadrosaur has a particularly bizarre crest, consisting of a single 'horn' nearly 1m long, emerging from a point between the eyes. When the first fossilized skull was found, the crest was thought to be an accidental result of preservation. However, further finds showing the same feature proved that this was not the case. The crest is usually shown as jutting forwards, but no one knows exactly how it was positioned in life. It may have been an isolated structure – making *Tsintaosaurus* look like the dinosaur equivalent of a unicorn – but it is also possible that it was connected to flaps of skin. Otherwise, *Tsintaosaurus* seems to have had a typical hadrosaur build, with relatively small front legs, but much larger hind ones.

MAXIMUM LENGTH	10m
TIME	Late Cretaceous
FOSSIL FINDS	Asia (China)

CORYTHOSAURUS

Corythosaurus – meaning 'helmet lizard' – was a large hadrosaur with a dome-shaped crest. The crest was hollow, and it contained spaces that were connected to its nasal passages. The crest's size varied from one animal to another, and was probably biggest in mature males. This size difference makes it likely that the crest was used in courtship displays, but it may also have played a part in helping *Corythosaurus* to keep cool. Fossilized impressions of this animal's skin show that it had a pebbly texture.

MAXIMUM LENGTH	9m
TIME	Late Cretaceous
FOSSIL FINDS	North America (Alberta, Canada, and Montana, USA)

EDMONTOSAURUS

Hadrosaurs were the only dinosaurs that could chew their food, thanks to their unusual teeth, which were arranged in several interlocking rows at the back of their jaws. *Edmontosaurus* – one of the largest of the family – had up to 1,000 teeth, which were brought together by powerful cheek muscles. Fossils of mummified animals show that *Edmontosaurus* had raised nodules on the surface of its skin, and many scientists think that it had loose skin around its nose. It may have been able to inflate this like a balloon, either as a mating ritual or as a warning to rivals. Like other hadrosaurs, its only real defence was to run away from danger on its back legs, although it might have been able to swim. Its size meant that it was no sprinter, leaving it vulnerable to tyrannosaurs and other giant predators.

MAXIMUM LENGTH	13m
TIME	Late Cretaceous
FOSSIL FINDS	North America (Alberta, Canada, and Montana, USA)

KRITOSAURUS

Very similar in size and appearance to *Hadrosaurus*, this crestless hadrosaur may have been one of its closest relatives. Like *Hadrosaurus*, it had a bony lump on its snout, making it look as if it had a broken nose. It probably weighed between 2 and 3 tonnes. Its remains were found in 1910 by Barnum Brown, a great collector from the American Museum of Natural History in New York.

MAXIMUM LENGTH	13m
TIME	Late Cretaceous
FOSSIL FINDS	North America (Texas, New Mexico)

▽ *The hadrosaur family divided into two groups.* Tstintaosaurus *and* Corythosaurus *belonged to the lambeosaurine group, containing species with flamboyant crests.* Edmontosaurus *and* Kritosaurus *belonged to the hadrosaurine group – their crests were either small or non-existent.*

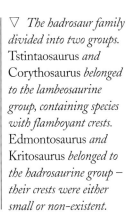

Corythosaurus

Tstintaosaurus

Edmontosaurus

Kritosaurus

ORNITHOPODS

▷ Fossils of Lambeosaurus magnicristatus *have been found in Alberta, Canada and Montana in the USA. The animal's helmet-shaped crest had a small, backward-pointing spike, but this was probably covered by a flap of skin which merged with the neck. This illustration shows an adult male.*

LAMBEOSAURUS

Lambeosaurus is the largest duck-billed dinosaur so far discovered. One species, *Lambeosaurus lambei*, had a bizarre two-part crest (page 92), consisting of a backward-pointing spike, and a forward-pointing part that looked like the blade of a hatchet, emerging from between its eyes. Another species, *Lambeosaurus magnicristatus*, looked more like *Corythosaurus* (page 105), with a dome-shaped crest. At one time, it was thought that *Lambeosaurus* and its relatives fed in water, using their tails as paddles, but most palaeontologists are now convinced that they lived on land.

MAXIMUM LENGTH	15m
TIME	Late Cretaceous
FOSSIL FINDS	North America

▷ Saurolophus *had a long, flattened head ending in a horn-like crest. Unusually, it also had a ring of bones around its eyes – a feature common in reptiles, but absent from many other members of the hadrosaur family. Its long 'beak' was toothless, but hundreds of teeth were packed together towards the rear of the animal's jaws.*

SAUROLOPHUS

Found in North America and Asia, *Saurolophus* had a solid bony crest, about 15cm long, on top of its head. Some palaeontologists think that the crest may have been connected to a flap of skin that could be inflated with air. If this is true, *Saurolophus* could have used it to produce honking sounds, which would have carried far and wide to attract mates, or warn the rest of the herd of danger. Many fossils have been found, the largest specimens coming from Asia.

MAXIMUM LENGTH	14m
TIME	Late Cretaceous
FOSSIL FINDS	North America, Asia (Mongolia)

▷ Parasaurolophus' *crest was the longest of all the hadrosaurs. Males had larger crests than females, giving strength to the theory that their elongated crests were primarily used in courtship, either through their appearance, or by making sounds.*

PARASAUROLOPHUS

With its extraordinary crest, this dinosaur was one of the most remarkable products of the dinosaur age. The crest was up to 1.8m long and it swept backwards from the animal's head, ending in a bony knob. The nostrils were connected to the crest by hollow tubes, which ran all the way along the crest, and then back down. At first sight, this bizarre structure looks like some kind of snorkel, but because it was not open-ended, it could not have worked in this way. Instead, it may have been used during courtship displays, and could have produced calls as deep as a foghorn, which would have been audible many kilometres away. *Parasaurolophus* had well-developed front legs, suggesting that it spent most of its time on all fours.

MAXIMUM LENGTH	10m
TIME	Late Cretaceous
FOSSIL FINDS	North America

ANATOSAURUS

A lot is known about *Anatosaurus* because some exceptionally well-preserved fossils have been found, as well as some 'mummified' specimens that reveal details of skin and internal organs. Weighing over 3 tonnes, it was a classic duck-billed dinosaur, with a wide head ending in a beak-like mouth (*Anatosaurus* means 'duck lizard'). As in other hadrosaurs, its beak had no teeth. These were located further back in its jaws. Stomach remains show that it ate pine needles, twigs, seeds and fruit. It was once thought to be semi-aquatic, because some foot remains seem to show webbing between the toes. Experts have since concluded that these flaps of skin were the remains of pads that bore the animal's weight on land.

MAXIMUM LENGTH	13m
TIME	Late Cretaceous
FOSSIL FINDS	North America

SHANTUNGOSAURUS

Shantungosaurus was one of the largest of the hadrosaurs, and one of the largest plant-eating dinosaurs capable of walking on two legs. It weighed about 7 tonnes, and when standing on its back legs, would have been about 7m tall. Half its length was made up by its huge tail, which would have acted as a counterweight when it walked upright. It did not have a crest, but it did have the beak-like mouth typical of its family, with teeth positioned at the back of the jaws. Even though it was a bird-hipped dinosaur, rather than a lizard-hipped sauropod, *Shantungosaurus* would have had almost as much effect on plant life as they did, thanks to its immense size. *Shantungosaurus* gets its name from Shandong, in eastern China, where an almost complete skeleton was found in 1973.

MAXIMUM LENGTH 15m

TIME Late Cretaceous

FOSSIL FINDS North America, Central Asia

▽ Hypacrosaurus *had a prominent hollow crest, rather like some ground-dwelling birds have today. It would have been useful for pushing through vegetation, but its true function will probably never be known.*

HYPACROSAURUS

Like *Corythosaurus* (page 105), this dinosaur had a hollow, helmet-like crest, with an almost identical internal structure. It also had a ridged back, and lived in herds, feeding on all fours. An insight into this dinosaur's family life has come from a nest of eight large fossilized eggs, discovered in Alberta, Canada. The eggs were the size of melons, and contained fossilized embryos. Arranged in rows, they were probably buried until they were ready to hatch. The eggs may have been covered with earth and vegetation – a mixture that would have produced heat as the plants rotted, helping the young dinosaurs to develop. Like *Maiasaura*, the parents probably guarded their nests.

MAXIMUM LENGTH 9m

TIME Late Cretaceous

FOSSIL FINDS North America (Alberta, Canada, and Montana, USA)

FOSSIL-HUNTING IN ASIA

STRETCHING ALMOST HALFWAY AROUND THE GLOBE, ASIA CONTAINS SOME OF THE BEST FOSSIL-HUNTING SITES IN THE WORLD. PALAEONTOLOGISTS HAVE UNEARTHED A WEALTH OF SPECTACULAR FINDS.

Southern Asia has seen a number of important dinosaur discoveries, but perhaps the most interesting finds have been further north, in Russia, Mongolia and China. During the 20th century, political problems meant access for western experts was limited, but this did not stop research. Russian scientists have built up the largest museum collections of fossils in the world, while in China, recent discoveries have thrown new light on the evolution of birds.

FOSSIL EVIDENCE

With its giant jaws gaping wide, this fully assembled fossil of Tarbosaurus *gives a spine-chilling impression of Asia's largest land predator. The first remains of* Tarbosaurus *were found in the Gobi region in 1955, and since then, about a dozen skeletons have been found. Some are almost complete, showing the huge difference in size between the animal's back legs and its tiny arms.*

DESERT RICHES

The Gobi Desert, in the heart of Central Asia, is a harsh but spectacular region that attracts many fossil-hunters. It contains vast deposits of rocks dating back to the time of the dinosaurs, and because it lies so far from the sea, rainfall is very low and so much of the rock is bare. This is the kind of landscape where fossilized remains literally stick out of the ground. However, finding them needs keen eyesight and dedication – particularly when the hot summer wind hurls stinging sand through the air.

During the 1920s, the American Museum of Natural History mounted

△ *The Bayn Dzag, or Flaming Cliffs, of southern Mongolia were laid down during the Cretaceous. The cliffs are being slowly eaten away by wind and sporadic desert storms.*

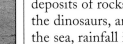

▷ *Using a pocket knife, a Mongolian palaeontologist carefully chips away at the bedrock surrounding a fossilized* Protoceratops *skull revealed beneath the surface of the cliffs.*

several large-scale expeditions to this isolated region, using trucks and camels to transport their supplies. Initially, the aim was to unearth fossils of early humans, but none were found. However, other fossils were there in abundance. At a site known as the Bayn Dzak, or Flaming Cliffs, in southern Mongolia, one team discovered large numbers of fossilized eggs, and the remains of over 100 *Protoceratops* – animals that probably died after they and their eggs were buried by sand. These expeditions also uncovered remains of *Velociraptor* and *Oviraptor*, small predatory theropods.

During the Soviet era, the Gobi was closed to western scientists, but since Mongolia became independent in the early 1990s, entry to the area has become easier and expeditions have been undertaken by experts from all over the world.

DEATH ON DUTY

Over the years, dozens of species of dinosaur have been found in the Gobi, including heavyweight plant-eaters such as *Saurolophus*, and fearsome predators such as *Tarbosaurus* – a close relative of *Tyrannosaurus*, which rivalled it in size. Researchers have also found the fragmentary remains of several species of segnosaurs – mysterious dinosaurs unique to central Asia that might have been predators, plant-eaters or perhaps even a mixture of the two. As well as unearthing fossils that 'paint portraits' of these extinct animals, palaeontologists have also made some finds that show how they behaved.

One of the most famous of these fossils was found in 1923 – an *Oviraptor* apparently smothered by sand while in the process of stealing another dinosaur's eggs. For several decades, the 'egg thief's' guilt seemed to be beyond doubt. But the accusation has turned out to be based on false evidence, because further fossils have been found. In one of

them, the remains of a smashed egg include tiny *Oviraptor* bones. These show that the adult *Oviraptors* were actually incubating eggs of their own.

Together with fossils from other parts of the world, these finds have helped to undermine the long-held idea that dinosaurs played little or no part in raising their young. Instead, *Oviraptor* seems to have been a devoted parent, doggedly remaining with its eggs, even when the sandstorms threatened its life.

FOSSILS FROM THE FAR NORTH

Three thousand kilometres north of the Gobi, the forests of Siberia flank the Arctic Circle. During the height of the last Ice Age, about 20,000 years ago, this area lay under a continental ice cap, but as the ice retreated, the ground turned to tundra – a treeless landscape of low-growing plants that provided food for mammoths, woolly rhinos and the so-called 'Irish elk'. It was an icy version of today's African plains, with large herds of plant-eating mammals and predators such as wolves migrating with the seasons.

Compared to dinosaurs, these animals became extinct in the recent past: the last woolly mammoth, for example, may have been alive on Wrangel Island, off the northest coast of Siberia, just 6,000 years ago. As a result, the fossilized remains of these creatures sometimes include traces of skin and hair, and in the case of deep-frozen animals (page 17), even flesh.

△ In 1971, one expedition to the Gobi region unearthed something quite unique – a fossil of two dinosaurs that had both died while locked together in combat. The attacker was Velociraptor, *and its intended victim was* Protoceratops. *In Mongolia, this extraordinary relic from the dinosaur age has been designated a national treasure.*

◁ Discovered in 1994, *this* Oviraptor *was probably smothered by sand while sitting on its eggs. If the parent was cold-blooded, sitting on the eggs would have protected them against marauders, but if it was warm-blooded – as seems likely – incubation would have helped the eggs to develop. From the fossil, it is not possible to say whether the adult was male or female.*

▽ *Two Chinese palaeontologists examine a fossilized dinosaur egg in Hubei Province, in central China. Matching an egg to a particular dinosaur is very difficult, and instead eggs – just like dinosaur tracks – are often given their own scientific names. Dinosaur eggs fetch high prices, and every year hundreds of Chinese ones are smuggled abroad.*

FOSSILS FROM THE EAST

During the 1920s, palaeontologists working at Zhoukoudian, in northeast China, discovered the remains of 'Peking Man', a human ancestor who lived over 400,000 years ago. As well as fossil bones and tools, the excavators also found deposits of ash deep inside caves – one of the earliest known examples of the deliberate use of fire. Peking Man was very similar to a modern human, but it belonged to a species called *Homo erectus* (page 216), which disappeared about 200,000 years ago.

Northern China is still an important area for fossil-hunting today, but for many scientists the focus is not so much on the ancestors of our own species, as on dinosaurs – and in particular, the ancestors of birds.

MILLION-YEAR-OLD EGGS

Some historians believe that dinosaur fossils, or 'dragon bones', were known about in China over 2,000 years ago. But scientific fossil-hunting did not begin in earnest until the 20th century,

The history of fossil-hunting is peppered with 'finds' that later turn out to be fakes. People make fake fossils for several reasons: some enjoy fooling the experts, but others do it to make money. The fossil shown here is a particularly skilful one which was 'unearthed' in China in 1997. Named Archaeoraptor liaoningensis, *it looks like a link between feathered dinosaurs and flying birds. It convinced several leading palaeontologists, and also* National Geographic *magazine, but on close inspection, it turned out to be mixture of two different animals – a bird and a small theropod dinosaur.*

when western palaeontologists embarked on lengthy expeditions in search of animal remains. However, the people who worked on the fossils were not always from abroad. China had its own experts, foremost among them being Yang Zhong-jian (also known as C.C.Young). He studied fossils in Europe and North America, before returning to China in the late 1920s.

Most of the early fossil-hunting in China concentrated on the northwest of the country – the area that borders Mongolia and includes part of the Gobi Desert. Finds here have included a wide range of armoured dinosaurs, which lived during Cretaceous times, and also a number of other large plant-eaters. Among them were *Shantungosaurus* and *Tsintaosaurus* – two of the largest duck-billed dinosaurs or

▷ *Watched by a large crowd, scientists work on an unusual find – a collection of fossilized eggs, together with dinosaur bones. If the bones and eggs are of the same age, this suggests that some disaster overtook the adult animal while it was at the nest.*

hadrosaurs – as well as *Tuojiangosaurus* and *Huayangosaurus*, two stegosaurs, both from the Jurassic, which were very different in size. The fossil-hunting expeditions also unearthed remains of *Mamenchisaurus*, a sauropod that was Asia's largest dinosaur, and had a spectacularly long neck.

China has also proved to be a treasure trove for dinosaur nests and eggs. The nests include one find nearly 3m across – a world record. There are some containing the remains of embryos, and others with more than a litre of rock-hard, fossilized yolk.

FEATHERED DINOSAURS

The first fossil to link dinosaurs and birds was *Archaeopteryx*, discovered in southern Germany in 1861. Although it was a bird, it clearly had some reptilian features, such as wing claws and a long bony tail. But before birds like *Archaeopteryx* evolved, there must have been earlier forms that looked more like 'normal' dinosaurs. In the last decade, palaeontologists sifting through layers of soft rock in Liaoning Province, northeast China, have helped fill in the missing links.

Sinosauropteryx, discovered in 1996, was one of these. A small theropod, or bipedal carnivore, it had strong back legs, but short arms ending in small clawed hands. It is certain that it could not fly, as it did not have even the beginnings of wings, but even so, its body was covered in downy plumage, which helped it to keep warm (page 148).

Liaoning has produced several other fossils. Among them are *Protarchaeopteryx* and *Caudipteryx*, both found roughly a year after *Sinosauropteryx*, and also feathered-but-flightless theropods. These discoveries make it likely that, far from being unusual, feathers were common in small theropods, and maybe other dinosaurs as well, although unlike birds, these animals used them for insulation rather than flight.

But why has this one part of China yielded so many fossils of these feathered theropods? One reason is that, like southern Germany, this region was covered with shallow lakes and lagoons at the time when the ancestors of birds were alive. In southern Germany, *Archaeopteryx* probably crashed into the water and drowned, sinking to the bottom and becoming covered in fine silt. In Liaoning, small feathered theropods probably fell in after a natural disaster, such as a volcanic eruption. As with *Archaeopteryx*, lake silt created superbly detailed fossils, allowing the outline of feathers to be seen today.

EARLY VERTEBRATES

Compared to feathered dinosaurs, tiny fish do not sound like the most exciting of fossil finds. But in 1999, Chinese researchers announced that they had found the fossils of two species over 500 million years old (page 30). This is an exciting breakthrough, because it pushes back the date when animals with backbones first appeared.

The finger-sized fossils were found in Yunnan Province, in the far south of China. One of the animals, *Myllokunmingia*, had gill pouches and a sail-like fin along its back, while the other, *Haikouichthys*, was more slender and may have had slime-producing glands, like a modern hagfish. The search is now on for further finds of these ancient but important animals.

△ Sinosauropteryx *was a feathered but flightless dinosaur that lived about 140 million years ago. It was unlikely to have been a direct ancestor of modern birds, but it shows some of the features that would have been present during the early stages of bird evolution.*

▽ *Measuring 7m long,* Tuojiangosaurus *was a stegosaur that lived in eastern Asia. China has produced a greater range of stegosaur fossil finds than anywhere else in the world.*

SOUNDS

TODAY'S REPTILES ARE LARGELY SILENT, BUT
DINOSAURS MAY HAVE COMMUNICATED WITH
GRUNTS AND ROARS THAT COULD BE HEARD
MANY KILOMETRES AWAY. THE EVIDENCE FOR
THIS COMES LARGELY FROM THEIR SKULLS.

Animals use sound mainly to keep in touch, and to ward off their rivals and enemies. For dinosaurs – particularly herd-forming plant-eaters – this kind of communication could have been a valuable aid to survival. Periodic contact calls, made by animals as they fed, would have helped the herd to stay together. Much louder alarm calls, produced when a predator was spotted, would let other herd members know that they were in imminent danger of attack. And for dinosaurs as a whole, far-carrying courtship calls would have allowed males to attract mates.

ECHOES FROM THE PAST
Animals make sounds in two different ways: by rubbing body parts together, or by using their vocal cords to make air vibrate when they breathe. Most dinosaurs probably had vocal cords, but none have survived in fossils.

Other soft parts, such as cheeks and lips, modify the sound that is made, but few signs of these survive. Fossil skeletons do show the air spaces in the skull, and the length of the trachea, or windpipe. As with wind instruments, the bigger these are, the deeper the sound that would be made.

If they did make sounds, the smallest dinosaurs, such as *Saltopus*, would probably have produced a high-pitched piping like birdsong. Giant sauropods would have made deep sounds too low for the human ear to hear. Each species would have had its own calls, and within each species, individuals would have had their own distinctive 'voice'.

COMPUTING A CALL
For sound specialists, hadrosaurs (pages 104–7) are particularly interesting, because their crests look as though they might have evolved partly as a way of producing calls. The crests contain extensions of the nasal tubes, leading between the nose and lungs. In *Parasaurolophus*, the tubes double back on themselves – a feature similar to the coiled airways of cranes.

In 1997, a group of American scientists used a medical scanner on a *Parasaurolophus* skull to identify the exact shape of the air passages that were preserved as solid rock. They were able to generate sounds that the dinosaur might have made. The result was a collection of low-pitched rumblings – the first dinosaur 'calls' to be heard on Earth for over 65 million years.

▷ Parasaurolophus' *crest, with its
trombone-like arrangement
of airways, was a natural
resonating chamber. In this artist's
impression, a male is calling by
inflating his cheeks and blowing
air out of his nose. His nostrils
may have acted like valves,
allowing it to alter the sound.*

THE MEAT-EATERS

The theropods – a word that means 'beast-footed' were distant cousins of the sauropods (page 71), but their shape and way of life could hardly have been more different. Instead of walking slowly on all fours, most theropods ran on two, and they fed not on plants, but on meat. This large and varied group of carnivores included some early species that were not much bigger than a cat, as well as – later – the largest predators that have ever lived on dry land. Most giant theropods hunted alone, but the smaller species, covered in this chapter, were quick-witted killers that worked in packs.

HUNTERS ON THE RUN

Sprinting across a late Triassic landscape, a pack of Coelophysis *approach a cetiosaur feeding in the marshy shallows of a lake. They usually hunt much smaller prey, but the plant-eater is at a disadvantage in the soft ground, and the pack may stand a chance of making a kill.*

THE MEAT-EATERS

CERATOSAURS

The earliest carnivorous dinosaurs evolved in the late Triassic, about 220 million years ago. Contrary to popular belief, few of these meat-eaters were giants, but what they lacked in size they made up for in speed and agility. Sprinting on their back legs, and balancing with their long tails, lightweight species called ceratosaurs could snap at animals on the ground, or even leap after insects in the air. Many had beak-like jaws armed with small but needle-like teeth, and slender hands with sharp claws – ideal implements for gripping and holding down struggling prey.

△ Procompsognathus *(above left and centre)* and Compsognathus *(above right) lived over 50 million years apart, but they had many features in common. Among these were a slim body, a long, stiff tail and a slender head on a flexible neck. Both dinosaurs would have had good eyesight, essential for catching fast-moving prey.*

PROCOMPSOGNATHUS
One of the oldest theropods yet discovered – and one of the earliest dinosaurs – *Procompsognathus* is known from a single skeleton, which is far from complete. However, judging from the remains of its badly crushed skull, it seems to have had a long, pointed snout and sharp teeth. It probably lived on a diet of insects and small lizards, which it caught either in its jaws, or with its large, five-fingered, clawed hands.

MAXIMUM LENGTH	1.2m
TIME	Late Triassic
FOSSIL FINDS	Europe (Germany)

COMPSOGNATHUS
Lightly built and highly agile, *Compsognathus* probably weighed up to 3kg, which is about as much as a large chicken. Its name means 'elegant jaw' – a flattering description of a narrow mouth that was packed with small but sharp teeth. Like its relatives, it was bird-like in appearance, with long back legs, three-toed feet and hollow bones. Fossilized stomach remains show that it ate lizards, and it also may have been cannibalistic.

MAXIMUM LENGTH	60cm–1.4m
TIME	Late Jurassic
FOSSIL FINDS	Europe (Germany, France)

SALTOPUS
Saltopus is one of the smallest dinosaurs known, weighing about 1kg – the same as a large domestic cat. Fossil evidence is a little scanty, making an accurate reconstruction impossible, but remains show that this tiny hunter had five-fingered hands – a primitive feature that changed as theropods evolved. Some scientists have suggested that *Saltopus* may have hopped, like some rodents and marsupials do today, but this interesting idea cannot be proved. Given its small size, insects were probably an important part of its diet, although it may also have scavenged on animals killed by larger dinosaurs.

MAXIMUM LENGTH	0.7m
TIME	Late Triassic
FOSSIL FINDS	Europe (Scotland)

COELURUS
Another small predatory dinosaur of similar stature and behaviour to *Compsognathus*, *Coelurus* lived in the swamps and forests of Jurassic North America. Unlike earlier theropods, it had only three fingers on each hand, each armed with sharp, curved claws. Its head was relatively small – about the size of a human hand – with a narrow but blunt-ended snout. When fully grown, *Coelurus* probably weighed up to 20kg.

MAXIMUM LENGTH	2m
TIME	Late Jurassic
FOSSIL FINDS	North America (Wyoming, USA)

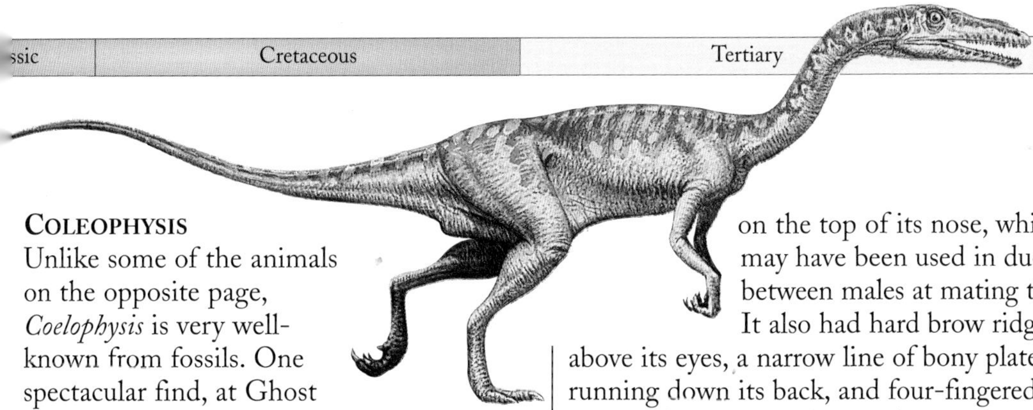

COLEOPHYSIS

Unlike some of the animals on the opposite page, *Coelophysis* is very well-known from fossils. One spectacular find, at Ghost Ranch in Colorado, USA, has yielded the remains of about 1,000 specimens, from juveniles to adults, making this one of the best-known Triassic dinosaurs. This mass grave strongly suggests that *Coelophysis* was sociable, although the discovery of fossilized bones inside larger specimens may well mean that they were not averse to eating each other's young. From this wealth of fossils, two types have been identified, known as 'robust' and 'gracile' forms. Palaeontologists think that these are males and females, rather than members of two separate species.

MAXIMUM LENGTH 3m

TIME Late Triassic

FOSSIL FINDS North America (Arizona, Colorado, New Mexico)

CERATOSAURUS

Weighing up to 1 tonne, *Ceratosaurus* was a sizeable hunter, although not as big as the true giants of the theropod world. Its most characteristic feature was a horn on the top of its nose, which may have been used in duels between males at mating time. It also had hard brow ridges above its eyes, a narrow line of bony plates running down its back, and four-fingered hands. The first nearly complete remains of *Ceratosaurus* were found alongside those of *Allosaurus* in a quarry in Colorado, USA, in 1883, and fossilized footprints discovered since then show that it may have hunted in packs. Unlike packs of smaller theropods, *Ceratosaurus* packs would have been able to attack and kill plant-eaters weighing many tonnes.

MAXIMUM LENGTH 6m

TIME Late Jurassic

FOSSIL FINDS North America (Colorado), Africa (Tanzania)

◁ Coelophysis *was a medium-sized predator, standing about as high as an adult man. When running at speed, it would have probably have stablilized itself by lowering its neck and holding its tail almost horizontally. Its small, serrated teeth were designed mainly for dealing with prey smaller than itself.*

▽ Ceratosaurus *attacks a* Brachiosaurus. *On its own,* Ceratosaurus *would have been a serious threat to large sauropods, but it would have been deadly if, as seems likely, it also hunted in packs.*

MOVING ON TWO LEGS

THE WORLD'S LARGEST DINOSAURS WALKED ON FOUR LEGS, BUT THE FASTEST AND MOST AGILE SPECIES – INCLUDING ALMOST ALL OF THE HUNTERS – WALKED OR RAN ON TWO.

Dinosaurs evolved from reptiles that walked and ran on all fours, but many of them moved on their back legs alone (pages 64–65). This way of moving brought three advantages – two-legged reptiles could often run faster, they could see further, and because their front legs were not needed for moving, they became free to carry out other tasks instead. The disadvantages of this way of moving was that, at high speed, a single misplaced step could send a dinosaur crashing to the ground.

△ Moving at full speed, tyrannosaurs held their tails high to balance the weight of their heads. When standing still, they kept their bodies upright.

BIPEDAL DINOSAURS
Two groups of dinosaurs walked partly or wholly on two legs: the theropods (both light- and heavyweight hunters) and the plant-eating ornithopods (pages 91–112). Many of the ornithopods were 'facultative bipeds', which means that they walked on all fours most of the time, but could switch to two legs to get at food, to defend themselves or to get away from danger. Their front and back legs differed in size, but their front legs were strong enough to support their body weight.

In theropods, the two-legged lifestyle went much further. Most of these dinosaurs always stood on their back legs, and were incapable of walking on all fours. Their front legs were much less powerful than their back legs, but they often had long fingers armed with sharp claws, which could be used for unearthing eggs, gripping food or slashing at their prey.

Tyrannosaurs – the biggest of these bipedal hunters – had back legs that could be twice the height of an adult human, but front legs that were not much longer than a human arm. These tiny front legs could have played no part in moving about, and would not have been much use for feeding. Some experts think that they may have been used as props when lying down, or perhaps when mating, but they remain a mystery.

SPRINTERS AND PLODDERS
Moving on two legs made small hunters fast and very manoeuvrable. One of the speediest of them all, the bird mimic *Dromiceiomimus*, had very long bones in the lower part of its back legs – the ideal shape for running. It could reach a speed of over 60km/h, fast enough to overtake most land animals today.

But not all two-legged dinosaurs were good long-distance runners. With its massive back legs and 7-tonne body, *Tyrannosaurus* was probably too heavy to keep up the chase for long, and when it was running, it would have found it almost impossible to twist and turn after its prey. Many palaeontologists believe that it was more likely to have been a 'stand-and-wait' predator, lurking among vegetation, and bursting out of cover once its prey was within striking range.

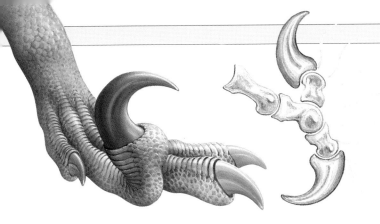

△ Deinonychus *had a retractable toe on the inside of each hind foot, armed with a giant sickle-shaped claw.*

The claw swivelled downwards when the animal was about to launch an attack.

STAYING BALANCED

For animals that move on two legs, staying balanced is vital. This would have been true for large hunters like *Tyrannosaurus*, because once it was in motion, it developed an almost unstoppable momentum. If it tripped, it risked a dangerous accident, with only its tiny front legs to break its fall. For lightweight hunters, such as *Deinonychus*, falls were less critical.

The human body is vertical, so our centre of gravity is above our legs – the right position for staying balanced. In theropods, the head and trunk leaned forwards in one direction and the tail in another. To keep their centre of gravity above their back legs, they had to make sure that these two parts of the body were balanced. For the largest hunters, having

▷ *Measuring about 4m long,* Deinonychus *was a middleweight bipedal hunter, but one with well-developed front legs. Like other theropods, it used its tail partly as a counterweight and partly as a stabilizer to absorb energy – rather like kangaroos do today.*

a huge head was a problem – it threatened to topple them over. To avoid this, they probably leaned forwards only when they ran.

BACK TO ALL FOURS

Many palaeontologists believe that sauropods – the largest plant-eaters of the dinosaur world – evolved from bipedal ancestors. But as they evolved and grew in size, this two-legged lifestyle was soon abandoned. Some sauropods could probably stand on their hind legs, propped up by their tails, but with their huge and heavy digestive systems, it is highly unlikely that they could have taken a single step on their back legs alone.

STUDYING DINOSAUR TRACKS

BECAUSE DINOSAURS DIED OUT SO LONG AGO, WE HAVE VERY LITTLE IDEA OF HOW THEY BEHAVED. FOSSILIZED TRACKS ARE VALUABLE EVIDENCE IN THIS AREA OF RESEARCH.

Although fossilized dinosaur tracks have been found all over the world, they are rarer than fossilized bones. This is because footprints are preserved only when conditions are exactly right. The ground must be soft, but not so soft that the prints soon fill in, and the prints must be covered by something that protects them – such as sediment or sand – not long after they are made. Most dinosaur tracks belong to single animals, but in some places entire herds have left their imprint on the ground.

◁ *Tracks at Lark Quarry in Australia show the world's largest fossilized stampede. About 150 small theropods and ornithopods seem to have been running for their lives from a large carnosaur. The tracks do not show if the predator managed to make a kill.*

IDENTIFYING FOOTPRINTS

With living animals, it is often quite easy to match footprints with the animals that made them. But with dinosaurs, it is usually more difficult. From a print's shape, experts can generally tell what type of dinosaur left it – for example, the prints left by sauropods and theropods look different, because sauropods had rounded or oval feet, while theropods had bird-like feet, with long toes and large claws. However, deciding which kind of sauropod or theropod left a set of prints is much harder. To avoid guesswork, tracks are often given their own scientific names.

▽ *Walking slowly in the heat of the midday sun, a small herd of* Iguanodon *make their way along a beach. Damp sand sometimes produced clear fossil prints, whereas sticky mud would blur the shape.*

GAUGING SPEEDS

As well as showing where a dinosaur went, tracks can often give an idea of its speed. To calculate this, a track expert needs to know two measurements – the length of the dinosaur's leg, and the length of its stride. These measurements show that ornithomimids – the fastest dinosaurs – could probably reach about 60km/h, and because they were light, they would have been able to accelerate and brake quite quickly. The largest sauropods and carnosaurs were much slower, and would have taken longer to build up speed. They probably had a maximum speed of about 30km/h – roughly twice as fast as a human on the run. For giant sauropods, such as *Seismosaurus*, true running is likely to have been impossible, because it would have put immense strain on their legs. These animals probably broke into an accelerated walk if threatened, moving one foot at a time, with the other three in contact with the ground.

Like other animals, dinosaurs did not waste energy unnecessarily, so tracks that show running are rare. Lark Quarry in Queensland, Australia, is one of the few sites where the track-makers – a group of small theropods and ornithopods – seem to be moving at top speed. It is believed that the animals were escaping from a predator.

TRACKWAYS

Collections of footpints – called trackways – can reveal a lot about dinosaurs on the move. Some trackways contain prints formed by several animals in a herd, but occasionally, trackways contain prints from more than one species. One of the most famous examples, at the Paluxy River in Texas, USA, shows the three-toed footprints of a large predatory theropod apparently stalking its sauropod prey. Trackways also indicate social interactions, such as the large adult dinosaurs walking on the outside of a herd to protect the young in the middle.

Like today's animals, dinosaurs gathered at particular places to feed or to drink. Where this happened, the ground became trampled, leaving a confusing jumble of tracks. Track experts – or ichnologists – call this kind of trampling 'dinoturbation'. Dinoturbation is common in rocks that have formed from ancient lake shores, where dinosaurs left their footprints in the mud. In other places, called megatrack sites, dinosaurs have left tell-tale footprints across huge areas of ground. Some palaeontologists think that these were migration routes – prehistoric dinosaur paths that may have been used for thousands of years.

FOSSIL EVIDENCE

This collection of footprints in Utah, USA, was left by several dinosaurs walking over the same patch of damp ground. Dinosaurs sometimes stepped in each other's prints, so track experts can often tell the order in which the tracks were made. This provides useful evidence about whether the dinosaurs were interacting with each other at the time. Utah is rich in fossilized tracks. Some prints, left by a hadrosaur, hold the world record at 1.35m.

△ *Closing in on a slow-moving sauropod, a theropod moves in for the attack. This scene – and events leading up to it – is recorded in tracks discovered in the bed of the Paluxy River in Texas, USA. The predator left the typical three-toed footprints of a theropod, while the sauropod's prints were rounded, with small claw marks visible at the front. Shortly after the attack, the prints were covered by sediment. Millions of years later, they were revealed as fossils.*

THE MEAT-EATERS

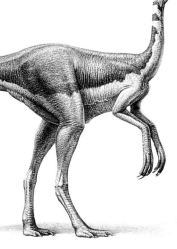

▷ *With its long neck and slender body and slender body and back legs,* Dromiceiomimus *bears a startling resemblance to a present-day flightless bird. Birds almost certainly evolved from close relatives of these animals (page 134).*

BIRD MIMICS

Bird mimics, or ornithomimids, were long-legged, slender-bodied dinosaurs that probably lived and hunted in small packs. They fed on smaller reptiles and insects, as well as plants and eggs, and behaved like today's large flightless birds, running at up to 70km/h to escape danger. Bird mimics had beak-like jaws without teeth, and slender 'arms' for picking up food. They were quick-witted, having large brains relative to their size.

▽ *Running for their lives, a herd of* Struthiomimus *quickly outpace a lumbering* Tyrannosaurus.

DROMICEIOMIMUS
Studies of *Dromiceiomimus* fossils show that this animal must have been one of the most intelligent dinosaurs of its time. Its large eye sockets make it likely that it hunted at night, and its relatively long lower leg bones show that it would have been exceptionally swift, perhaps reaching speeds of 65km/h. Its jaws were weak, and it probably snapped up insects and other small items of food, perhaps digging them out with its three-fingered hands. Its wide pelvis could be a sign that it gave birth to live young, or laid very large eggs.

MAXIMUM LENGTH 3.5m

TIME Late Cretaceous

FOSSIL FINDS North America (Alberta, Canada)

STRUTHIOMIMUS
Struthiomimus means 'ostrich mimic' – an appropriate name for a dinosaur with slender legs and large bird-like eyes. It had long, gangly arms, and well-developed claws on its fingers. It also had a remnant fourth toe in its hind feet. Its tail kept it balanced as it ran, and as it swerved to avoid attack. *Struthiomimus* was probably carnivorous, but its lack of teeth would have restricted it to small prey. This dinosaur was originally classified as a form of *Ornithomimus*, and some experts think that, as further fossils are found, it may turn out to be the same animal. All bird mimics look very similar – apart from the giant *Deinocheirus* – so classifying them has proved difficult.

MAXIMUM LENGTH 4m

TIME Late Cretaceous

FOSSIL FINDS North America

BIRD MIMICS

ORNITHOMIMUS

Bird mimics were built for speed, and *Ornithomimus* was no exception to this rule. It had light, hollow bones and long, powerful, bird-like legs with clawed feet. With its good eyesight and quick reactions, it is likely to have been an efficient hunter, and also a successful scavenger. However, recent studies of this dinosaur's skull suggest that it – and perhaps other bird mimics – were cold-blooded, which means that they would only have been able to run in short bursts. *Ornithomimus* was initially known only from feet and legs – the first complete skeleton was found after a gap of 30 years, in 1917.

MAXIMUM LENGTH 4m

TIME Late Cretaceous

FOSSIL FINDS North America (Alberta, Canada, and Colorado, Montana, USA), Asia (Tibet)

ANSERIMIMUS

All that is known about *Anserimimus* – a name that means 'goose mimic' – comes from one fossilized skeleton found in Mongolia. Even though this lacks part of its head, this species seems to have been a typical ornithomimid, although one with particularly strong, short arms and long finger claws. This suggests that *Anserimimus* may have relied on digging for finding food.

MAXIMUM LENGTH 3m

TIME Late Cretaceous

FOSSIL FINDS Asia (Mongolia)

GALLIMIMUS

Despite its name, which means 'chicken mimic', *Gallimimus* may have been the largest member of the ornithomimid family. It stood about twice as high as an adult man, but even so was relatively light for its size, enabling it to run at speed. Its face and beak were elongated, and its hands were shovel-like, indicating that it dug for food.

MAXIMUM LENGTH 6m

TIME Late Cretaceous

FOSSIL FINDS Asia (Mongolia)

DEINOCHEIRUS

Known only from a pair of arms and some shoulder bones, *Deinocheirus* is one of the great mysteries of the dinosaur world. If it was an ornithomimid, it was certainly the giant of the family, since its arms were 2.5m in length. They were armed with claws over 25cm long, which could have made formidable weapons.

MAXIMUM LENGTH Up to 20m

TIME Late Cretaceous

FOSSIL FINDS Asia (Mongolia)

◁ Ornithomimus *was a typically athletic member of the bird mimic family, running quickly whenever food beckoned or danger threatened. It would have run with its head held high, giving it a good view of its surroundings. Its long, stiff tail acted as a counterbalance.*

▽ *Running with its head up,* Gallimimus *was like a mobile lookout-post with a far-reaching view of its surroundings. Its eyes faced sideways, just like those of ostriches and other flightless birds. This arrangement is not good for judging depth, but it is ideal for spotting possible danger from any direction.*

△ Dromeosaurus *(top)*, Deinonychus *(centre) and* Velociraptor *(bottom)* were highly efficient predators, all armed with a single retractable claw on each foot. The claw stayed off the ground when the animal was moving, keeping its point needle-sharp.

DROMAEOSAURS

Fast and ferocious, dromeosaurs were killers of other dinosaurs. They were perfectly built for speed and slaughter, with light bodies, athletic legs, and sharp, sickle-like claws. Their heads were relatively large, and their long jaws were armed with sharp curved teeth. They had well-developed brains, and they often worked in packs to hunt down animals several times their own size.

DEINONYCHUS
Although it was far smaller than many other predators that lived during the Cretaceous Period, *Deinonychus* – meaning 'terrible claw' – was a serious threat even to the largest

plant-eating dinosaurs. By operating in packs, rather like modern-day wolves, it would harass and exhaust its prey before closing in for the final attack. When the moment came to make the kill, the members of the pack would jump at their victim and slash at it with their retractable sickle-shaped claws – formidable weapons that were up to 12cm long. As the pack members leaped and ripped into their prey, they used their stiff tails as counterweights to prevent themselves losing their balance. Like other dromeosaurs, *Deinonychus* had a large brain for its size, giving it the intelligence and rapid reactions needed in a hunter that operated in groups. *Deinonychus* was such an active and energetic predator that some experts think it may have been warm-blooded (page 148–150), a theory that has yet to be proved.

MAXIMUM LENGTH 4m

TIME Early Cretaceous

FOSSIL FINDS North America

DROMAEOSAURUS

Half the size of *Deinonychus*, but built along very similar lines, *Dromaeosaurus* was another fast-footed predator, probably able to reach speeds of around 60km/h. It also had a sickle-like claw on the inner toe, which could be retracted when not in use. Fossils of this animal were discovered 50 years before its larger relative, which is how the dromaeosaur family got its name. The remains that were found were only partial, and palaeontologists could not interpret them fully until they had studied *Deinonychus*, and seen the similarities.

MAXIMUM LENGTH 1.8m

TIME Late Cretaceous

FOSSIL FINDS North America

VELOCIRAPTOR

Similar in size and body shape to *Dromaeosaurus*, although with a longer and flatter head, *Velociraptor* was first discovered in Mongolia in the 1920s. Its way of life was vividly illustrated when, many years later, an expedition uncovered the fossilized remains of a *Velociraptor* that had been killed while attacking a *Protoceratops* (page 155). *Velociraptor* means 'speedy thief' – a good description of a small, fast-moving and intelligent hunter that could probably reach speeds of 60 km/h. Although it could run at this speed only in short bursts, *Velociraptor* may have been second only to the bird mimics (page 122) in top speed. Like other dromaeosaurs, little is known about its breeding habits and whether it laid eggs.

MAXIMUM LENGTH 1.8m

TIME Late Cretaceous

FOSSIL FINDS Asia (Mongolia, China)

SAURORNITHOLESTES

Uncertainty surrounds *Saurornitholestes*, since knowledge of it is limited to remnants of a skull, some teeth, and arm bones found in Alberta, Canada, in 1978. Based on this slender evidence, palaeontologists have classified it as a dromaeosaur, but it may have been a 'bird lizard' or saurornithoid (page 126). An agile hunter, it had large hands with grasping fingers.

MAXIMUM LENGTH 1.8m

TIME Late Cretaceous

FOSSIL FINDS North America (Alberta, Canada)

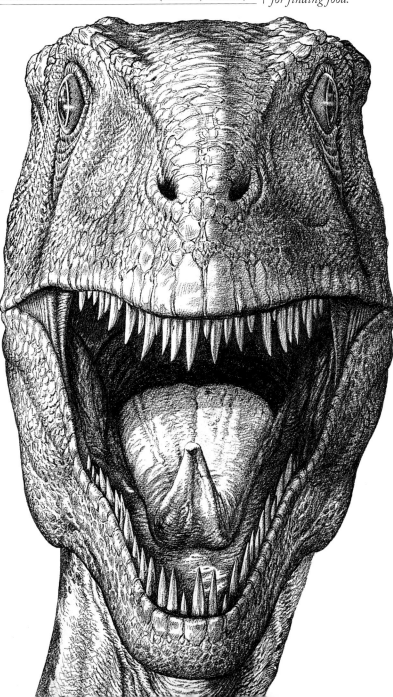

▽ *Like other predatory dinosaurs, Deinonychus could not slice into its prey, and instead it used its backwardly curving teeth to rip away chunks of flesh. It also had large eyes, and it would have relied mainly on its sharp eyesight to spot potential prey when hunting. Its sense of smell was probably less important for finding food.*

THE MEAT-EATERS

TROODONTS

The animals on these two pages belonged to several families, but most were lightweight theropods with unusually large brains. The troodonts, in particular, were highly intelligent by dinosaur standards, with large eyes that suggest they hunted at night. Fast and agile, some of them may have been warm-blooded, keeping in their body heat with a layer of insulating feathers. *Baryonyx* – on the far right – was a much larger animal and probably not much brighter than other theropods of its time.

▷ Oviraptor *made up for its lack of teeth by having sharp shearing edges on its 'beak'. Because its beak was short, it would have closed with considerable force – enough to break open bones. The size of the crest probably varied according to sex and age.*

▽ *Lean and energetic,* Troodon *was one of the most intelligent land animals of the late Cretaceous. This artist's impression shows it with bare skin, but it is possible that it had a covering of downy, heat-retaining plumage.*

OVIRAPTOR
With its bird-like head and short, toothless beak, *Oviraptor* – meaning 'egg thief' – was an unusual and distinctive animal. Standing about the same height as an adult man, it had thin but well-developed arms, and fingers that were equipped with slender claws. Its beak was hooked and had sharp edges for slicing through food. Recent fossil discoveries show that, although it may have eaten other dinosaur eggs, it was careful with its own (page 109).

MAXIMUM LENGTH	2.5m
TIME	Late Cretaceous
FOSSIL FINDS	Asia (Mongolia)

TROODON
From a distance, *Troodon* looked like a bird mimic (page 122), but it shared the same kind of weaponry as the dromaeosaurs – a lethal claw on each of its second toes, which could be swivelled upwards when it ran. Some palaeontologists think that it may actually have been a dromaeosaur, but it is possible that these swivelling claws evolved more than once. It also had large, serrated teeth, grasping hands, and eyes that faced partly forwards – a combination that would have made it a very effective hunter. If *Troodon* did hunt after dark, as the size of its eyes suggests, its main prey might have been mammals, which were almost all nocturnal in the Cretaceous. *Troodon* teeth were first discovered nearly 150 years ago, but nothing was known about the animal itself until the 1980s.

MAXIMUM LENGTH	1.8m
TIME	Late Cretaceous
FOSSIL FINDS	North America (Alberta,Canada and Wyoming, Montana, USA)

SINORNITHOIDES
Another member of the troodont family, *Sinornithoides* is the only one known from a complete fossil skeleton. It was a small and very slender animal, weighing perhaps just 3kg when fully grown, and its food is likely to have consisted of insects and other small animals, which it may have found by scratching with its front claws.

MAXIMUM LENGTH	1.2m
TIME	Early Cretaceous
FOSSIL FINDS	Asia (China)

BARYONYX
Discovered in an English clay pit in the early 1980s, *Baryonyx* – meaning 'heavy claw' – was one of the most intriguing European dinosaurs to surface in recent times. For a theropod, its skull had a very unusual shape, ending in a flattened, crocodile-like snout. Its teeth were conical rather than blade-like, packed in dense rows along its jaws. It had at least two very large claws, about 30cm long. No close relatives of this animal have yet been found, and it is classified in a family of its own.

MAXIMUM LENGTH	9m
TIME	Early Cretaceous
FOSSIL FINDS	Europe (England)

TROODONTS

Standing in shallow water, Baryonyx *uses its extra-large front claws to grab unsuspecting fish. Two* Brachiosaurus, *in the background, know that this specialized predator does not present a threat.*

DINOSAUR BRAINS

DINOSAURS WERE THE PROVERBIAL DIM-WITS OF THE PREHISTORIC WORLD. BUT IS IT A REPUTATION THEY REALLY DESERVED, AND IF SO, HOW DID THEY MANAGE TO SURVIVE?

Myths abound about dinosaurs' supposed stupidity. One is that they had two brains, while another is that their lack of brain-power helped to make them extinct. But as living animals prove, large brains are not an essential for biological success. Research shows that brain size and intelligence varied greatly from one group of dinosaurs to another. Some were slow on the uptake, but others were just as intelligent as many mammals alive today.

NERVOUS SYSTEMS

Because dinosaurs were vertebrates, their nervous systems would have been similar to those of other vertebrates alive today. In a vertebrate, the 'headquarters' of the system is the brain, which merges with the spinal cord – a long filament of nervous tissue that runs through the hollow core of the

△ *Stegosaurus had a brain about the size of a walnut, weighing roughly 75g, but some of its nerve cells supplying distant parts of its body were over 3m long. How fast its nerves worked would have depended on whether it was cold-blooded – a matter for debate.*

backbone. Nerves lead away from the spinal cord to reach all parts of the body, collecting information from the sense organs, and also sending signals to trigger muscles into action.

In all vertebrates, the brain plays a key role in initiating movement and making sure the body works in a coordinated way. But some movements, called reflex reactions, are triggered without the brain being directly involved. If you tread on something sharp, for example, your leg will immediately pull back, because an automatic response has been triggered by your spinal cord.

Reactions like these are potential lifesavers and they have to be fast, but the larger an animal is, the further the signals have to travel. In today's reptiles, signals move along nerves at up to 40m per second, which is quick enough to produce an almost instant

◁ *This diagram (above left) shows the brain cavity of a* Stegosaurus, *and other structures close to it. The ear opening is shown in black; the circular objects above it are part of the inner ear, which played a part in controlling balance.*

◁ *Dome-headed dinosaurs, or pachycephalosaurs, looked as though they had large brains, but this was because their small brain cavity was covered by a mound of bone.*

response. But in large dinosaurs, nerve signals would often have had to travel several metres, creating a significant time-lag.

This time-lag effect may help to explain the so-called 'second brain', which is seen in stegosaurs and some other dinosaurs. Instead of being a true brain, this was actually an enlarged relay centre that dealt with these automatic reactions.

RELATIVE BRAIN SIZE

Dinosaur skulls often contain the remains of a brain cavity, allowing their brain volume to be measured by computerized imaging, or by the more simple technique of filling the cavity with fluid, and then measuring the fluid when it is poured out.

Dinosaur brains varied between the size of a grape and a grapefruit. But the size of the body also has to be taken into account, because the larger an animal, the more nerves were needed to control it.

With living animals, researchers have made detailed studies of the ratio between brain weight and the total weight of the body. For humans, the figure comes out at about about 1:40, while for an average dog it is about 1:125. For a stegosaur, the figure was about 1:50000 – indicating that these

animals were very dim indeed. But body size and brain size do not alter in step. In small birds, for example, the ratio can be as high as 1:12, making them 'brainier' than humans.

In gauging the relative intelligence of related animals, a more useful figure is an 'encephalization quotient' or EQ, which gives an idea of relative brain development. As the chart below shows, sauropods had the lowest figure among dinosaurs, with values of about 0.2, whereas small theropods did well, with scores of above 5.5. Among mammals, humans have an EQ of about 7.4, but this does not tell us much about dinosaur brainpower, as figures from very different groups cannot be directly compared.

INSTINCT AND LEARNING

Given their way of life, it is no surprise that plant-eating dinosaurs come bottom on the EQ list. Unlike hunting species, these animals did not need to stalk or ambush their food, and their daily life consisted largely of eating and digesting. By contrast, small hunters such as *Dromiceiomimus* survived by learning from experience, which gave them the best chance of making successful kills. For them, intelligence was essential for survival.

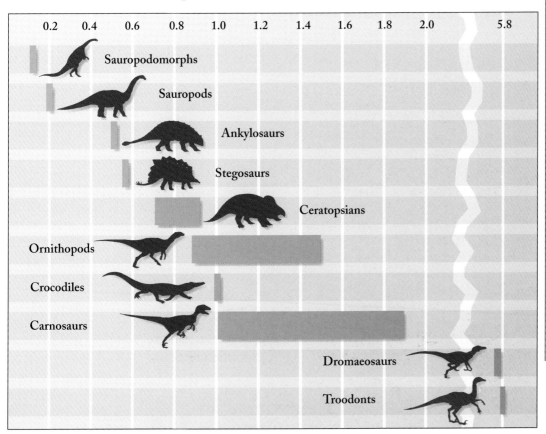

◁ *This chart shows typical encephalization quotients, EQs, for dinosaurs and crocodilians. EQ, not to be confused with IQ, is the ratio of actual brain weight to the expected brain weight, given an animal's size and type. For dinosaurs, the expected brain weight is based on measurements of living reptiles. EQ gives a general indication of brain development, and therefore of an animal's intelligence. An EQ of more than 1 shows that an animal has a brain weight above average for its class, while an EQ below 1 shows the reverse.*

EGGS AND PARENTAL CARE

AS FAR AS IS KNOWN, ALL DINOSAURS
REPRODUCED BY LAYING EGGS. FOSSILIZED
NESTS SHOW THAT SOME WERE CAREFUL
PARENTS, LOOKING AFTER THEIR EGGS
AND ALSO THEIR YOUNG.

People have unearthed fossilized dinosaur eggs for centuries without realizing what they are. The first to be correctly identified were in France, just over 150 years ago. Since then, many different types have been found, often exactly as they were laid. Dinosaur eggs were surprisingly small. The largest discovered is only about twice the length of an ostrich egg. They could not be larger because the thick shells would have stopped the embryos inside from getting enough oxygen, and the baby dinosaurs would have been unable to break the shell when they hatched.

Dinosaur eggs came in a wide variety of shapes. Some of them looked like overstuffed sausages, while others were round, and their shells could be pitted or smooth.
1 *Modern day hen's egg – 7.5cm long*
2 *Maiasaura egg – 15cm long*
3 *Protoceratops egg – 20cm long*
4 *Hypselosaurus egg – 30cm long*

DINOSAUR EGGS
Many of today's reptiles lay their eggs in shallow holes, which they scrape out in loose soil or mud. Fossilized nests – which have been discovered in many different parts of the world – suggest that most dinosaurs behaved in the same way. By scraping the ground with their feet, or perhaps their snouts, they excavated hollows or craters that could be over 1m across. Like modern reptiles, the number of eggs laid by the dinosaurs varied. Some laid fewer than 10 eggs at a time, but some giant nests recently discovered in China contain 40 eggs or more.

FOSSIL EVIDENCE

Complete dinosaur nests – like the one shown here – are a rare and exciting discovery. Most nests leave few remains, and for an entire nest to become fossilized before the young dinosaurs can hatch, something had to go badly wrong. This nest, which is being excavated by scientists in Argentina, was probably covered by a sudden sandstorm. The dinosaur embryos would have died through lack of oxygen, allowing the egg clutch to be preserved whole.

INCUBATION
What happened after egg-laying is more difficult to piece together. At one time, palaeontologists assumed that female dinosaurs covered their eggs and left them to develop on their own, but some fossils have shown that this may not always have been true. In the 1920s, a fossil *Oviraptor* was found, apparently caught in the act of stealing eggs from a nest. However, more recent fossils (page 109) have shown *Oviraptor* sitting on its own eggs, probably to protect them, and perhaps to keep them warm. If *Oviraptor* did incubate its eggs, it is unlikely to have been the only dinosaur that behaved in this way.

Some dinosaurs may have incubated their eggs by covering them with fresh vegetation. As the plants rotted, they generated warmth like a compost heap. The warmth would

▷ *Dinosaur eggs were packed with nutrients, which would have made them a useful source of food for omnivores such as Oviraptor. Here, one has been caught trying to raid a Protoceratops nest, and the nest's owner has gone on the attack with its beak-like jaws.*

▽ *By nesting together, herd-forming species such as Maiasaura had a better chance of fighting off nest raiders. Each female – perhaps helped by her mate – built a crater-shaped nest of mud, up to 2m wide. The female then laid about 20 eggs, and covered the clutch with a mixture of foliage and sand. The eggs probably took about a month to hatch.*

have enabled the eggs to develop even if the outside temperature was low.

LEAVING THE NEST

By examining the shells of empty eggs, researchers can work out how young dinosaurs behaved immediately after they hatched. In many nests, the shells are open at one end but largely intact. This suggests that the young moved out of their nest soon after hatching, or the empty shells would have been crushed by the young dinosaurs.

To leave the nest this early, these young animals must have been well-developed. Their parents may have watched over them, but they were more likely to have been left to fend for themselves.

STAYING PUT

Other dinosaur nests tell a quite different story. At a nest-site in Montana, USA, crushed eggshells have been found with the fossilized remains of young nestlings. The nests were made by *Maiasaura*, a duck-billed dinosaur (page 104) that nested in groups. The recently hatched *Maiasaura* were still poorly developed, which makes it unlikely that they were about to leave the nest. They probably relied on their parents to bring them food. Once the young left the nest, they were protected by being part of a herd, and by growing extremely rapidly. Even so, many young dinosaurs failed to survive their first year – which is why large families were an essential part of dinosaur life.

Carnivorous dinosaurs would have easily carried dead animal prey back to the nests. But plant food is harder to carry. *Maiasaura* probably brought plants back to its young, but other plant-eaters may have fed their young with regurgitated, semi-digested food.

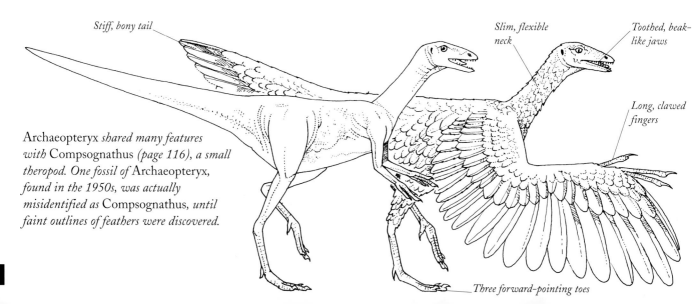

Longisquama's *feather-like scales may have been used for gliding, but they are unlikely to have had any direct connection with the feathers evolved by birds.*

THE ORIGIN OF BIRDS

MOST SCIENTISTS BELIEVE THAT BIRDS EVOLVED FROM SMALL THEROPOD DINOSAURS. THE KEY STEP WAS THE DEVELOPMENT OF FEATHERS, TURNING ANIMALS THAT COULD RUN OR CLIMB INTO ONES THAT COULD FLY.

The earliest true bird known to science is *Archaeopteryx*, which lived in the late Jurassic Period, over 150 million years ago. Discovered in 1861, it looked like a cross between a reptile and a bird, with a toothed beak, a long bony tail, and the unmistakable outline of feathers. In recent years, other 'feathered reptiles' have been found.

THE FIRST FEATHERS

Birds use feathers for two quite different things – to keep themselves warm and to fly. Feathers that are used for insulation are usually short and fluffy, while ones used for flight are much larger, and have a curved surface or vane. These two kinds of feathers are very unlikely to have evolved at the same time. Insulating feathers almost certainly came first, and then, over millions of years, some developed into specialized feathers that could be used for flight.

No one knows when feathers first appeared. Some palaeontologists have claimed that they can be seen in *Longisquama*, a reptile that dates back to Triassic times, but the majority of experts are not convinced. The best evidence for feather evolution comes from small theropods recently discovered in China. One of these, *Sinosauropteryx*, had short downy plumage, and a feathery crest running down its neck and back. It was a feathered dinosaur, but it would not have been able to fly.

INTO THE AIR

Sinosauropteryx lived slightly later than *Archaeopteryx*, which means that it could not have been its direct ancestor. However, its downy plumage shows what the forebears of flying birds may have looked like, before they evolved fully feathered wings. But how did wings develop and, more important, why?

One theory is that the ancestors of birds evolved wings as an adaptation for hunting insects and other small animals. According to this idea, these 'proto-birds' chased their

Stiff, bony tail

Slim, flexible neck

Toothed, beak-like jaws

Long, clawed fingers

Archaeopteryx *shared many features with* Compsognathus *(page 116), a small theropod. One fossil of* Archaeopteryx, *found in the 1950s, was actually misidentified as* Compsognathus, *until faint outlines of feathers were discovered.*

Three forward-pointing toes

prey across the ground, leaping into the air to catch small animals as they tried to escape. Over a long period of time, the argument goes, they developed extra-large feathers on their front legs to help them stay balanced, and also perhaps to help them scoop up their prey. The feathers gradually became longer, while the muscles that worked the front legs became stronger. Eventually, this created animals that could flap their way off the ground.

GLIDERS IN THE TREES?

This ground-based theory is borne out by some features shown by *Archaeopteryx*, such as its strong legs. But most palaeontologists believe that birds actually evolved from reptiles that lived not on the ground, but in trees. By evolving extra-large feathers, these animals would have developed the ability to glide, so that they could travel through woodlands and forests without having to go on the ground. From this, flapping flight would have gradually developed.

Gliding is something that has cropped up many times in reptile evolution. It was used by *Coelurosauravus* (page 170), and a range of other tree-dwellers, and it can be seen in several species of lizards alive today. For supporters of the 'tree-based' theory, this makes it all the more likely that birds began in a similar way.

LIGHT FOR FLIGHT

Gliding uses up very little energy, but flapping flight is strenuous business. To stay airborne, early birds had to undergo some important 'design changes' that made them increasingly different from their dinosaur ancestors. Evolution cannot look ahead, so these changes were not planned. Instead, they built up slowly over a long period as birds spent more and more of their time in the air.

Many of these changes helped birds to lose weight – 'excess baggage' that made it harder to stay aloft. Many of their bones fused so their skeletons became lighter. Like their theropod ancestors, they had hollow, air-filled bones, but the air spaces became larger and more extensive, reaching most of the way down their wings and legs. They also developed enlarged breastbones, which anchored the powerful chest muscles that were needed for flight, and a V-shaped furcula, or wishbone, that braced the chest during flight.

These changes proved to be a winning combination. Birds became increasingly common in Cretaceous times, and when the Age of Reptiles came to its cataclysmic end, they were the only dinosaur descendants that managed to survive.

▷ Archaeopteryx *had asymmetrical or 'lopsided' wing feathers, like those of modern birds. Feathers like these generate lift when air flows over them, and they are evidence that* Archaeopteryx *could fly.*

▽ Avimimus *(far left) was a feathered theropod that was not able to fly.* Archaeopteryx *(centre) was smaller and lighter, with well-developed flight feathers.*

Pigeon

△ *Compared to* Archaeopteryx, *modern birds like this pigeon have no teeth, short tails and – with a handful of exceptions, such as the hoatzin – they have no wing claws.*

Archaeopteryx

Avimimus

THE MEAT-EATERS

EARLY BIRDS

Despite the discovery of many fossils, there are still plenty of unanswered questions about how the first birds evolved. Some researchers think that they may have split into two groups early in their history. According to this theory, the first group contained *Archaeopteryx* and other long-tailed species, while the second contained short-tailed birds – the direct ancestors of the ones alive today. Not all palaeontologists are convinced, but one fact is certain: by late Cretaceous times, birds were very successful, and lived all over the Earth.

△ *Apart from its toothed beak,* Ichthyornis *(above right) looked like a modern tern, and probably had a very similar way of life. The evidence for* its *diet comes from large numbers of fish bones found near its fossilized remains.*

▷ Hesperornis *(centre) swam by paddling with its webbed feet, while using its stubby wings to steer. Compared to flying birds, diving species like* Hesperornis *have fewer air-cavities in their bones. This helped them to stay submerged.*

ARCHAEOPTERYX
Archaeopteryx is probably the most famous prehistoric animal known. Only six fossil specimens have been found – all from Solnhöfen in southern Germany. In most of them, the imprint of feathers can be clearly seen. *Archaeopteryx* was about the size of a crow, but had toothed jaws and a long reptile-like tail. Its legs were long, and its wings had three claws at their 'elbows', which might have been used in climbing. Like today's birds, it almost certainly reproduced by laying and incubating eggs, although no fossils of these have been found.

MAXIMUM LENGTH	35cm
TIME	Late Jurassic
FOSSIL FINDS	Europe (Germany)

▷ Archaeopteryx *is a classic example of an evolutionary link between two groups of animals. It was discovered just two years after Charles Darwin published his theory of evolution.*

ICHTHYORNIS
With a name meaning 'fish bird', *Ichthyornis* was similar to some seabirds alive today, although it still had one primitive feature – a beak lined with sharp teeth. Unlike *Archaeopteryx*, the bony part of its tail was very short, and its wings did not have claws. Internally, it had two other features that are found in all modern flying birds: many of its bones contained large air spaces, which helped to reduce its overall weight, and it also had a narrow forward-pointing flap, called a keel, that protruded from its breastbone. This flap, which is missing in *Archaeopteryx*, anchored the large chest muscles that powered its wings.

MAXIMUM LENGTH	35cm
TIME	Late Cretaceous
FOSSIL FINDS	North America (Kansas, Texas in USA)

HESPERORNIS
The earliest true birds were flying species, but as birds evolved, some species lost the power of flight. *Hesperornis* was one of them – a large, fish-eating diver with tiny wings, and legs placed far back along its body, near its tail. On land, *Hesperornis* may have lumbered along like a seal, but its streamlined shape and webbed feet made it fast and manoeuvrable underwater, like today's grebes. Becoming flightless may seem like a backward step, but during bird evolution, many other species have followed this path. They include many land-dwelling species, including the largest birds that have ever lived (page 213).

MAXIMUM LENGTH	1.75m
TIME	Late Cretaceous
FOSSIL FINDS	North America (Kansas, USA)

GIANT MEAT-EATERS

During the Jurassic and Cretaceous Periods, predatory theropods evolved in step with their prey. Some species, such as *Deinonychus*, tackled large animals by hunting in packs, but others relied on their individual size and power to make a kill. These giant meat-eaters were the super-predators of the reptile age, able to topple plant-eaters that could weigh more than 30 tonnes. *Tyrannosaurus* is by far the most famous among them, but recent discoveries have shown that, in Cretaceous times, other predatory theropods may have been larger still.

PACK ATTACK

Launching a deadly ambush, a group of Deinonychus *attack a plant-eating hypsilophodont several times their own size. For Cretaceous plant-eaters, packs of these small and highly agile hunters would have been just as dangerous as much larger predators that stalked prey on their own.*

CARNOSAURS

AT ONE TIME, ALL LARGE PREDATORY
DINOSAURS WERE CLASSIFIED IN A GROUP
CALLED THE CARNOSAURS, MEANING 'FLESH
REPTILES'. SINCE THEN, RESEARCH HAS
SHOWN THAT GIANT MEAT-EATERS WERE
NOT NECESSARILY CLOSE RELATIVES.

Unlike the smaller theropods, which often used their claws to attack their prey, the largest meat-eaters of the dinosaur world used their teeth to attack their victims. Their arms were often puny, but their skulls were huge – a feature that *Carcharodontosaurus* (page 160), shows in a particularly chilling way. For hunting, this kind of anatomy proved to be lethally effective, and it probably evolved separately in several different theropod groups.

▽ *This cladogram
shows the possible links
between tetanurans, or
advanced theropods.
Each branch forms a
clade which includes an
ancestral species, together
with its descendants.*

FAMILY FEATURES
At first glance, giant theropods, such as *Allosaurus* and *Tyrannosaurus*, look very similar. All of them had powerful hind legs, small arms, and narrow skulls with immense tooth-filled jaws. They may not have been as fast on their feet as palaeontologists once supposed, and it is quite likely that some of

them were scavengers as well as hunters, but their reputation as the ultimate terrestrial killers is still well deserved.

It seems only common sense that these massively built hunters were as closely related as, for example, tigers and lions are today. But for palaeontologists trying to work out the evolutionary history of dinosaurs, outward similarities can cause problems. Animals often develop similar adaptations if they have similar lifestyles, through convergent evolution. If they are already quite similar to begin with, convergence can make true family relationships extremely difficult to unravel. This is the position with large theropods.

UNRAVELLING THE PAST
To get a true picture of how closely different species are related, palaeontologists and biologists use a system called cladistics. This involves comparing animals in detail, and seeing how many 'derived features' they share. A derived feature is one that develops in an ancestral species, and which is then handed on to all its descendants. Because ancestors have ancestors themselves, derived features steadily build up as time goes by. The more derived features two species share, the more closely they must be related. This information can be used to construct a cladogram, a chart that shows the branches in evolution that divide one group of species from another.

The cladogram on this page shows one idea of how all the advanced theropods might have been related. The allosaurs and tyrannosaurs are far apart, and belong to two separate 'clades': the carnosaurs, a group that contains some of the largest theropods, and the coelurosaurs, which contains some of the smallest. Through convergent

TETANURANS   **CARNOSAURS**   **COELUROSAURS**

Megalosaurs

Allosaurs

Carcharo-
dontosaurs

Coelurus

Compsognathus

Bird mimics

Segnosaurs

Oviraptor

Dromaeosaurs

Tyrannosaurs

evolution, tyrannosaurs developed giant bodies and tiny arms, just like the allosaurs, 50 million years before.

LIMITS TO GROWTH

Like the plant-eating sauropods (page 84), giant theropods enjoyed some obvious advantages because of their size. Weighing up to 6 or 7 tonnes, and with bodies up to 14m long, they would have developed a nearly unstoppable momentum as they slammed into prey. As sauropods increased in size, these hunters did as well, although the increase happened at different times in different groups, with the megalosaurs being the first to enter the heavyweight class.

But if large size was such an asset, why did theropods stop at the 7-tonne mark, when plant-eating dinosaurs evolved bodies that were perhaps ten times heavier still? The chief reason is that, unlike plant-eaters, predators rely on speed and agility to survive. Compared to smaller theropods, animals like *Allosaurus* were already slow and lumbering, and it is quite likely that if they had evolved much larger bodies, they would not have been able to function as predators that pursued their prey.

▽ *Large theropods like* Tyrannosaurus *evolved extreme differences in size between the front and back limbs. Their heads were the largest of all the dinosaurs, apart from some ceratopsians.* Tyrannosaurus *may have ambushed animals rather than chasing them. It may also have obtained a proportion of its food from carrion – an efficient form of nutrition.*

GIANT MEAT-EATERS

MEGALOSAURS AND SEGNOSAURS

The megalosaurs were the earliest of the giant bipedal hunters. Megalosaurs had small front legs with three-fingered hands, massively built skulls and, in some cases, horns or crests. Segnosaurs, also known as therizinosaurs, are known only from fragmentary remains. They were unrelated to megalosaurs, and experts have had great difficulty deciding where they fit into the dinosaur world. Some believe they were plant-eating sauropods, but others think they were highly specialized large theropods.

DILOPHOSAURUS

The earliest known megalosaur, *Dilophosaurus*, was an agile hunter, despite weighing up to half a tonne. Its most conspicuous feature was its double crest, which was positioned over its forehead and muzzle, with a central furrow running down its length. Its function is unclear – it may have been used in courtship displays, and is likely to have been larger in males than in females. The remains of three *Dilophosaurus*, found together in Arizona, suggest that this species may have hunted in packs. From its long, thin teeth, some scientists have concluded that *Dilophosaurus* was more likely to have used its clawed hands, rather than its teeth, to grab its prey and rip it apart.

MAXIMUM LENGTH	6m
TIME	Early Jurassic
FOSSIL FINDS	North America (Arizona, USA), Asia (China)

△ Dilophosaurus' *double head crest was partly hollow, so it is unlikely that it was used for self-defence. It may have been for display and unique to males.*

▷ Eustreptospondylus *was first mistaken for* Megalosaurus, *since the two animals were similar in many ways. However, it was about 2m shorter, with a much smaller body weight.*

EUSTREPTOSPONDYLUS

Only one specimen of *Eustreptospondylus* has ever been found. Unusually for a land animal, it was discovered in marine sediments, leading scientists to conclude that its carcass was washed out to sea. It may have reached the sea by a river, but it is possible that it lived on the shore, perhaps scavenging food from the remains of animals left stranded by the tide. Although incomplete, the fossil is still the best-preserved carnosaur yet found in Europe. It had a typical megalosaur build, with large back legs, three-fingered hands, and a head without a crest. Some of the bones show signs of not being fully developed, which makes it likely that it was not fully grown when it died.

MAXIMUM LENGTH	7m
TIME	Mid Jurassic to late Cretaceous
FOSSIL FINDS	Europe (England)

MEGALOSAURUS

Standing 3m tall, and weighing about a tonne, *Megalosaurus* – 'great lizard' – was an animal that more than lived up to its name. A *Megalosaurus* thighbone, found in England in 1676, was the first dinosaur bone to come to the attention of European science. At the time, no one correctly guessed what it was, and over 150 years passed before Richard Owen, the pioneering anatomist and palaeontologist, included *Megalosaurus* in a new category of extinct reptiles – the dinosaurs. Since then, *Megalosaurus* remains have been found in several different countries, although none of them is complete. However, they show that it was one of the largest predators of the Jurassic, with a head nearly 1m long. Fossilized trackways, found in southern England, show that it had a 'pigeon-toed' gait, with its tail held off the ground when moving at speed. It was probably a rapid runner, but not built for a drawn-out chase.

MAXIMUM LENGTH 9m
TIME Jurassic
FOSSIL FINDS Europe (UK, France), Africa (Morocco)

ERLIKOSAURUS

Erlikosaurus belonged to the segnosaur or therizinosaur family – an obscure group of less than a dozen known species, all from central Asia or the Far East. Although segnosaurs are generally classified as theropods, *Erlikosaurus*'s skull – the only segnosaur example so far discovered – looks quite unlike those of other predatory dinosaurs, with small teeth overall, but an upper jaw that ends in a toothless beak. It had unusually large claws and probably stood on two legs. From studies of its teeth and skeleton, it seems possible that *Erlikosaurus* and other segnosaurs may have been fish-eaters.

MAXIMUM LENGTH 6m
TIME Mid Cretaceous
FOSSIL FINDS Asia (Mongolia)

NANSHIUNGOSAURUS

Like *Erlikosaurus*, this animal was also a segnosaur, but knowledge about it is based on a handful of very incomplete remains. Nothing is known about its head, as its skull has not been found, but it had a long neck and tail. Its front legs were well-developed, and it may have moved on all fours. Enlarged finger claws seem to have been a feature of *Nanshiungosaurus* and its

relatives. One species, called *Alxasaurus*, had finger claws up to 70cm long, making them probably the largest of any dinosaur.

MAXIMUM LENGTH 5m
TIME Mid to late Cretaceous
FOSSIL FINDS Asia (China)

PROCERATOSAURUS

The most unusual feature of *Proceratosaurus* was the horn on the top of its snout. This was thought to be evidence that it was a forerunner of the ceratosaurs (page 116), which is how it got its name. It is often classified as a megalosaur but its place is open to doubt since the only remains found so far have been part of the skull and jaw. Apart from its horn, *Proceratosaurus* seems to have been a typical mid-Jurassic hunter, although a fairly small one, with a maximum weight of perhaps 100kg.

MAXIMUM LENGTH 4m
TIME Mid Jurassic
FOSSIL FINDS Europe (UK)

◁ Megalosaurus *was a successful 'prototype' version of the giant bipedal predator – a body form that persisted among various groups of theropods right until the Age of Reptiles ended.*

◁ Proceratosaurus *is known from a single skull, which makes it difficult to judge exactly how it looked. This reconstruction shows it as a typical theropod, with small front legs.*

▽ *Looking more like a sauropod than a theropod,* Nanshiungosaurus *is a mystifying animal. It may have led an amphibious existence, feeding on fish, but its large size, long neck and small head make it just as likely that it was a browser.*

GIANT MEAT-EATERS

ALLOSAURS

Appearing 50 million years before the tyrannosaurs, the allosaurs may have included the largest carnivores ever to have lived on land. Found throughout the world, they were bipedal predators, with immense heads, very large back legs, but relatively short arms with three-fingered hands. No dinosaur – no matter how big – would have been able to withstand allosaur packs.

▽ *An* Allosaurus *attacks a* Diplodocus *several times its own size.* Allosaurus *may have hunted individually – on their own they would have been fearsome – or in packs.*

CARCHARODONTOSAURUS
Meaning 'shark-toothed lizard', *Carcharodontosaurus* was first discovered in the 1920s, but these remains were destroyed during World War 2, and some new ones have only recently come to light (pages 160–161). This massively built hunter – and possibly scavenger – may have weighed as much as 8 tonnes, and had teeth up to 20cm long. Its skull measured about 1.6m from front to back, and it is possible that the entire animal may have been bigger than *Tyrannosaurus* (page 144), even though its brain was only about half the size.

MAXIMUM LENGTH 13.5m

TIME Early Cretaceous

FOSSIL FINDS North Africa

ALLOSAURUS
Allosaurus was a common and widespread predator 150 million years ago, hunting or scavenging for a living. It weighed up to 3 tonnes, and scientists are far from agreed how a predator this large would have moved, or whether it would have been able to chase and catch fast-moving prey. Despite its powerful hind legs, it is doubtful that it would have been able to run faster than 30km/h, and skeletal injuries in some *Allosaurus* remains suggest that it was often injured in hunting mishaps – whether in falls, or by its prey fighting back.

MAXIMUM LENGTH 12m

TIME Late Jurassic

FOSSIL FINDS North America (western USA), Australia

NEOVENATOR

Discovered on the Isle of Wight in 1978, but not excavated until the 1980s, *Neovenator* – meaning 'new hunter' – was a smaller and more agile predator than its cousin *Allosaurus*. The single fossil found so far shows that *Neovenator* had a strongly curved forehead, and large nostrils, indicating that it had a good sense of smell. During Cretaceous times, it was probably the largest flesh-eating dinosaur in what is now northern Europe.

MAXIMUM LENGTH	8m
TIME	Early Cretaceous
FOSSIL FINDS	Europe (UK)

GIGANOTOSAURUS

Found in 1994 by an amateur palaeontologist in Patagonia, *Giganotosaurus* may have been the largest predatory dinosaur ever. Its skull alone was nearly as long as a man is tall, and its body was as long as a bus. Estimates of its weight vary, with the highest figure – about 8 tonnes – putting it among the real heavyweights of the theropod world. Unlike

△ *Striding across a marshy landscape, Neovenator sniffs the air for prey. This recently discovered allosaur had a muzzle shaped like a giant beak.*

Tyrannosaurus, *Giganotosaurus* had a relatively narrow head, and teeth that were shaped for slicing through flesh, rather than for breaking bones. Its name means 'giant southern lizard'.

MAXIMUM LENGTH	13m
TIME	Late Cretaceous
FOSSIL FINDS	South America (Argentina)

◁ *With its right shoulder seriously injured, the* Apatosaurus *risks crashing to the ground. If it does, it cannot escape, and the* Allosaurus *can make an easy kill.*

GIANT MEAT-EATERS

◁ *Two young* Albertosaurus *race past a*
Daspletosaurus, *which has waded into water to feed on a carcass. If the* Daspletosaurus *had been on land, the smaller animals would not have risked venturing so close.*

DASPLETOSAURUS

Only a handful of specimens of this dinosaur have been found, but its fossilized remains suggest that it may have been a direct ancestor of *Tyrannosaurus*. It probably weighed up to 3 tonnes, and would have been about 5m tall. Like other tyrannosaurs, *Daspletosaurus* had an extra set of ribs, called gastralia, between its true ribs and its pelvis. These helped to support its intestines, and may have protected them when resting on the ground.

MAXIMUM LENGTH	8m
TIME	Late Cretaceous
FOSSIL FINDS	North America (Alberta, Canada)

TYRANNOSAURS

Although they existed for only 15 million years, the tyrannosaurs are among the most fascinating and awe-inspiring animals from the dinosaur age. Their huge heads were armed with immense serrated teeth, and they stood on pillar-like back legs that could be twice as tall as an adult man. Their front legs were even smaller that those of the allosaurs, and they ended in two-fingered hands not much bigger than our own. Tyrannosaurs were undoubtedly meat-eaters, and probably lived mainly by hunting. They may also have scavenged for dead remains.

TARBOSAURUS

This Asian tyrannosaur looks very much like *Tyrannosaurus*, but had a longer skull and was not so heavily built. Like *Tyrannosaurus*, it was unlikely to have survived solely by hunting, and probably scavenged dead remains. It lived in Asia, where it would have been the largest land predator. Fossil remains of *Tarbosaurus* were first discovered in 1948, and since then, experts have been divided on exactly where it fits into the tyrannosaur family. Because it is so similar to *Tyrannosaurus*, some experts think that it might actually be the same animal.

MAXIMUM LENGTH	14m
TIME	Late Cretaceous
FOSSIL FINDS	Asia (Mongolia)

ALBERTOSAURUS

Weighing about 3 tonnes, *Albertosaurus* was small compared to its relatives, but still much larger than any predatory land animal alive today. It had the typical tyrannosaur build, with an outsize head, long hind legs and a muscular tail that helped it balance. Each of its jaws had a single row of serrated teeth, which were gradually shed and replaced throughout its lifetime. It shared its habitat with plant-eaters such as hadrosaurs (pages 104–107) and ankylosaurs (pages 164–165), that would also have been its prey.

▽ *For tyrannosaurs, life was a constant balancing act. As it strides along, this* Tarbosaurus *holds its tail high, so that it acts as a counterweight for its enormous head.*

MAXIMUM LENGTH	8m
TIME	Late Cretaceous
FOSSIL FINDS	North America (Canada, USA)

▽ *With a menacing lunge of its head, a Tyrannosaurus threatens a* Troodon *which has just stolen part of its meal. The subject of the feast is a hadrosaur, which has died from natural causes. Remains like these probably made up an important part of* Tyrannosaurus' *diet. Like scavengers today,* Tyrannosaurus *would have found this kind of food partly by smell, and partly by looking to see where other scavengers had gathered.*

TYRANNOSAURUS

After *Carcharodontosaurus* (page 142), this huge animal was probably the largest land-based predator that has ever lived on Earth. Several superbly preserved fossil skeletons have been found, most notably 'Sue' (page 147), which was discovered in 1990. These fossils show that *Tyrannosaurus* weighed up to 7 tonnes, and towered up to 6m high. It took paces nearly 5m long – further than most people can long-jump – and dealt with its food using 15cm-long teeth with serrated edges like steak knives. Some scientists have suggested that it was too big to pursue its prey in the open, because its tiny arms could not have broken its fall if it tripped and fell.

Instead, it may have hunted by lurking among trees, launching an attack when its prey was close by.

MAXIMUM LENGTH 14m

TIME Late Cretaceous

FOSSIL FINDS North America (Canada and USA), Asia (Mongolia)

ALIORAMUS

Most tyrannosaurs had deep skulls and jaws that were flattened from side to side. *Alioramus* and its relatives were different, because their skulls had elongated snouts with weaker jaws. *Alioramus* also had about six bony knobs located between its nostrils and eyes. These knobs were too small to have been weapons, and it is possible that they played a part in courtship, rather like the 'horns' some lizards have today. If this is true, they may have been present only in the males.

MAXIMUM LENGTH 6m

TIME Late Cretaceous

FOSSIL FINDS Asia (Mongolia)

FOSSIL-HUNTING IN NORTH AMERICA

THE FIRST DINOSAUR FOSSILS WERE FOUND IN EUROPE, BUT NORTH AMERICA IS THE PLACE WHERE 'DINOMANIA' REALLY GOT UNDERWAY – PARTLY AS A RESULT OF A BITTER FEUD BETWEEN TWO LEADING PALAEONTOLOGISTS.

I n 1858, the zoologist Joseph Leidy described the first dinosaur skeleton found in North America as *Hadrosaurus*. But during the late 1800s, two much more forceful characters dominated the fossil-hunting stage: Edward Drinker Cope and Othniel Charles Marsh. They discovered huge numbers of fossils, and their rivalry ignited public interest in North America's fascinating prehistoric life.

Dry places are particularly good for finding fossils. Over millions of years, wind and rain scour the surface of the ground, revealing fossils entombed in the underlying rock. This tree trunk is one of hundreds in Arizona's Petrified Forest National Park. This particular trunk has broken into sections, as the rock that supported it has slowly crumbled away.

COLLECTING THE PAST
By the time Cope and Marsh died, they had accumulated an extraordinary variety of fossil remains. These included the first skeleton of a giant plant-eating sauropod – *Apatosaurus* (known at the time as *Brontosaurus*) – and a wide array of others, including predators such as allosaurs and tyrannosaurs, as well as the horned dinosaurs, or ceratopsids, which were unique to North America. They also helped to trace the path that evolution had followed. Marsh, for example, assembled a

△▷ *Edward Drinker Cope (above) and Othniel Charles Marsh (right) were pioneering North American palaeontologists.*

complete series of fossil horses, showing how these animals had slowly adapted to a life on North America's open plains.

TREASURE TROVES

Because of its size and varied geography, North America is a palaeontologist's paradise. Many of the best finds have been made in the 'badlands' and deserts of the American Midwest, where ancient sedimentary rocks have been slowly eroded by rivers, rain and wind. Some of these sites have produced an enormous number of fossils: at Ghost Ranch in New Mexico, for example, the remains of over 1,000 *Coelophysis* – a small bipedal predator – are possible evidence that these agile animals hunted in packs. Another site, the Red Deer River in Alberta, Canada, has produced more types of dinosaur than any equivalent area in the world, while further west, and further back in time, Canada is also the site of one of the most important fossil formations revealing early animal life – the Burgess Shale (pages 32–35).

Not all North American fossil finds consist of remains that were once buried in rock. The famous La Brea tar pits, outside Los Angeles, are deposits of sticky tar that has seeped upwards from natural springs since prehistoric times. From these treacherous pools, the fossilized remains of thousands of trapped animals have been recovered (page 212).

Palaeontologists work on the fossilized skeleton of a Tyrannosaurus, *cleaning and stabilizing the remains before they are removed from the site where they have lain for over 60 million years .*

RECENT DISCOVERIES

North America is famous for giant fossils, and in recent years, there have been spectacular discoveries. One of the most exciting came in 1990, when the remains of

a gigantic *Tyrannosaurus rex* were found in South Dakota. The fossil – named Sue, after its finder Sue Hendrickson – is now displayed in the Field Museum, Chicago, and is the largest and most complete *Tyrannosaurus* on display n the world. Unlike previous finds, Sue's skeleton includes a wishbone or furcula – evidence that backs up the widespread belief that birds evolved from predatory dinosaurs.

Some finds are accidental. In 1979, two hikers in New Mexico came across the fossilized tail of *Seismosaurus*. The tail led palaeontologists to the rest of this plant-eater's skeleton, which is still being unearthed.

▽ *Soft sedimentary rocks are a prime source of fossils. These rocks in Arizona were laid down during the Triassic.*

△ *Excavating fossils is a delicate business. A wooden frame is used to protect the pelvis of a* Tyrannosaurus *before it is winched away from the surrounding bedrock.*

◁ *The completed mount of 'Sue's' fossilized skeleton, at the Field Museum in Chicago. This massive animal weighed about 6.5 tonnes, and was nearly 13m long.*

WERE DINOSAURS WARM-BLOODED?

BECAUSE DINOSAURS WERE REPTILES, IT IS EASY TO IMAGINE THAT THEIR BODIES WORKED LIKE REPTILES TODAY. BUT IN ONE KEY AREA, THEY MAY HAVE BEEN QUITE DIFFERENT.

At one time, scientists assumed that dinosaurs were cold-blooded, which means that their temperature depended on their surroundings. But in the early 1970s, an American biologist, Robert Bakker (page 84), argued that they might have been warm-blooded, like mammals and birds. This controversial theory has radically altered ideas about dinosaur biology.

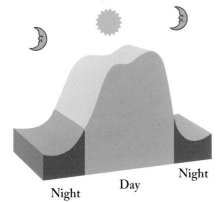

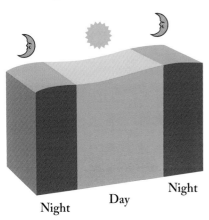

Lizards are cold-blooded. Their temperature rises as the day warms, and then falls at night.

Walruses are warm-blooded. They keep their body temperature at 35°C day and night.

WARMTH FROM WITHIN

Living vertebrates (animals with backbones) can be divided into two overall groups. Animals in the first group – amphibians, fish, reptiles – are cold-blooded or ectothermic. Their body temperature rises and falls according to the temperature around them. Birds and mammals, on the other hand, are warm-blooded or endothermic. An inbuilt 'thermostat' keeps their body temperature almost constant – and usually much higher than that of their surroundings. Warm-blooded animals generate more heat by breaking down more food, and they keep hold of it by having an insulating layer of feathers, fat or fur.

These two different systems have some far-reaching effects on the way animals live, because bodies work more efficiently at high temperatures. When it is hot, cold-blooded animals are hot as well, and they can move quickly. But when it turns cool, the same animals become slow and sluggish. In really cold conditions they have difficulty moving at all. Warm-blooded animals stay warm whatever the conditions outside, so birds and mammals can remain active and busy during the coldest winters, and some of them are quite comfortable on polar ice.

WRAPPING UP

Dinosaur remains do contain some clues that hint at a warm-blooded lifestyle. For many palaeontologists, one of the most convincing is feathery insulation – something that has only been seen in the very recent past. The first 'feathered dinosaur', *Sinosauropteryx*, was discovered in northeast China in 1996, revealing patches of feathery filaments around its fossilized skeleton. In 2000, an even clearer example of primitive plumage – this time in a dromaeosaur – was unearthed in the same region (page 111). Neither of these Chinese dinosaurs could fly, and the only conceivable function for their feathers was to keep in body heat. Both were small predatory theropods, and if they had feathers, it is quite likely that other theropods did as well. They were not the only insulated reptiles of prehistoric times: some pterosaurs, such as

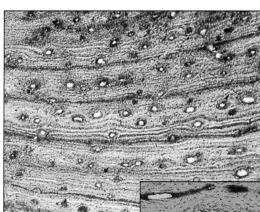

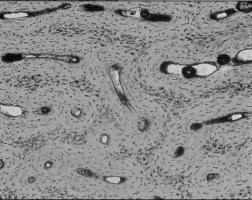

Sordes (page 174), seem to have had the equivalent of closely-cropped fur.

Another factor that points to warm-bloodedness was their way of life. Like other small theropods, *Sinosauropteryx* had a relatively large brain, and its skeleton shows that it would have been an agile and fast-footed hunter. This kind of lifestyle would have called for rapid reactions – a characteristic feature of warm-blooded animals.

EVIDENCE IN BONE

Some experts also believe that signs of warm-bloodedness can be seen in dinosaur skeletons. In the 1970s, Robert Bakker pointed out that, when looked at under a microscope, dinosaur bone shows signs of sustained rapid growth. This feature is common in warm-blooded animals, but rarer in cold-blooded ones, except in times when there is a particularly good supply of food.

But many palaeontologists today find this 'evidence' rather doubtful, and recent research into dinosaur breathing has prompted different conclusions. The palaeontologists looked at dinosaur noses with X-ray scanners, searching for turbinal bones inside the nasal cavity. In birds and mammals, these bones form a complicated collection of paper-thin scrolls that allow warmth and moisture to be collected and recycled from outgoing air. But if dinosaurs were cold-blooded, their

breath would also have been cold, so there would have been no warmth to recycle, and probably no turbinal bones. The results so far show that dinosaurs did not have them.

DINOSAUR HEARTS

If dinosaurs were warm-blooded, their circulatory systems would have been modified to produce a higher rate of oxygen flow. They would have needed larger hearts than their cold-blooded relatives, and their blood would almost certainly have flowed in a figure-of-eight circuit. This double circulation system allows oxygen-rich blood to be pumped at high pressure and high speed.

Unfortunately, soft organs, such as dinosaur hearts, hardly ever fossilize, but in 2000, the remains of what looked like a heart were found in a fossil of *Thescelosaurus*, a small plant-eating hypsilophodont. Using medical scanning techniques, researchers concluded that it did have a double circulation, meaning that it could have been warm-blooded.

◁ *The photograph (far left) shows growth rings in dinosaur bone. Growth rings like these are usually found in cold-blooded animals, and they show spurts of growth that occur during warm conditions, when there is plenty of food.*

◁ *Dinosaurs also have fibro-lamellar bone (centre left), which is found in warm-blooded animals. This kind of bone grows quickly, and is not usually found in cold-blooded animals, although there are some exceptions to this rule.*

DOUBLE CIRCULATION SYSTEM

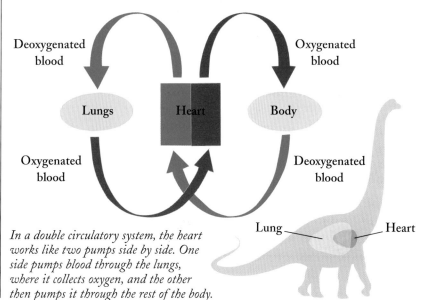

Deoxygenated blood

Oxygenated blood

Lungs   Heart   Body

Oxygenated blood

Deoxygenated blood

Lung   Heart

In a double circulatory system, the heart works like two pumps side by side. One side pumps blood through the lungs, where it collects oxygen, and the other then pumps it through the rest of the body.

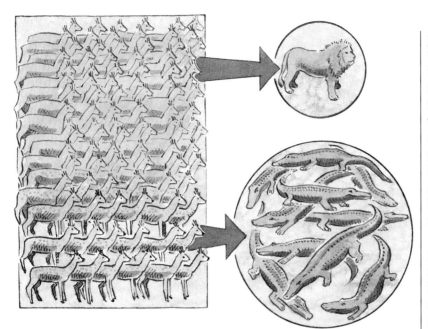

△ *A warm-blooded predator needs about ten times as much food as a cold-blooded one, so 100 antelope could keep 1 lion, or 10 crocodiles, fed for a year.*

▽ *Warm-blooded hunters need a high intake of food to keep their bodies working, and to make up for heat loss.*

ENERGY FROM FOOD

In the debate about whether dinosaurs were warm-blooded, the search for anatomical clues continues. But palaeontologists also have another line of evidence – the relative numbers of predators and their prey.

Cold-blooded predators, which include all of today's reptiles, can survive on a small amount of food. Crocodiles, for example, can go for weeks between meals, because they need only a small amount of energy to keep their bodies ticking over, while some snakes can last over a year. Warm-blooded predators, on the other hand, use up about ten times as much energy simply running their bodies and keeping them warm, which means that they need to take in about ten times as much food per kilogram of body weight. A lion can survive without eating for a few days, but if this hungry period stretches to much more than a week, it runs the serious risk of starving to death. For smaller warm-blooded animals, things become critical even more rapidly, because their body warmth quickly drains away.

This difference means that the same numbers of prey can support ten times as many cold-blooded hunters as warm-blooded ones. Assuming that hunters and their prey fossilize at the same rate (which may or may not be true), palaeontologists should be able to tell if a predatory dinosaur was warm-blooded simply by counting fossils, and doing some simple mathematics.

At present, this work on prehistoric ecology is still underway. Some researchers claim to have found a 'warm-blooded' ratio, but the overall picture is far from clear.

MIX AND MATCH

Faced with this confusing and sometimes contradictory evidence, palaeontologists have come to a variety of conclusions. Some think that all dinosaurs were warm-blooded, while others believe that they were cold-blooded, like reptiles today. But a growing number are convinced that different groups of dinosaurs worked in different ways.

According to this idea, small highly active predators, such as *Sinosauropteryx*, were fully warm-blooded like birds, while some of the smaller plant-eaters may have been cold-blooded like modern reptiles. But the largest dinosaurs – particularly the sauropods – may have been somewhere in between, simply because they were so big. Like giant fermentation tanks on legs, these animals would have absorbed heat energy as their internal microbes broke down their food, but their massive bulk would have meant that this heat would have been very slow to drain away. They would have been 'lukewarm-blooded' – a curious situation that has no equivalent in animals alive today.

ARMOURED DINOSAURS

In the early stages of dinosaur evolution, plant-eating species often relied on their great size to protect them from predators. But during the Jurassic Period, different ways of protecting herbivores from attack evolved. One of these was body armour, a defensive system that allowed plant-eaters to stand their ground. Most armoured dinosaurs belonged to the ornithischian, or bird-hipped, branch of the dinosaur world. They included animals with massive head-shields and gigantic horns, as well as ones that carried their own armour plating on their backs.

DINOSAUR DEFENCES

FOR PLANT-EATING DINOSAURS, RESISTING
ATTACK RATHER THAN RUNNING AWAY WAS
A HIGH-RISK STRATEGY. IN A WORLD FULL
OF PREDATORS, THEY NEEDED THE BEST
DEFENCES THAT EVOLUTION COULD PROVIDE.

I t is hard to imagine what it feels like to be approached
by a hungry carnivore weighing 6 or 7 tonnes. In normal
circumstances, most plant-eating dinosaurs did their
very best to prevent this happening, by being constantly
on the alert for danger, and ready to walk or run away. But
for armoured dinosaurs, different instincts applied. These
animals evolved a strategy which meant standing their
ground. Their bodies were designed to withstand a direct
assault but, to increase their chances of survival, many of
them tried to land the first blow by going on the attack.

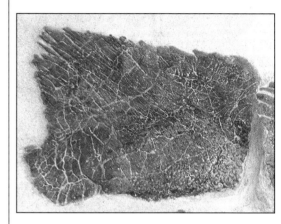

*Dinosaur 'defences' are not always what they
seem.* Stegosaurus *had a row of bony plates
along its back, which were once thought to
be armour against attack. However, detailed
examination of fossilized plates – like the one
shown here – has revealed that they were
made of relatively soft bone. Instead of being
a form of armour, they are more likely to have
been used to control body temperature.*

JAWS AND CLAWS

Unlike predatory theropods, most plant-
eating dinosaurs were unable to do much
damage with their teeth. This was either
because they did not have any, or because
their teeth were shaped for collecting and
crushing plants, rather than for stabbing
flesh. Some armoured species had toothless
beaks that could deliver a dangerous bite
(page 155), but jaws played little part
in plant-eaters' self-defence.

Feet and claws were another
matter. Many sauropods could
rear up on their hind legs to
stamp on an attacker –
something that was
made even more
effective by a single
sharp 'thumb

claw' on each front foot. Although they were much smaller, many ornithopods also had these claws, and because they often moved on their hind legs alone, they would have been able to carry out 'hand-to-hand' combat. These thumb claws were especially large in iguanodonts (page 100).

WHIPS AND CLUBS

But with some plant-eaters, the part that a predator had to watch out for was the tail. The 10m-long tail of an adult *Diplodocus* had the same sort of strength and flexibility as a tyre rubber, reinforced by strands of steel wire. If it was given a sudden flick, the tip would reach supersonic speeds, wrapping around an enemy's body like a whip. A well-aimed blow against a predator's eyes or legs would leave it temporarily blinded, or reeling on the ground.

Some sauropods, such as *Shunosaurus* (page 75), had tails with bony tips, which turned them into clubs. The real specialists at this form of defence were the ankylosaurs (page 165). Their tails were not particularly long by dinosaur standards, but they carried a more substantial weight. In *Euoplocephalus*, one of the largest species, the weight could probably reach a speed of over 50km/h by the end of a full 180-degree swing, landing with enough force to inflict a skull-cracking blow.

SPINES AND HORNS

Clubbing the enemy was one way to fight back; stabbing it was another. Stegosaurs and nodosaurs both used this kind of defence, one group fielding spines on their tails, and the other having them on their shoulders. It is not always easy to distinguish true weapons from ornaments (pages 162-163), but a sideways slant is often a clue that a spine could be used in earnest – vertical

ones were more likely to be for show.

Ceratopsians, which included *Triceratops* and its relatives, often had giant head shields, and horns projecting from their muzzles and brows. These were probably used partly for impressing rivals, and partly for self-defence.

ARMOUR PLATING

If all else failed, and a predator pressed home its attack, armoured dinosaurs relied on their body plating to save the day. This consisted of flat pieces or raised nodules of bone, which developed in the skin, rather than being attached directly to the skeleton. Bony growths like this, called osteoderms, also formed the ankylosaurs' clubs.

Interestingly, osteoderms are one of the oldest forms of self-defence in the vertebrate world, dating back to the first armoured fish, 400 million years ago. Unfortunately, osteoderms – and the spines attached to them – usually became scattered when an animal died. So it is often difficult to decide exactly how they would have been arranged in life. However, they were usually separated by small areas of skin, which allowed the armoured layer to bend. Many armoured dinosaurs had well-protected backs, but relatively vulnerable undersides – a weak point that their enemies would have exploited if they got the opportunity.

△ *These three tails show different adaptations for defence. In Ankylosaurus (left) the tail ends in a body club, while Stegosaurus' tail (centre) is armed with spikes. Diplodocus' tail (right) had neither, but was extremely strong, and could be slapped into an enemy like a whip.*

◁ *A Stegosaurus fossil from the Morrison Formation, Wyoming, USA, shows what look like defensive plates. The true function of these plates may actually have been quite different.*

◁ *Crouching down to protect its vulnerable underside (far left), a Euoplocephalus lashes out at a Tyrannosaurus with its tail-club. To be really effective, the blow needed to be well-aimed – not an easy matter as the animal was inevitably facing the other way.*

CERATOPSIDS

Often known as 'horned dinosaurs', most members of this family were distinguished by armour-plated skulls and formidable horns. Their armour would have been used for defending themselves against predators, and perhaps in courtship, much as rhinoceroses do today. The ceratopsids were one of the last families of dinosaurs to evolve before the great extinction 66 million years ago. They were plant-eaters, and ranged from the size of a big dog to larger than a bull elephant. They almost certainly foraged in herds, and lived across the northern hemisphere.

PSITTACOSAURUS
Named 'parrot lizard' because of its parrot-like beak, *Psittacosaurus* walked on two legs, and was once classified as an early iguanodont. However, it is now thought to have been a primitive ceratopsid. It lacked the horns and frills of true horned dinosaurs, but it did have a ridge of bone at the top of its skull to which its jaw muscles were attached, and small horny projections on its cheeks. *Psittacosaurus* stood about 1m

▽ Psittacosaurus *ate cycads and other tough plants, and it balanced itself with its tail.*

◁ Leptoceratops *would probably have been able to move on either two or four legs. Its front feet had five clawed, prehensile fingers for grasping vegetation and pulling it towards its 'beak'.*

high at the shoulder, and probably had a lifespan of 10 to 15 years.

MAXIMUM LENGTH	2.5m
TIME	Early Cretaceous
FOSSIL FINDS	Asia (Mongolia, China, Thailand)

LEPTOCERATOPS
This small dinosaur represents a halfway stage between the 'parrot' dinosaurs, such as *Psittacosaurus*, and the later horned dinosaurs. Like *Psittacosaurus*, it had a parrot-like beak, although with some teeth in the upper jaw. However, the fringed projection at the back of the skull is more evident, without being as exaggerated as it was in later ceratopsids. Unlike its later relatives, it did not have any horns. With its well-developed back legs, *Leptoceratops* was a good runner – an essential feature for a plant-eater with no other way of defending itself. It probably fed on all fours, but reared up when it needed to move at any speed.

MAXIMUM LENGTH	2.7m
TIME	Late Cretaceous
FOSSIL FINDS	North America, Asia (Mongolia), Australia

MICROCERATOPS
The midget of the ceratopsid family, *Microceratops* was lightly built and probably quick on its feet, judging from its long, athletically built hind legs. However, it would almost certainly have grazed on all fours, keeping an eye out for potential predators and taking flight if one was spotted. The back of its skull had the raised fringe typical of this dinosaur family.

MAXIMUM LENGTH	80cm
TIME	Late Cretaceous
FOSSIL FINDS	Asia (Mongolia, China)

BAGACERATOPS

Bagaceratops represents another step along, or divergence from, the evolutionary line for the ceratopsids. It was small but heavily built, with a solid body and stout legs, and would have moved on all fours. It had the beginnings of a skull crest, with bony ridges leading up from its sharp bird-like beak. It also had a blunt, stubby horn on the top of its nose, and ear-like horny projections on each cheek. It would have used its beak to tear off vegetation and its cheek teeth to grind it up. Well-preserved fossils of *Bagaceratops* have been found. From their posture, some may belong to animals that were in underground nests when they died.

MAXIMUM LENGTH 1m

TIME Late Cretaceous

FOSSIL FINDS Asia (Mongolia)

PROTOCERATOPS

Some excellent fossil finds have given palaeontologists a good picture of what *Protoceratops* looked like and how it lived. It was a heavily built creature, weighing about 200kg, although it stood less than 1m tall. It normally moved on all fours, but it may have been able to raise itself up and run on two. It had a pronounced shield-like projection at the back of its head, which anchored some of the muscles that worked its powerful beak. When this dinosaur was discovered, in the 1920s, palaeontologists also found nests and fossilized eggs. The eggs had remarkably thin shells, and were laid in groups of over a dozen, in spirals in the sand.

MAXIMUM LENGTH 2.7m

TIME Late Cretaceous

FOSSIL FINDS Asia (Mongolia, China)

▽ *The fossilized remains of a fight to the death between a* Protoceratops *and a* Velociraptor *were found in 1971.* Velociraptor *had vicious claws to slash its prey, but despite being a plant-eater,* Protoceratops *was able to hit back with its powerful beak. The desperate duel seems to have ended in stalemate, leaving both dinosaurs mortally wounded. Their remains were probably engulfed by sand.*

ARMOURED DINOSAURS

STYRACOSAURUS

The most formidably armed of the horned dinosaurs, *Styracosaurus* fully lived up to its name, which means 'spiked lizard'. It was actually far bigger than any lizard alive today, with a single 60cm long horn on the tip of its nose, and a ring of equally impressive spikes around its head shield. It weighed about 3 tonnes, and it probably defended itself like a modern-day rhinoceros, using its horns and spikes to inflict serious injuries. Studies of this dinosaur's body shape and fossilized tracks indicate that it ran on all fours at speeds of up to 32km/h. A find of about 100 fossilized specimens in Arizona, USA, makes it look very likely that *Styracosaurus* lived in herds.

The dinosaurs probably fed on cycads and palms, grinding up the tough leaves with their cheek teeth.

MAXIMUM LENGTH 5.5m

TIME Late Cretaceous

FOSSIL FINDS North America (Alberta, Canada, and Arizona, Montana, USA)

PACHYRHINOSAURUS

Scientists are unsure whether this ceratopsid had a nose horn or not, since the fossil evidence consists of about a dozen incomplete skulls. The skulls have a thick ridge of bone between the eyes, and this may have formed the base of a horn which later fell away, or it may have been a weapon in its own right. However, both sexes certainly had a large frilled head shield, which was armed with horns and spikes. *Pachyrhinosaurus* weighed over 2.5 tonnes, and

▽ *During their relatively short history, ceratopsids developed an amazing variety of head shields and horns. From the left, the trio shown below are* Styracosaurus *and* Pachyrhinosaurus, *and behind them, the massively built* Triceratops. *These animals' shields and horns had a dual purpose – they were used to fend off predators, but they were also used in real or mock fights with rivals. The horns and frills may also have been used to help them cool down when necessary.*

its arched back was almost twice the height of an adult human being.

MAXIMUM LENGTH 7m

TIME Late Cretaceous

FOSSIL FINDS North America (Alberta, Canada, and Alaska, USA)

TRICERATOPS

The most famous of the horned dinosaurs, *Triceratops* gets its name from its three-horned head. It was the giant of its family, weighing up to 10 tonnes. The two horns on its brow were 1m or more in length, while its entire skull was up to 3m long, making it one of the largest of the dinosaurs. Its skull shield was remarkable for its size and because it consisted of a solid sheet of bone. Hundreds of fossils show that this huge plant-eater roamed North America in large herds. Some skulls show major injuries, suggesting that these animals engaged in fierce contests, probably over mates. *Triceratops* was one of the last of its line, evolving a few million years before the dinosaurs disappeared.

MAXIMUM LENGTH 9m

TIME Late Cretaceous

FOSSIL FINDS Western North America

△ *Like other ceratopsids,* Anchiceratops *was a variable animal, with no two individuals having exactly the same shield and horn shape. Some scientists think that these differences would have enabled these dinosaurs to recognize each other as they mingled in herds.*

ANCHICERATOPS

Considerably smaller than *Triceratops*, this animal had a long and narrow head shield, with a serrated edge of backward-pointing spines. Its shield also had a pronounced central dividing ridge. *Anchiceratops* was a swamp dweller, and lived on lush vegetation, gathering it up with its parrot-like beak. It could weigh over 5 tonnes, and probably spent much of its time wading through shallow water and wet mud.

MAXIMUM LENGTH 6m

TIME Late Cretaceous

FOSSIL FINDS North America (Alberta, Canada)

CENTROSAURUS

Looking like a gigantic rhinoceros – although from a totally different line of the animal world – *Centrosaurus* was a heavy, powerful, thick-set animal with a large horn on top of its beak-like snout. Unlike many other ceratopsids, it had a relatively short head shield, although it was edged with tooth-like horns. The frill was not made of solid bone, but had two openings, reducing its weight. In Canada, a find of about 50 specimens close together points to their being herd animals.

MAXIMUM LENGTH 6m

TIME Late Cretaceous

FOSSIL FINDS North America (Alberta, Canada and Montana, USA)

ARMOURED DINOSAURS

STEGOSAURS

Stegosaurs were slow-moving plant-eaters with a double row of bony plates or spines protruding from their backs. These plates were attached to their skin, rather than their skeletons, making it difficult to establish exactly how they were positioned in life. Opinions differ about their purpose. They may have been used for self-defence, but they could also have played a part in heat regulation, helping to warm up or cool down the animal's blood. If so, the plates may have been able to 'blush' – something that could have been used as part of a mating ritual, or as a warning signal. Stegosaurs were also armed with vicious spikes on their tails, which would have been wielded like medieval weapons to stab their enemies.

STEGOSAURUS
Stegosaurus weighed about 3 tonnes, and was the largest member of its family. It had a strangely proportioned body, with its hind legs much larger than its front ones, giving it a massively humped back. Its remarkably small head was held low and housed a tiny brain, which was not much bigger than a walnut (page 128). Like other stegosaurs, it had a beak-like snout, and chewing teeth at the back of its mouth. *Stegosaurus* probably fed on all fours, although some experts think it could have reared up to reach its food.

MAXIMUM LENGTH	9m
TIME	Late Jurassic
FOSSIL FINDS	Western North America, Europe (UK)

▷ *One of the oldest known stegosaurs,* Huayangosaurus *was also one of the smallest, standing only about 1.8m at the hips – roughly the height of a man – and weighing just over 1 tonne. It may have been the ancestor of other later members of the stegosaur family.*

◁ *The five animals shown here give an idea of how stegosaur 'armour' varied.* Tuojiangosaurus *(top left) and* Stegosaurus *(top right) had two rows of broad, flat plates. The plates look impressive, but many palaeontologists think that they were actually too thin to have been used in self-defence.* Dacentrurus *(bottom left),* Lexovisaurus *(bottom centre) and* Kentrosaurus *(bottom right) had narrower plates, graded into spines on their tails. These five animals shared several features typical of their family – elephant-like legs, an arched back and a relatively tiny head.*

HUAYANGOSAURUS

Like the rest of the family, *Huayangosaurus* was equipped with a paired row of pointed back plates, and a further elongated and horn-like pair on its hips. Its tail was armed with two pairs of pointed horns. Unusually for a stegosaur, it had teeth in its beak, rather than just in its cheeks. *Huayangosaurus* is one of several species that have been unearthed in China, making this region the best part of the world for stegosaur remains.

MAXIMUM LENGTH	4m
TIME	Mid Jurassic
FOSSIL FINDS	Asia (China)

TUOJIANGOSAURUS

A good picture of this dinosaur comes from the discovery of two sets of fossilized remains found in China. It had pairs of V-shaped plates running along its spine, which were biggest in the middle of its back, and decreased in size towards its neck and tail. Just like *Stegosaurus*, it had two pairs of long spiky horns on its tail, and a steeply arched back. At its tallest point – over its hips – it was about 2m high.

MAXIMUM LENGTH	7m
TIME	Late Jurassic
FOSSIL FINDS	Asia (China)

KENTROSAURUS

First discovered in the early 1900s, during the German fossil-hunting expeditions to Tanzania (page 160), *Kentrosaurus* is one of Africa's best-known stegosaurs, with dozens of additional specimens being unearthed in recent times. Although similar in shape to *Stegosaurus*, *Kentrosaurus* was much smaller. The pairs of plates on its back gave way to spiky horns, some 60cm long, from midway down its back to the tip of its tail. It was believed to have had a long spike protruding sideways from each of its hips, or perhaps from each of its shoulders. These spikes would have been useful in self-defence. Like other stegosaurs, it had relatively small teeth for a plant-eater, and may have swallowed stones to help it grind up its food (page 79).

MAXIMUM LENGTH	5m
TIME	Late Jurassic
FOSSIL FINDS	Africa (Tanzania)

LEXOVISAURUS

Named after an ancient tribe from France, where some of the earliest remains were found, *Lexovisaurus* was a typical stegosaur with pairs of narrow pointed plates down its back, as well as an additional pair of spikes, up to 1.2m long, thought to have been located on its shoulders. Weighing up to 2 tonnes, it was probably faster than some of the larger stegosaurs, and may have been able to run at speeds of up to 30km/h.

MAXIMUM LENGTH	5m
TIME	Mid Jurassic
FOSSIL FINDS	Europe (England, France)

DACENTRURUS

One of the smaller stegosaurs, and also one of the earliest, *Dacentrurus* weighed about 1 tonne, and was well-armed with sharply pointed back and tail plates up to 45cm long. Its remains have been found in several locations in western Europe, and they include what may have been one of its eggs.

MAXIMUM LENGTH	4.5m
TIME	Mid Jurassic
FOSSIL FINDS	Europe (England, France, Portugal)

FOSSIL-HUNTING IN AFRICA

AFTER SOME SPECTACULAR DISCOVERIES
DURING THE LAST 100 YEARS, AFRICA IS A
KEY DESTINATION FOR PALAEONTOLOGISTS.
FAMOUS FOR FOSSILS OF HUMAN ANCESTORS,
ITS PREHISTORIC INHABITANTS INCLUDED
THE LARGEST LAND PREDATORS EVER.

Fossil collecting in Africa began on a truly grand scale, with the discovery of an immense 'dinosaur graveyard' in Tanzania in 1907. Since the 1920s, East and South Africa have produced finds that help to map out human evolution, and recently, major dinosaur finds have been made on the edges of the Sahara Desert and in Madagascar.

△ Afrovenator –
'African hunter' – was an
allosaur that lived in the
early Cretaceous. It was
up to 9m long, and
weighed up to 2 tonnes.

THE HUNTER-KILLERS

Ask anyone to name a giant predatory dinosaur and the chances are that they will think of *Tyrannosaurus rex*. Far less well known, although probably even larger, was an immense allosaur that lived in North Africa in early Cretaceous times. Called *Carcharodontosaurus*, which literally means 'shark-toothed lizard', this awe-inspiring predator was first discovered in the 1920s, when European palaeontologists found parts of its skull and a small number of other bones. These remains were eventually taken to a

Paul Sereno, seen here during his 1993 expedition to Niger, has been one of the most successful fossil-hunters of recent years. As well as discovering Afrovenator *and rediscovering* Carcharodontosaurus, *he has made some major breakthroughs in the study of early dinosaurs in South America. His finds here include* Eoraptor, *and the most complete specimens so far collected of* Herrerasaurus.

museum in southern Germany, but in 1944 the building was damaged by Allied bombers, and its unique fossils destroyed.

For the next five decades, it remained on the list of dinosaurs that had been found and then lost. That was the situation in 1996, when a team from the University of Chicago, led by palaeontologist Paul Sereno, carried out a prospecting trip in Morocco's Atlas Mountains. Working on a ridge of eroded

▽ *Seen next to the extraordinarily large skull of* Carcharodontosaurus, *a human skull looks like little more than a bite-sized snack.*

sandstone, they extracted a skull measuring 1.6m long: *Carcharodontosaurus* had been rediscovered, and the new specimen was even larger than the one that vanished during World War II. For Paul Sereno, this discovery was both a first and a second, because he had already found another African allosaur – which he named *Afrovenator* – during an expedition to Niger, in 1993.

Off the coast of Africa, Madagascar is also the scene of great interest in the dinosaur world. In 1999, remains of primitive plant-eating dinosaurs were found to be over 230 million years old, making them the most ancient species yet discovered.

THE FOSSILS OF TENDAGURU HILL

Palaeontologists in Africa often work in remote locations, but they do have the benefit of modern transport. Things were not so easy in the early 1900s, when the German naturalist Eberhard Fraas travelled through Tanzania – then known as Tanganyika – following up information about fossil finds at a site called Tendaguru Hill. On arrival, Fraas found that Tendaguru contained a vast array of remains. Between 1909 and 1913, German palaeontologists carried out four expeditions to the area, collecting over 200 tonnes of fossils. These were coated in plaster, packaged up and then carried all the way to the coast, to be shipped back to Europe.

Among this extraordinary haul were the remains of a large range of plant-eaters, including stegosaurs, hypsilophodonts and diplodocids. But in terms of size, the most impressive finds were several partial *Brachiosaurus* skeletons, including –

unusually for a sauropod – an almost complete skull. When these eventually arrived in Germany, a complete *Brachiosaurus* skeleton was assembled, creating the largest 'articulated' dinosaur fossil in the world. The skeleton is still housed in Berlin's Humboldt Museum.

HUMAN ORIGINS

One visitor to Tendaguru, after the German excavations were over, was the British anthropologist Louis Leakey. At the time of Leakey's visit, most anthropologists believed that human evolution had begun in Asia – an idea that American fossil-hunting expeditions hoped to prove when they

visited the Gobi Desert (page 108). But during his long career, spent largely in Tanzania and neighbouring Kenya, Louis Leakey and his wife Mary helped to show that this was not true. Among their fossil finds was *Homo habilis*, a human-like primate that was a direct ancestor of our own species, living about 2 million years ago.

Following Louis Leakey's death in 1972, his son Richard continued the family tradition, making several important finds.

◁ *Standing next to the remains of a* Brachiosaurus, *these Tanzanian labourers were some of hundreds who excavated and carried fossils during the German expeditions to Tendaguru Hill, in the early 1900s.*

◁ *The Tendaguru* Brachiosaurus – *the world's largest dinosaur exhibit – stands in the Humboldt Museum in Berlin. When this skeleton was prepared,* Brachiosaurus *was the tallest dinosaur known, but the number one position has since been taken by* Sauroposeidon.

◁ *A group of American and British palaeontologists at work, cleaning sauropod remains in Niger. Once exposed at the surface, fossils like these slowly fracture as they warm up and expand in the desert sunshine, and then cool and contract after dark. Some of the resulting fragments can be seen on the ground.*

WEAPONS AND ORNAMENTS

IN THE DINOSAUR WORLD SOME BODY PARTS, SUCH AS HORNS AND SPINES, EVOLVED AS MUCH FOR IMPRESSING RIVALS AS FOR FENDING OFF PREDATORS.

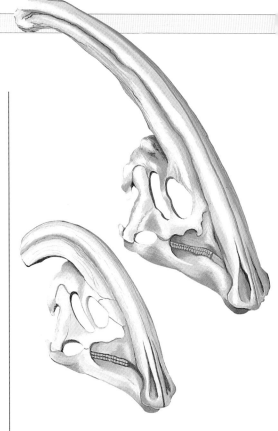

A t first glance, the huge horns of a *Triceratops* look as though they were designed for one thing only: keeping carnivores at bay. The same is true of their head-shields, and of the spines, lumps and bumps that many armoured dinosaurs possessed. But studies of living animals show that structures like these are not always quite what they seem. In modern mammals, horns and antlers are often used by males as badges of rank, as well as for self-defence.

SEXUAL SELECTION

In the living world, animals evolve because ones that are best adapted for survival have the most young, which inherit their characteristics. This is called natural selection. But in many species, another kind of selection is at work as well – sexual selection. It occurs when females decide which males to choose as mates.

Imagine a species of bird in which males have red tails. If the females find red tails attractive, the males with the biggest and reddest tails will stand the best chance of mating. Those males will father more young, and the proportion of males with large red tails will slowly increase.

◁ *From relatively modest beginnings, shown here by* Protoceratops *(top), the head-shields of ceratopsians became increasingly elaborate.* Styracosaurus *(middle) had holes in its spine-edged frill, but in* Triceratops *(left) the frill was solid and extremely heavy.*

△ *The crests of hadrosaurs are typical examples of structures that evolved through sexual selection. This shows two* Parasaurolophus *skulls; the male's crest is longer than the female's.*

Tails will get larger and redder, making males increasingly different from their mates.

What is true of tails is also true of any other feature that females find impressive, whether it is bright plumage, large horns, or the strength and skill to push rivals out of the way. Sexual selection can help to exaggerate any of these as time goes by.

Sexual selection is something that palaeontologists have to bear in mind when looking at dinosaur armour and weapons. For example, the elaborate head-shields of *Triceratops* and its relatives almost certainly started out as a straightforward form of defence. But over millions of years, they became suspiciously large in males, and highly elaborate. They also varied enormously from one species to another. To experts in animal evolution, this suggests one thing: sexual selection was at work. As these animals evolved, it slowly turned their head-shields into ornaments as well as armour, helping the males to win mates.

Sometimes, these ornaments were simply shown off, making their owner look more striking and desirable. The crests of some hadrosaurs, for example, probably functioned in this way. But fossil remains show that head-shields and horns of ceratopsids were used in ritual combat between rival males.

LOCKING HORNS

At the beginning of the breeding season, *Triceratops* and its relatives probably behaved like many grassland animals today, with males sparring with each other for the right

features that had this kind of drawback. A *Triceratops* head-shield, for example, was an enormous and extremely heavy 'attraction' that would have taken a large amount of energy to grow, and even more to carry around. To a lesser extent, the thickened brain-cases of dome-headed dinosaurs, or pachycephalosaurs, fell into the same category. But one of the best examples of an animal with burdensome body parts is the

▽ *In* Triceratops. *the head-shield and horns were status symbols that were shown off in male-to-male confrontations. However, when turned against predators, they made effective weapons. Here a mature male sees off a* Tyrannosaurus.

to mate. One of the key features of this kind of fighting is that it looks more dangerous than it really is. The two rivals square up to each other in a threatening way, but when they clash, they do so in a fashion that prevents either of them becoming seriously injured. Like today's buffalo and antelopes, ceratopsids had large air spaces in the front of their skulls. This helped to cushion the impact of a head-on clash, protecting their brains from damage.

However, injuries did sometimes occur. Many *Triceratops* skulls show shallow nicks in their surface – evidence of painful gouges where an opponent's horns hit home.

GOING TO EXTREMES

An interesting feature of sexual selection is that it can make some body parts so large that they verge on being a handicap. Dinosaurs and other prehistoric animals showed

Irish elk – a prehistoric deer from the Pleistocene Epoch (page 211). Males had antlers more than 3m wide, which weighed nearly 50kg. Antlers this large were so cumbersome that they were almost useless as weapons, but amazingly – as in today's deer – they were shed and regrown each year.

▽ *Rhinoceroses use their horns in the same way as dinosaurs. With their horns locked together, these males are unlikely to do each other harm, but one will yield to the other.*

ARMOURED DINOSAURS

NODOSAURS AND ANKYLOSAURS

Ankylosaurids first appeared in the late Jurassic, but their heyday was during the Cretaceous. First to evolve were the nodosaurs, which spread across the northern hemisphere. They were heavily built, slow-moving plant-eaters, equipped with body armour of horns and bony plates. Towards the end of the Cretaceous, the nodosaurs gave way to the ankylosaurs proper, which had even tougher armour, and a bony club at the end of their tail.

△ Nodosaurus *(top)*, Hylaeosaurus *(middle)* and Silvisaurus *(bottom)* were all typical nodosaurs with extensive protective body armour of horny plates and spikes running over their backs. Only their legs and undersides lacked this protection, but incomplete fossils mean that their exact appearance is still a matter of conjecture.

HYLAEOSAURUS
Hylaeosaurus was first discovered in about 1830 by the famous British palaeontologist Gideon Mantell. It was only the third dinosaur to be identified, and only a few isolated fragments of its skeleton have come to light since. As a result, its exact appearance is difficult to establish, but it is likely to have shared a range of typical nodosaur features, including armour plating, perhaps backed up by rows of horns projecting sideways from its flanks and along its tail. Like other nodosaurs, its front legs were probably shorter than its hind legs,

giving it a humped profile, and they would have been stoutly built to carry the weight of its armour.

MAXIMUM LENGTH	6m
TIME	Early Cretaceous
FOSSIL FINDS	Europe (England, France)

SILVISAURUS
Like *Hylaeosaurus*, this was an early nodosaur with a range of primitive features. These included small pointed teeth in its upper jaw, in contrast with later species, which typically had toothless beaks. It also had a relatively long neck, which makes it possible that it browsed on tall shrubs, as well as eating plants closer to the ground. It was armoured with large bony plates, and also with spikes, although incomplete fossils make it difficult to tell how these were arranged on the living animal.

MAXIMUM LENGTH	4m
TIME	Early Cretaceous
FOSSIL FINDS	North America (Kansas)

NODOSAURUS
With an arched back covered in bands of small bony plates, stretching from behind its neck right down its tail, *Nodosaurus* – 'lumpy lizard' – looked like a huge prehistoric armadillo. No skulls have yet been found, but its head was likely to have been small, with narrow jaws. Like all ankylosaurids, it fed on low-growing plants, and had leaf-shaped teeth. Its heavy build and small brain were typical of an animal that relied on armour to avoid attack, and its lifestyle and diet make it probable that it lived in herds.

MAXIMUM LENGTH	6m
TIME	Late Cretaceous
FOSSIL FINDS	North America (Kansas, Wyoming)

EDMONTONIA
Edmontonia was one of the largest nodosaurs – an ankylosaur that lacked a clubbed tail. Several almost complete fossil skeletons have been found, and they show that it was built even more solidly than a rhinoceros, with a band of bony plates extending all the

way to the tip of its tail, and additional plates over its neck and its skull. The two vertebrae that joined its head to its spine were fused together, which means that it would have had difficulty bending its neck. Once it reached adulthood, *Edmontonia* was so well armoured that it was unlikely to be attacked. It had several pairs of giant spikes protruding from its shoulders, which would have been an effective deterrent against predators. It lived in the same time and place as *Euoplocephalus*, but its narrower jaws imply that it had a different diet, reducing direct competition between the two.

MAXIMUM LENGTH 7m

TIME Late Cretaceous

FOSSIL FINDS North America (Alberta in Canada, Alaska, Montana in USA)

EUOPLOCEPHALUS

With body armour extending even in front of its eyelids, and a tail ending in a heavy club, *Euoplocephalus* was a typical true ankylosaur. It had a large head with protective spikes, and further spikes and nodules arranged in rows down its back and the base of its tail. Over 40 fossil finds have been made so far, including several skulls, which show that it had a broad, toothless muzzle – a kind that would have been good at cropping swathes of low-growing plants. *Euoplocephalus* probably weighed about 2 tonnes, and although it was solidly built, its tail-club suggests that it was quite nimble on its feet in the event of an attack by a predator.

MAXIMUM LENGTH 7m

TIME Late Cretaceous

FOSSIL FINDS North America (Alberta in Canada, Montana in USA)

ANKYLOSAURUS

Largest of the true ankylosaurs, and almost the last of its line, *Ankylosaurus* was a massively built plant-eater. It weighed up to 4 tonnes, but its club weighed over 50kg and could be swung quickly to smash a predator's teeth or skull. It had armour plating embedded in its skin, and the rows of spikes and raised nodules that characterize ankylosaurs. It may have been a herding animal, like many of its relatives, but its size means it would have been safe feeding on its own.

MAXIMUM LENGTH 10m

TIME Late Cretaceous

FOSSIL FINDS North America (Montana in USA, Alberta in Canada)

△ Euoplocephalus *(top) with its distinctive club-ended tail and* Edmontonia *(bottom), co-existed in late Cretaceous North America. Although they had the same general build, differences in their jaw structure suggest that they fed on different plants.*

◁ *Weighing as much as one of today's elephants, but with its own built-in weaponry and armour,* Ankylosaurus *was one of the best protected plant-eaters during the Age of the Reptiles, but it failed to survive when the Cretaceous Period came to an end.*

ARMOURED DINOSAURS

DOME-HEADED DINOSAURS

In the dinosaur world, a large head was not necessarily a sign of great intelligence. This is particularly true with the pachycephalosaurs, or bone-headed dinosaurs. These remarkable animals get their name from their reinforced brain-case, which in some cases was over 20cm thick. Scientists believe that male bone-headed dinosaurs used their skulls in head-to-head clashes, in much the same way as sheep or goats do today. Alternatively, they may have used their heads as battering rams to butt rivals in the side.

▽ Homalocephale *(top) and* Stegoceras *(bottom) were both small, bipedal, grazing dinosaurs with thickened tops to their skulls.* Homalocephale *had a flat top to its skull, while* Stegoceras *had a dome. Both lived in herds, and used speed and agility to escape predators.*

HOMALOCEPHALE
Homalocephale's head had a thick, flat top of bone, with bony protrusions around the edge like a crown. The thick skull bones were flexible, and relatively porous. Some experts think that this is evidence against the head-butting theory, because a skull like this would not have been able to withstand a massive impact. Certainly, no evidence of skull damage has been discovered. *Homalocephale* had small, leaf-shaped teeth, which indicates that it would have lived on a diet of plants, fruit and seeds.

MAXIMUM LENGTH	3m
TIME	Late Cretaceous
FOSSIL FINDS	Asia (Mongolia)

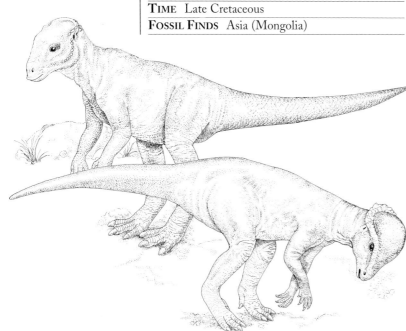

STEGOCERAS
In size, body shape and behaviour, *Stegoceras* was probably very like *Homalocephale*. It too was a small, bipedal plant-eater, with a steeply sloping snout, and serrated teeth shaped for chewing low-growing plants. The most obvious difference was its head – a raised dome adorned with a prominent crown of bony growths, the largest of which was at the back of the skull. The dome probably got bigger as the animal reached maturity, and it seems to have been more pronounced in males. For males, a large head would have been a sign of importance, in the same way that large tusks are a badge of rank in bull elephants. *Stegoceras* would have been a fast runner, and like other bone-heads, it lived in herds. Although it ran on two legs, it probably dropped onto all fours to feed.

MAXIMUM LENGTH	2m
TIME	Late Cretaceous
FOSSIL FINDS	North America (Alberta, Canada, and Montana, USA)

166

DOME-HEADED DINOSAURS

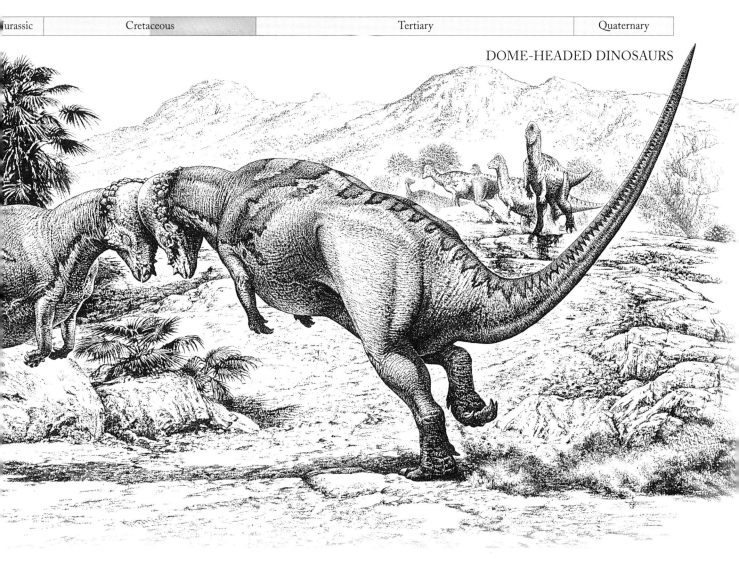

PRENOCEPHALE

In 1974, a superbly preserved skull of *Prenocephale* was found in Mongolia. It had a large bulbous head with a knobbly ridge running around the edge, and looked like a small-scale *Pachycephalosaurus*. *Prenocephale* probably lived by browsing on leaves and fruit and, like its relatives, almost certainly lived in herds. It shared another family feature: a mesh of bone-like tendons in the rear half of its tail, which would have held its tail rigid.

MAXIMUM LENGTH 2.5m

TIME Late Cretaceous

FOSSIL FINDS Asia (Mongolia), western North America

PACHYCEPHALOSAURUS

The biggest of the 'bone heads', this dinosaur weighed nearly half a tonne. It had a very large skull, topped with a solid dome up to 25cm thick. Running around the outside of its head, at the base of the dome, was a ring of bony knobs. For its size, *Pachycephalosaurus* had tiny teeth. Like other bone-heads, it probably had a good sense of smell, which would have been useful for detecting predators. As the only fossil finds have been skull remains, scientists have had to guess what the rest of its body looked like. This dome-headed giant was one of the last of its line, surviving until the mass extinction that wiped out all the dinosaurs 66 million years ago.

MAXIMUM LENGTH 4.6m

TIME Late Cretaceous

FOSSIL FINDS Western North America

▽△ Pachycephalosaurus *would have used its 'bone head' to win in clashes with male rivals.*

DINOSAUR DROPPINGS

WITH THEIR OFTEN HUGE APPETITES, DINOSAURS PRODUCED IMMENSE AMOUNTS OF DROPPINGS. SOME HAVE SURVIVED AS FOSSILS, GIVING PALAEONTOLOGISTS A DIRECT INSIGHT INTO WHAT DINOSAURS ATE.

Coprolites – fossilized droppings – are discovered much less often than fossilized bones. One reason for this is that they have an irregular shape, which means that even expert eyes find them difficult to spot. Another factor is that droppings are much softer than bones, which means that they have much less chance of being preserved. Rain washes them away, and scavenging animals – such as insects – often break them apart. Just occasionally, genuine 'dino dung' does come to light, millions of years after it dropped to the ground.

△ *Fossilized droppings are often difficult to identify. The one on the left came from a dinosaur, and the one on the right may have been produced by a marine reptile.*

REMAINS OF A KILL
In 1995, a group of scientists working in Saskatchewan, Canada, took a stroll from a site where a *Tyrannosaurus* was being excavated. One of the team noticed some pale round objects that were slowly eroding from a layer of hard mud. These came from a giant dinosaur coprolite, the largest that has ever been found. Roughly cyclindrical, it measured about 45cm long and up to 16cm across, and when it was fresh, probably weighed about 2.5kg.

The fossil was taken back to the lab, where paper-thin slices were shaved off it and viewed under a microscope. These revealed pieces of broken bone, which had been partially digested. By looking at the pattern of blood vessels inside the bone fragments, researchers were able to tell that the victim was a young dinosaur and probably a plant-eater. The animal that produced the coprolite, on the other hand, was undoubtedly a carnivore, the most likely candidate being *Tyrannosaurus* itself.

PLANT-EATERS' COPROLITES
Plant-eating dinosaurs outnumbered meat-eaters and ate more food. Some herbivores had quite modest food requirements, but giant sauropods, such as *Argentinosaurus*, probably consumed about 3 or 4 tonnes of food a week, which translates into about 1 tonne of droppings – enormous potential source of evidence about dinosaur diets.

Unfortunately, compared to carnivores, plant-eaters' droppings fossilized more rarely, mainly because they contained no hard fragments of bone. The few sauropod droppings that have been found include specimens from Utah, USA, which look like squashed footballs up to 40cm across. Their shape is explained by the fact they originally contained water, and hit the ground from a height of several metres. Some of these coprolites contain pieces of conifer stems.

At the other end of the scale, geologists in England have discovered large numbers of coin-sized coprolites, thought to have been produced by a plant-eating dinosaur. What the droppings lacked in size, they made up for in numbers. One deposit contained nearly 300 of these pellets, and a close examination showed that they contained the undigested remains of cycad leaves – a common ingredient of dinosaur diets.

AT HOME IN DINO DUNG
Some coprolites of plant-eating dinosaurs are riddled with fossilized burrows, each up to the thickness of a finger. These burrows were created by dung beetles, which 'mined' the giant droppings as a source of food. Just like dung beetles today, some would have shaped pieces of the dung into balls and rolled them away to make nurseries for their young. By dismantling and scattering piles of dung, these scavenging insects helped to return nutrients to the soil – ones that plants need to grow.

REPTILES IN THE AIR

Before birds evolved, reptiles were the only backboned animals that had successfully taken up life in the air. Initially, reptiles were gliders rather than true fliers, using specialized scales or skin-flaps to cushion their fall as they leaped from tree to tree. But by the end of the Triassic, a completely new group of flying reptiles evolved, equipped with muscle-powered wings. These were the pterosaurs – a collection of quick-witted and sometimes gigantic aviators that soared and flapped their way through the skies. They flourished for over 150 million years, and left a great treasury of fossils.

WINGS OF SKIN

GLIDING OR FLYING REPTILES EVOLVED ON AT LEAST FOUR SEPARATE OCCASIONS IN THE DISTANT PAST. THE MOST SUCCESSFUL BY FAR WERE THE PTEROSAURS, WHICH TOOK TO THE AIR ON WINGS MADE OF SKIN.

The first flying reptiles appeared towards the end of the Permian Period, over 240 million years ago. These early aviators were all gliders, speeding between trees on wing-like flaps that they opened just before take-off. They included *Coelurosauravus*, which had foldaway wing flaps along its sides, and *Longisquama* (page 62), a Triassic animal with elongated scales down its back. One of the strangest, a tiny animal called *Sharovipteryx* (page 60) had two pairs of flaps. But none of these animals could stay airborne for long for more than a few seconds, because their wings could not be flapped up and down.

▽ *Coelurosauravus was an early glider, from the late Permian. About 40cm long, it had elongated ribs that could hinge outwards to form a pair of skin-covered wings. Some of today's lizards glide in exactly the same way.*

FIRST FLAPPERS

With the evolution of the pterosaurs in the Late Triassic, reptiles stopped being simple gliders, and developed real mastery of the skies. Pterosaurs are sometimes confused with dinosaurs, but while they were a distinct group, they did share the same direct ancestors. Not only did they appear at the same time as the dinosaurs, they also became extinct at the same time as well.

(page 62)

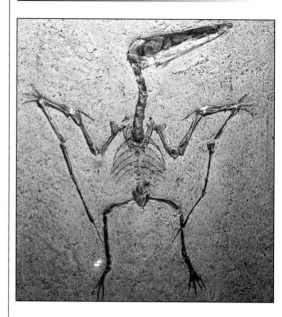

FOSSIL EVIDENCE

Many pterosaurs fed on fish or squid, catching prey by swimming close to the water's surface. If they crashed, their remains sank to the bottom, where they stood a good chance of becoming fossilized. This Pterodactylus *fossil is a typical example, showing the entire skeleton in superb detail. By contrast, species that lived over land, such as* Quetzalcoatlus, *left a meagre amount of fossil evidence.*

Until the global disaster that brought the Age of Reptiles to an end, pterosaurs were by far the largest animals that could fly. Unlike gliding reptiles, they could flap their wings to stay airborne, and they may have been as manoeuverable as today's birds.

DESIGN FOR FLIGHT

Few fossils exist of the earliest pterosaurs, but later forms, particularly from near the end of the Jurassic, have left a wealth of well-preserved remains. They show that pterosaurs had very specialized arms, featuring an immensely elongated fourth finger, often as long as the rest of the limb. When the wing was extended, this finger stretched open a double-sided membrane of skin, which ran in a triangle between three points – the shoulder, the wingtip, and a

region near the hind leg. A second and much smaller membrane formed a forward part of the wing. It also started at the shoulder, but ran in front of the main arm bones to a point near the wrist, creating a straight edge in front of the elbow. The remaining fingers were far shorter, and clustered together at the wing's leading edge. They were probably used for walking and climbing, and perhaps tearing up food.

Unlike a bird's feathers, which consist of dead cells, a pterosaur's wing membranes were made of living tissue. They were reinforced by tough but elastic fibres, and they contained a network of blood vessels to keep them alive. Compared to feathers, they were simple structures, and did not need lots of preening to keep them in good condition. But, although minor damage could be repaired, a major tear was likely to be permanent, and therefore potentially fatal.

Apart from their wings, pterosaurs showed other physical modifications. Their skeletons were light, with a reduced number of bones, and the ribcage was deep but short. Early species, the rhamphorhynchoids, had long tails, but later ones, the pterodactyls, had tails that were reduced to a

short stub. In these pterosaurs, the head was often longer than the rest of the body.

ENERGY FOR FLIGHT

The shape of their beaks, together with the fossilized remains of meals, shows that pterosaurs were carnivorous, feeding on a range of animals from insects

to fish, or scavenging on dead remains. Strangely, once flowering plants evolved, pterosaurs do not seem to have branched out into eating fruit and seeds, although these are both packed with energy.

Giant pterosaurs, such as *Arambourgiana* (page 178), were experts at soaring, a highly efficient way of flying that uses very little muscle power. But smaller species would have needed to put a lot of effort into flapping, one of several reasons why palaeontologists think that most pterosaurs, or perhaps all of them, were warm-blooded.

◁ *Different tail lengths make it easy to tell rhamphorhynchoids and pterodactyls apart.*

◁ *The largest pterosaurs had a wingspan larger than a hang-glider, while the smallest were not much larger than a starling when fully grown.*

▽ *Pterosaur wings consisted of a double-sided sheet of skin, reinforced by tough fibres. As in birds, most of the bones contained air cavities to save weight.*

1 QUETZALCOATLUS
2 PTERANODON
3 DSUNGARIPTERUS
4 DIMORPHODON
5 PTERDACTYLUS
6 SORDES

REPTILES IN THE AIR

LONG-TAILED PTEROSAURS

The long-tailed pterosaurs were the first reptiles capable of true powered flight. They appeared in the late Triassic Period, and were widespread in the Jurassic. Like the pterodactyls, which eventually replaced them, they had leathery wings held open by a lengthened fourth finger, but they also had some more primitive features. These included sharply pointed teeth and slender tails that often ended in a diamond-shaped 'vane'. Many of these pterosaurs fed on fish, but they rarely landed on the water. Instead, they did all their hunting on the wing.

▽ *Clinging to rocks with wing claws and feet, two* Dimorphodon *bask in the morning sunshine, while another flies off to feed. Like other pterosaurs,* Dimorphodon *would have used a lot of energy in flight. It was probably warm-blooded, and insulated by fur-like scales.*

DIMORPHODON
Fossils of this animal were first found in 1828, by the British collector Mary Anning (page 198), and for over a century it remained the most primitive pterosaur known to science. With its bulky, puffin-like beak, *Dimorphodon* was one of the most distinctive long-tailed pterosaurs. Its head was almost as large as the central section of its body, but it was lighter than it looked, because the skull contained large spaces separated by thin struts of bone. Its front teeth were long, and protruded from its beak, but the teeth further back were much smaller. Its wings were equipped with three large, clawed fingers, while its tail was long but probably quite stiff, because it was reinforced by parallel rods of bone. Opinions are divided about how *Dimorphodon* lived, and why it had such a large beak. It may have fed on fish or small land animals, but its beak may have acted partly as display, in the same way that toucans' beaks do today.

WINGSPAN	1.4m
TIME	Early Jurassic
FOSSIL FINDS	Europe (England)

SCAPHOGNATHUS
This long-beaked pterosaur is one of several species that have been found in the Solnhöfen limestone of southern Germany – a geological formation famous as the source of *Archaeopteryx* fossils (page 134). It had the large protruding teeth typical of long-tailed pterosaurs, and short wings. Its tail ended in a diamond-shaped 'vane' – another feature common in early pterosaurs, which would have helped to improve its stability when on the wing. *Scaphognathus*' jaws would have enabled it to catch fish or insects, but there is no evidence whether or not it fed over water or on land.

WINGSPAN	90cm
TIME	Late Jurassic
FOSSIL FINDS	Europe (Germany)

LONG-TAILED PTEROSAURS

rest of the body. *Rhamphorhynchus'* jaws were slightly upturned at their tips, and they would have made a very effective fish trap. To feed, the animal probably skimmed close to the surface, with the lower half of its beak slicing through the water. If its beak made contact with a fish, it would have snapped shut instantly – a fishing technique still used by some birds today. Some *Rhamphorhynchus* fossils show the remains of fish in the stomach, in various stages of digestion.

WINGSPAN 1.75cm
TIME Late Jurassic
FOSSIL FINDS Europe (Germany, England), Africa (Tanzania)

PREONDACTYLUS

Preondactylus is one of the earliest known pterosaurs. It had several primitive features, including long legs and a short skull, but it was a capable flier, skimming over lakes and lagoons to catch fish. One fossil consists of a jumble of bones apparently regurgitated by a large fish; it may have been swallowed after it crash-landed.

WINGSPAN 1.5m
TIME Late Triassic
FOSSIL FINDS Europe (Italy)

◁ *With a fish clamped in its tooth-filled beak, a* Rhamphorhyncus *flies off to feed. Small fish would have been swallowed whole, while larger ones would be taken to a safe place and then torn apart – as shown by the animal in the background. Unlike today's birds, pterosaurs could hold their catch with their wing claws while they set about it with their teeth.*

▽ *Swinging its feet forward and cupping its wings, a* Preondactylus *comes in to land. For pterosaurs – just as for birds – good eyesight and coordination were essential for flight. Studies of pterosaur skulls showed that these animals had well-developed brains, allowing them to carry out precise manoeuvres in mid-air.*

ANUROGNATHUS

Anurognathus literally means 'without tail or jaws' – an understandable if misleading description of this unusual pterosaur. Known from just one specimen found in Germany in the 1920s, it had a tail that was little more than a stump, and a short, blunt head with only a few small teeth. Its legs and feet, however, were well developed. One possible explanation for these features is that the fossil is of a young animal, which would have changed shape as it became adult. Another possibility is that *Anurognathus* was a lightweight hunter of dragonflies and other insects, and may have used dinosaurs as living launch-pads to dart after its prey.

WINGSPAN 50cm
TIME Late Jurassic
FOSSIL FINDS Europe (Germany)

RHAMPHORHYNCHUS

Rhamphorhynchus is the best known of the long-tailed pterosaurs, thanks to some superbly preserved fossils in the Solnhöfen limestone of southern Germany. Several species have been identified, but they all have long, pointed jaws armed with large crisscrossing teeth. Their wingspan was among the largest of all tailed pterosaurs, but their legs were disproportionately short, suggesting that they were not very agile on the ground. The Solnhöfen fossils show the outlines of the wings, along with the vane-tipped tail, which was often longer than the

REPTILES IN THE AIR

EUDIMORPHODON

Fossils of this animal show a number of interesting details of pterosaur anatomy. Like most other long-tailed species, it had a long beak with large teeth at the front, and smaller teeth at the sides. Its large eyes were protected by a circle of thin bony plates, called a sclerotic ring, and it had thickened neck vertebrae to support the weight of its head. It also had gastralia, or stomach ribs, so its ribcage enclosed almost the whole of its underside. *Eudimorphodon* was a fish-eater, and is among the earliest pterosaurs known from the fossil record.

WINGSPAN	1m
TIME	Late Triassic
FOSSIL FINDS	Europe (Italy)

BATRACHOGNATHUS

Like *Rhamphorhynchus*, this pterosaur had a deep, blunt beak, and this, together with its small size, makes it likely that it fed on insects. Its skull was about 5cm long, and contained large spaces, covered by skin, that helped to save weight. Fossils show that, like many of its relatives, this species had a uropatagium – a flap of skin stretching between its legs and tail – as well as the flaps that formed its wings. Many of today's bats have a similar skin flap helping them fly.

WINGSPAN	50cm
TIME	Late Jurassic
FOSSIL FINDS	Asia (Kazakhstan)

SORDES

When the remains of this animal were first discovered, in the 1960s, it looked very much like a 'standard' pterosaur. But, under close examination, the fossil showed one astonishing feature – signs of what look like a coat of fur. As with bats, the fur seems to have covered the animal's head and most of its body, but not its wings or tail. Many palaeontologists take this as evidence that pterosaurs were warm-blooded – a theory that may explain their highly active way of life. If this is true, it is likely that many pterosaurs had 'fur', although it is rarely seen in fossil remains. Apart from its remarkable coat, *Sordes* had large eyes and a long, narrow beak, with large protruding teeth. As with *Batrachognathus*, its small size suggests that it fed on insects rather than fish.

WINGSPAN	60cm
TIME	Late Jurassic
FOSSIL FINDS	Asia (Kazakhstan)

▽ Sordes *(top and left), had a bat-like shape, with a flap of skin connecting its hind legs to the base of its tail. Its furry scales may have been a common feature in pterosaurs, but so far it is the only species that shows this clearly in fossils.*

▽ Batrachognathus *(bottom right) had well-developed wing claws useful for clinging to vegetation when it landed to swallow its catch.*

PTERODACTYLS

The pterodactyls were a group of pterosaurs widespread in the late Jurassic. By the Cretaceous, the long-tailed pterosaurs had died out, leaving the pterodactyls as the only reptiles in the skies. They had very short tails, and some were adorned with bizarre bony crests. Some species were not much bigger than pigeons, but others were the largest flying animals that have ever existed on Earth.

▷ *A number of pterosaurs had flattened crests at the tip of their beaks. This is Criorhynchus, which had a wingspan of over 5m. In flight, its trailing legs acted as a counterbalance for its head, and they may have helped it to steer.*

▷ *Seen from the front, Ornithodesmus' beak reveals its duck-like shape. This kind of beak may have helped Ornithodesmus to catch fish in muddy water, where it would have used touch rather than sight to find its prey.*

ORNITHOCHEIRUS

Up to 4m long, and with a wingspan three times the size of the largest flying bird alive today, *Ornithocheirus* (page 182) was a spectacular airborne reptile. Like other pterodactyls, it had a 'front-heavy' build, with a large head and neck, but only the shortest trace of a tail. In many species, the beak was distinctive, with a vertical crest at its tip. *Ornithocheirus* was not shaped for flapping flight. It travelled by seeking out thermals, or columns of warm rising air. Having reached the top of one thermal, it could then glide down to the next. This method of flight was highly energy-efficient, and it could travel great distances with little effort. It probably fed on squid and fish.

WINGSPAN 12m

TIME Early Cretaceous

FOSSIL FINDS Europe (England), South America (Brazil)

◁ *Circling over a lagoon, a small flock of* Dsungaripterus *soar upwards on rising air. Although they fed along the seashore, these pterosaurs would have visited freshwater to drink and to bathe.*

DSUNGARIPTERUS

This unusual pterosaur – the first one to be discovered in China – had a beak with a vertical crest at its base, and an upturned and sharply pointed tip. Its teeth were short, strong and effective at crushing food rather than grasping it. From these features, it seems likely that *Dsungaripterus* fed on molluscs and other hard-bodied seashore animals, prising them from rocks and then crushing them in its jaws. Its long legs would have been ideal for wading among rock pools as it searched for food.

WINGSPAN 3.5m

TIME Early Cretaceous

FOSSIL FINDS Asia (China)

ORNITHODESMUS

Ornithodesmus was one of several pterodactyls that had wide, duck-like beaks. Its beak looks heavy, but the tip was attached to the rest of its skull by remarkably narrow struts of bone, making it far lighter than it appears. It had short but effective teeth at the tip of its beak, making it likely that it fed on fish. The name *Ornithodesmus* is also used for a species of dinosaur; as this was named first, the pterosaur will eventually be renamed.

WINGSPAN 5m

TIME Early Cretaceous

FOSSIL FINDS Europe (England)

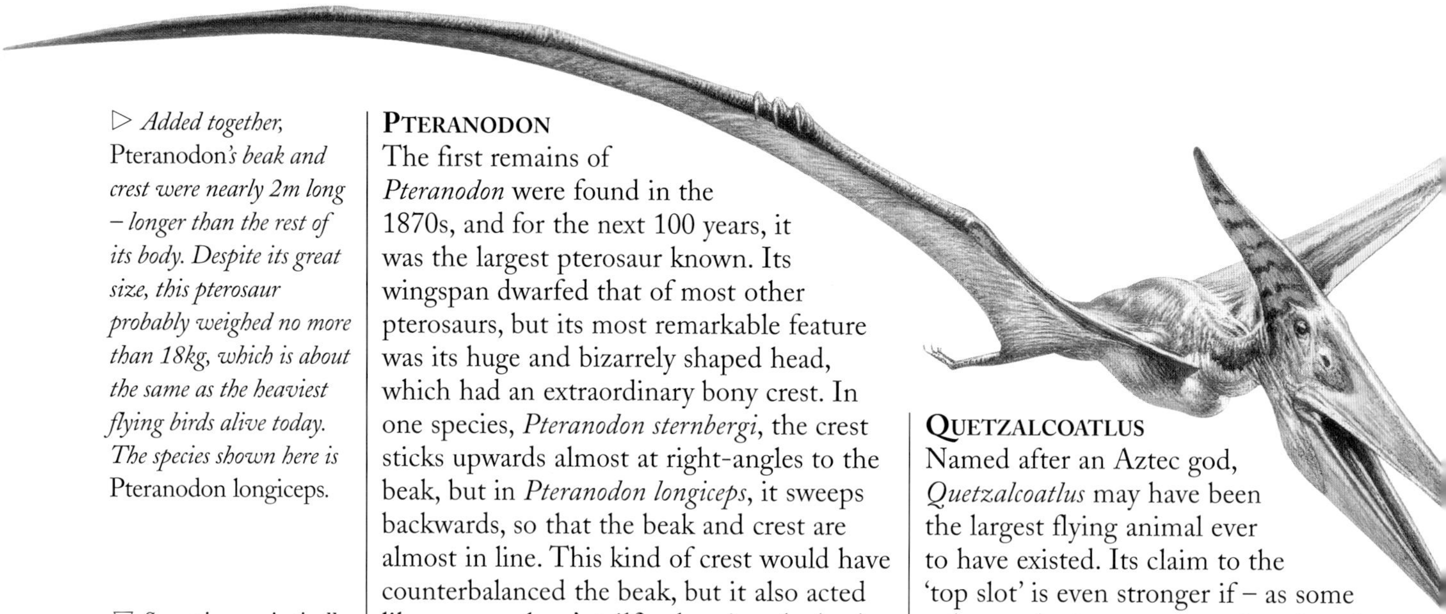

▷ *Added together,*
Pteranodon's beak and
crest were nearly 2m long
– longer than the rest of
its body. Despite its great
size, this pterosaur
probably weighed no more
than 18kg, which is about
the same as the heaviest
flying birds alive today.
The species shown here is
Pteranodon longiceps.

▽ *Sweeping majestically*
over a herd of sauropods, a
flock of Quetzalcoatlus
sets off to find food. These
huge pterosaurs could
have migrated immense
distances, and would
probably have been far
more widespread than the
few fossil finds suggest.

PTERANODON

The first remains of
Pteranodon were found in the
1870s, and for the next 100 years, it
was the largest pterosaur known. Its
wingspan dwarfed that of most other
pterosaurs, but its most remarkable feature
was its huge and bizarrely shaped head,
which had an extraordinary bony crest. In
one species, *Pteranodon sternbergi*, the crest
sticks upwards almost at right-angles to the
beak, but in *Pteranodon longiceps*, it sweeps
backwards, so that the beak and crest are
almost in line. This kind of crest would have
counterbalanced the beak, but it also acted
like an aeroplane's tailfin, keeping the beak
pointing into the oncoming air. The
stabilizing effect may have been an advantage,
but many other pterosaurs – including the
gigantic *Quetzalcoatlus* (below) – managed to
fly perfectly well without a crest. *Pteranodon*
probably caught fish by skimming close to
the waves. Like some of today's fishing
seabirds, it is unlikely to have landed on the
water because, with its immense wingspan, it
would have found it difficult to take off again.

WINGSPAN 9m
TIME Late Cretaceous
FOSSIL FINDS North America (South Dakota, Kansas, Oregon), Europe (England), Asia (Japan)

QUETZALCOATLUS

Named after an Aztec god,
Quetzalcoatlus may have been
the largest flying animal ever
to have existed. Its claim to the
'top slot' is even stronger if – as some
palaeontologists suggest – *Arambourgiana*
(pages 178–179) is simply a *Quetzalcoatlus*
that has been misidentified. The original
remains of *Quetzalcoatlus*, which were
unearthed in 1971, consist of wing bones
built on a gigantic scale. By comparing these
with complete skeletons of smaller species,
estimates of its wingspan have ranged as
high as 15m, although current figures are
generally smaller. Unlike most pterosaurs,
Quetzalcoatlus probably lived inland, and it
would have flown largely by soaring, like a
living glider. Its toothless beak suggests that
it was probably a scavenger, although it may
also have caught animals on the ground
(page 181).

WINGSPAN 12m
TIME Late Cretaceous
FOSSIL FINDS North America (Texas)

TROPEOGNATHUS

This large South American
pterosaur had a vertical crest
above and below the
tip of its beak, like
the one seen in
Ornithocheirus
(page 175). Its beak
was armed with
interlocking teeth,
showing that it was
a fish-eater, and it is
possible that the
crest may have

helped it to catch food. However, an alternative explanation is that the crest was used for display purposes during the animal's breeding season. If so, it probably varied in size between the sexes, although this has not been proved from fossil remains.

WINGSPAN 6m

TIME Early Cretaceous

FOSSIL FINDS South America (Brazil)

ANHANGUERA

Like *Tropeognathus*, *Anhanguera* is known from remains found in northeast Brazil. It had a typical fish-eater's beak, with interlocking teeth, and its complete skull was about 50cm long. Like other pterodactyls, its backbone was shaped in an unusual way, with the largest vertebrae in the neck, tapering to the smallest ones in its stumpy tail. By comparison, most terrestrial reptiles have their largest vertebrae in the central part of the body, where they carry the most weight. Pterodactyls needed their extra-large neck vertebrae to support their outsize heads.

WINGSPAN 4m

TIME Early Cretaceous

FOSSIL FINDS South America (Brazil)

CEARADACTYLUS

Another fish-eater from modern-day Brazil, *Cearadactylus* had about a dozen unusually long teeth at the tip of its beak, much smaller ones further back in the jaws, and no teeth at all at the point where its beak hinged. This kind of anatomy, which was common among pterodactyls, meant that *Cearadactylus* could not chew its prey. Instead, it would have swallowed small fish whole, or torn larger ones apart after landing with its catch.

WINGSPAN 4m

TIME Early Cretaceous

FOSSIL FINDS South America (Brazil)

PTERODACTYLUS

The first specimen of this well-known reptile came to light in 1784, making this the earliest pterosaur to be discovered. Its name means 'wing finger', and the word pterodactyl has often been used mistakenly for pterosaurs as a whole. *Pterodactylus* had a compact body with a small ribcage, long wings with three tiny clawed fingers, and a short tail. Its neck was well developed to support its large head and beak – but it did not have a crest. Over a dozen species of *Pterodactylus* have been identified, varying slightly in their anatomy and size. The largest species fed on fish, while the smallest probably ate insects.

WINGSPAN 2.5m

TIME Late Jurassic

FOSSIL FINDS Europe (England, France, Germany), Africa (Tanzania)

△ *On the ground, most pterodactyls walked on all fours, although some of them could stride on the hind legs alone. Here, a* Pterodactylus *shows how the wings folded back when not in use.*

▽ Tropeognathus *(top)*, Cearadactylus *(middle) and* Anhanguera *(bottom) were three large pterodactyls found in Brazil. When these animals were alive, South America and Africa were just beginning to drift apart as the Atlantic Ocean formed.*

GLIDING GIANTS

Gliding over a Late Cretaceous seascape, two Arambourgiana watch for fish swimming near the surface. These immense pterosaurs are known from the slenderest fossil remains – a single neck vertebra measuring 60cm long, which was found in Jordan in 1943. From this one bone, palaeontologists have deduced that Arambourgiana probably had a wingspan of 12m, making it perhaps the largest pterosaur of all time.

How PTEROSAURS FED

WITH THEIR WARM-BLOODED BODIES, PTEROSAURS NEEDED A PLENTIFUL SUPPLY OF FOOD. MANY WERE FISHERS OR INSECT-EATERS, BUT SOME HAD QUITE DIFFERENT WAYS OF KEEPING HUNGER AT BAY.

Fossilized pterosaur skulls provided plenty of evidence about their eating habits. Their beaks evolved to fit particular diets. Most seem to have fed over water, but land-based species had a smaller chance of being fossilized if they died.

△ Rhamphorhyncus *probably fed in just the same way as skimmers – living seabirds that fish from the water's surface.*

LIVING SIEVES

Of all the pterosaurs known from fossils, one stands out from all the rest. Called *Pterodaustro*, or 'southern wing', it was originally found in Argentina, and lived during the early Cretaceous. Unusually for a pterosaur, *Pterodaustro*'s beak had a strong upward curve, but its strangest feature was a set of about 500 wiry teeth on either side of the lower jaw. These teeth pointed upwards like the bristles of a toothbrush, and they were so long that they could not fit inside the beak when the upper jaw was closed.

Pterodaustro used its teeth to sieve food from shallow water. As water flowed past the bristles, tiny animals and plants became trapped by them. The pterosaur would then close its beak so that it could swallow its catch – a feeding system remarkably like the one used by flamingoes today.

As a rule, fish-eating pterosaurs hunted from the air, skimming the surface but rarely landing on the water. Some experts think that *Pterodaustro* also fed in this way, but another view is that it waded through the shallows with its wings folded back, sweeping its beak from side to side. If true it would have been an ungainly sight.

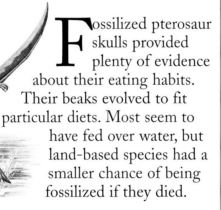

◁ Pterodaustro *uses its bristle-filled beak to feed. The bristles – actually highly modified teeth – were up to 4cm long, and were made of keratin, the same substance that forms hair and claws.*

GETTING A GRIP

Apart from *Pterodaustro*, pterosaurs either had widely spaced teeth, or no teeth at all. Unusually for reptiles, the toothy species sometimes had several types of tooth, including large single-pointed ones at the front of the jaws, and smaller ones with a number of points at the sides. This feature must have developed at an early stage in pterosaur evolution, because it is visible in some of the oldest species, such as *Eudimorphodon* (page 184).

For pterosaurs that caught fish from the air, spotting prey and snatching it up were the first two steps in a complex operation. Once a fish had been grabbed by the front teeth, it then had to be manoeuvred into a head-first position, so that it could be swallowed, or it had to be flicked from the front of the beak towards the back, so that it was secure for the journey back to land. This is where the small lateral teeth came in. Unlike the front teeth, they had a more powerful bite, and because they were short, the pterosaur could carry its victim without its beak gaping.

In some fossils, the outlines of what look like throat pouches can be seen. These handy devices would have allowed pterosaurs to carry food back to land without any risk of it wriggling free.

FEEDING ON LAND

Fish-eaters were not the only pterosaurs that had teeth. Smaller species, based on land, probably used their teeth to catch insects, both in the air and on the ground. At one time, pterosaurs were thought to be clumsy on land, moving with a scuttling walk, as many bats do today. More recent studies of pterosaur skeletons suggest that they might have been surprisingly agile. In some, the rear legs were straight and strong, and with their wings folded back, their wing claws would have given them a tenacious grip.

At a time when giant plant-eating dinosaurs were common, this four-legged stance could have been put to good use. Some pterosaurs might have probed damp ground for insect grubs but others probably followed dinosaur herds, watching for any insects as they fed. A dinosaur's back would have made a perfect platform for watching out for food, and with four sets of claws to keep them in position, pterosaurs would have been difficult to dislodge.

SOARING SCAVENGERS

During the Cretaceous, the giants of the pterosaur world dispensed with teeth altogether. Instead, species such as *Pteranodon* and *Quetzalcoatlus* had massive toothless beaks, sometimes over a metre long. *Pteranodon* was a fish-eater, but *Quetzalcoatlus* fossils come from rocks that formed inland.

One theory is that *Quetzalcoatlus* lived like some of today's cranes and storks, striding across the ground or through shallow water, snatching any small animals it found. But it is more likely that it was not a hunter at all, but a scavenger. Its huge wings, combined with its excellent eyesight, would have made it the 'super-vulture' of the late Cretaceous, soaring high over open landscapes in search of dinosaur remains.

For a scavenging *Quetzalcoatlus*, feeding often involved breaking through centimetres of dead dinosaur skin to reach the meat. Pterosaur teeth would not have been much help, but a dagger-like beak was perfect. With a few well-aimed blows, *Quetzalcoatlus* could have punctured the hardest of hides.

△ *Looked at anti-clockwise from the top right, this four-stage sequence shows* Anhanguera *catching a fish. Its catch is small enough to be swallowed on the wing – anything much larger than this would have had to be taken back to land and ripped apart.*

▷ *Probing into soft mud, a* Pterodactylus *catches a worm. Like today's birds, pterodactyls had very good eyesight, moderate hearing, but probably a poor sense of smell. They would have found worms by sight, and perhaps by touch.*

How PTEROSAURS BRED

FOR PTEROSAURS, RAISING YOUNG WAS A DEMANDING BUSINESS. INSTEAD OF LAYING EGGS AND THEN ABANDONING THEM — LIKE SOME REPTILES — THEY ALMOST CERTAINLY SPENT TIME LOOKING AFTER THEIR YOUNG.

Fossils reveal little about the family life of pterosaurs, but there are a few clues about how they bred. One is that female pterosaurs generally had a narrow pelvis, which makes it unlikely that they gave birth to live young, unless they were small and poorly developed. They are more likely to have laid eggs. They would have laid them in inaccessible places, such as cliffs and trees, away from predators.

▷ *Back from a fishing trip, an adult* Ornithocheirus *regurgitates food for one of its offspring.*

DELIVERING FOOD

Being warm-blooded, pterosaurs would almost certainly have incubated their eggs. The young hatchlings would have looked like miniature versions of their parents, but with shorter beaks and wings. They would not have been able to fly, which means that they would have depended on their parents for food. Some adult pterosaurs may have brought back pieces of food in their beaks, but for fishing species — which often wandered far out to sea — this would have been an inefficient method of delivery. Instead, they probably fed their nestlings on regurgitated and partly digested food, a system that allowed them to catch several fish before having to head back to the shore.

For most pterosaurs, the work of feeding and guarding the young is likely to have kept both parents fully occupied. Because they had to operate as a team, the two adults would have stayed together for the whole of the breeding season, or perhaps even for life.

FLYING LESSONS

Today's flying vertebrates — birds and bats — have to wait until they reach adult size, or very close to it, before they fly. A remarkable feature of pterosaurs is that the young seem to have begun flying when they were still a lot smaller than their parents. Evidence for this comes from fossils of *Pterodactylus*, which include some specimens less than 10cm long. These have well-developed wings, but some of their other features, such as the shape of their beaks, shows that they were juvenile animals.

This discovery has some intriguing implications for pterosaur family life. Young pterosaurs had to learn to fly, and they would almost certainly have been 'instructed' by their parents. But even when they were fully at home in the air, they may still have been partly dependent on their parents for food. While the parents hunted for prey, their youngsters may have flapped around them in a family flock, until the time came when they could catch all their own food.

REPTILES IN THE SEA

Although reptiles evolved on land, many slowly abandoned terrestrial life and moved into the sea. During the Mesozoic Era, these included dolphin-like ichthyosaurs, long-necked plesiosaurs, and a host of other predators, some almost as large as today's baleen whales, and far more dangerous. Together, they were the dominant marine animals, but their supremacy was not to last. The ichthyosaurs died out during the Cretaceous, and of the other animals featured in this chapter, only turtles survived into modern times.

ADAPTING TO LIFE IN WATER

FOR AIR-BREATHING, FOUR-LEGGED REPTILES, MOVING FROM LAND TO WATER MEANT SOME MAJOR CHANGES IN SHAPE, AND ALSO IN BEHAVIOUR. DIFFERENT GROUPS OF REPTILES MADE THE CHANGE IN DIFFERENT WAYS.

Because reptiles were so successful on land, it seems all the more remarkable that so many kinds took up life in the sea. But evolution does not work in a set direction, and if a change brings advantages, that change is likely to be made. For marine reptiles, the advantage was reduced competition for food – a factor that made life increasingly difficult on land. The ancestors of today's turtles were among the first to make the transition, followed by a variety of other groups. Interestingly, dinosaurs were not among them, although it is likely that most could swim.

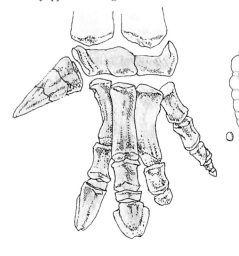

▽ The hand bones of an iguanodon (left) compared with those in the flipper of an ichthyosaur (right). Ichthyosaurs evolved large numbers of additional bones, which made their flippers more rigid.

SHAPES FOR SWIMMING

For land animals, gravity is a tiring fact of life, but air resistance is rarely a problem. In the sea, things are the other way around. Here, animals are buoyed up by the water around them, so they weigh little or nothing. But the moment they start to move, water resistance slows them down. The faster they swim, the more energy this resistance wastes.

The best way to minimize resistance is to have a streamlined body – something that all marine reptiles evolved at an early stage. Turtles developed flatter, smoother shells, while pliosaurs had bodies with long heads and short necks. The true

specialists, however, were the fastest-moving of all prehistoric marine reptiles – the ichthyosaurs. With their beak-like snouts and barrel-shaped bodies, they could swim as fast as dolphins.

As well as different body shapes, marine reptiles also had different swimming styles (pages 194–195). But while some wriggled their way through the water and others sped along with their flippers or tails, almost all had one thing in common – a large number of phalanges, the bones that make up fingers and toes. Typical land-dwelling reptiles, such as lizards, have 4 phalanges in each finger or toe, the same number as humans. Marine reptiles could have as many as 17, and some had extra fingers and toes. All these bones were bound together by strong ligaments, turning their feet into reptilian fins.

This proliferation of finger and toe bones is known as hyperphalangy. Millions of years after most marine reptiles died out, exactly the same adaptation evolved in the cetaceans, the group of mammals that includes today's dolphins and whales.

COMING UP FOR AIR

Despite some far-reaching changes in shape, marine reptiles still needed to breathe air. In fact, this is one area in which evolution has never quite managed to turn back the clock in reptiles or in sea-going mammals. Instead of losing lungs, marine reptiles developed ways of breathing more easily at sea.

One of the first and simplest adaptations was nostrils high up on the head, equipped with flaps that allowed them to be closed. Another was a secondary palate – a flap at the back of the mouth that could shut off the windpipe, or trachea. This would have been vital, because marine reptiles did not have lips, so they could not keep water out of their mouths while they were submerged. The palate prevented water flowing down the windpipe and into their lungs.

With the help of these two modifications, they could take a breath at the surface, and then dive down to search for prey. No one knows how long they could stay underwater, but today's crocodiles may provide a guide. When they are active, large species surface

Young ichthyosaur emerging tail-first

roughly every 5-10 minutes, but they can rest underwater for several hours. In prehistoric times, the deepest divers were the ichthyosaurs, and some, such as _Ophthalmosaurus_, may have been able to stay underwater for an hour or more, but much less if they were swimming at high speed.

EGGS OR LIVE BIRTH?

Apart from their need to breathe air, ichthyosaurs were fully equipped for life at sea. Fossils show that they gave birth to live young, which meant that they never had to return to land. But for other marine reptiles in these distant times, evidence about

reproduction is thin on the ground. No remains have ever been found of young animals developing inside their mothers, or of embryos inside eggs. As a result, palaeontologists can only guess how these animals might have bred.

It is possible that smaller species might have dragged themselves onto land to lay eggs, much as turtles do today. But with giant species, such as the whale-sized _Liopleurodon_ (page 191), this is likely to have been physically impossible. For this reason, most experts believe that animals like this gave birth, instead of laying eggs.

◁ _This fossil shows a female ichthyosaur in the act of giving birth. The young animal is emerging tail-first, and its head is partly hidden by its mother's hind flippers._

▽ _This 'family tree' shows how marine reptiles were related to other reptiles of the Mesozoic. Several marine groups died out well before the Age of Reptiles ended._

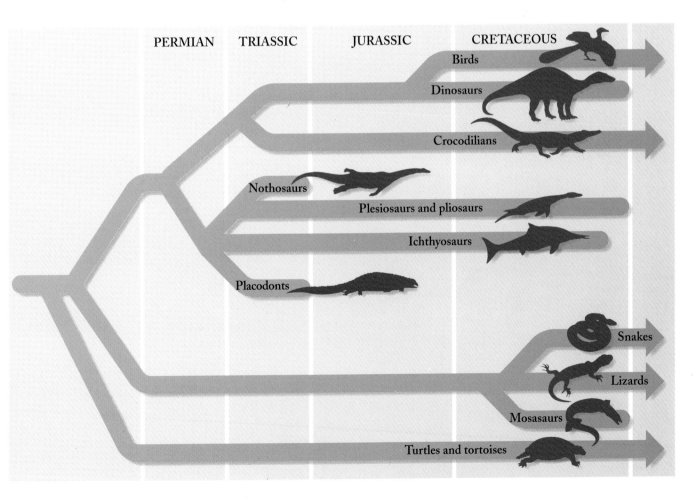

PERMIAN	TRIASSIC	JURASSIC	CRETACEOUS

Birds

Dinosaurs

Crocodilians

Nothosaurs

Plesiosaurs and pliosaurs

Ichthyosaurs

Placodonts

Snakes

Lizards

Mosasaurs

Turtles and tortoises

REPTILES IN THE SEA

NOTHOSAURS

The nothosaurs – with the unrelated placodonts – were early marine reptiles that showed different degrees of adaptation to life in water. Some of them lived in lagoons and along shallow shores, and spent much of their time on land, but others were sea-going creatures that may have wandered far into open water. A fossilized embryo, found in Switzerland, shows that some or perhaps all of these animals reproduced by laying eggs, a primitive characteristic that made them partly dependent on land.

MAXIMUM LENGTH	4m
TIME	Mid Triassic
FOSSIL FINDS	Europe (Italy, Switzerland)

PISTOSAURUS
Unlike *Ceresiosaurus*, *Pistosaurus* had some advanced features that made it even better equipped for life in open water. Its flipper-like legs were smooth and elliptical – without any visible toes – and its backbone was relatively stiff, allowing it to move by paddling instead of by waving its tail. Its head was small and almost cylindrical, another adaptation that would have helped to reduce energy-wasting turbulence as it slipped through the water. *Pistosaurus* is classified in the same order as the nothosaurs, but in a family of its own. It could clearly have ranged far out to sea, but if it laid eggs – as other nothosaurs seem to have done – it would have had to return to land to breed.

MAXIMUM LENGTH	3m
TIME	Mid Triassic
FOSSIL FINDS	Europe (France, Germany)

△ Pistosaurus *had well-developed flipper-like limbs, although the outlines of toes were probably evident beneath the surface of its skin. Its tail was cylindrical, and did not have a fin.*

▽ Ceresiosaurus *had a characteristic nothosaur body, with a long neck, finned tail and well-developed flippers with distinct toes. It probably hunted for fish in rocky crevices on the seabed, instead of in open water.*

CERESIOSAURUS
Ceresiosaurus was a typical nothosaur, with a slender, streamlined shape. It had a long, highly flexible tail, and extra bones in its toes – a feature that evolved on many separate occasions in marine reptiles and mammals. Its head was relatively small, but its jaws were armed with small, sharp teeth – the hallmark of a fish-eater. Opinions differ about how *Ceresiosaurus* swam. Instead of using only its tail, like the placodonts (see opposite), or its flippers, like the plesiosaurs (page 188), it may have used both, perhaps switching from one form of movement to the other as it adjusted its speed. Along with many other marine reptiles from the Triassic, its remains have been found in ancient marine sediments in the Alps of Europe, an area which once formed part of the Tethys Sea.

LARIOSAURUS
Only about half the size of an otter, *Lariosaurus* was much smaller than some of its nothosaur relatives, although at the other extreme, some other nothosaurs were not much bigger than a human hand. It had a lizard-like shape, with a short neck and toes, and its hind limbs still retained distinct toes and claws, although its feet would have been

webbed. It would probably have been amphibious, feeding in shallow water, but spending much of its time resting on the shore. Because they had small bodies, animals like *Lariosaurus* would have been quickly chilled by cool seawater. As a result, most of them were restricted to the tropics. Between swims, they would have basked on rocks to warm themselves up – very like marine iguanas do today.

MAXIMUM LENGTH 60cm
TIME Mid Triassic
FOSSIL FINDS Europe (Spain)

NOTHOSAURUS

Nothosaurus was a highly successful and widespread animal, appearing at the beginning of the Triassic Period, and surviving – with relatively few changes – for over 30 million years. Several particularly well-preserved specimens have been found,

clearly showing its webbed feet with five long toes. Its front legs were shorter than its hind ones – a characteristic that is more useful for moving on land than it is for swimming at sea. This reptile had a sinuous, streamlined body, and spines on its vertebrae make it likely that its tail had a vertical fin. *Nothosaurus* was a fish-eater, but its leg anatomy suggests that it spent a substantial amount of time on the shore, like modern seals do today.

MAXIMUM LENGTH 3m
TIME Triassic
FOSSIL FINDS Europe (Germany, Italy, Switzerland), north Africa, Asia (Russia, China)

PACHYPLEUROSAURUS

At one time, this animal and its relatives were thought by scientists to be nothosaurs, but they were probably close cousins, rather than members of the same family.

Pachypleurosaurus itself was slim and lizard-like, with paddles that worked like a seal's flippers, enabling it to haul itself out onto land. Compared to the rest of its body, its head was very small, perhaps allowing it to probe underwater crevices in search of fish to eat. There were several species of *Pachypleurosaurus*, and they varied a great deal in size. The smallest species were only about 60cm long.

MAXIMUM LENGTH 2.5m
TIME Mid Triassic
FOSSIL FINDS Europe (Italy, Switzerland)

PLACODUS

Looking like a large, humpbacked lizard, *Placodus* was one of the earliest marine reptiles. It had webbed feet and a flattened tail, but apart from this, it showed few modifications for life in the water. Its head was short, and it had three different types of teeth: protruding incisors at the front of its jaws, rounded molars along the sides, and a set of six flattened molars on the roof of its mouth. This suggests that it fed on molluscs in shallow water, prising them from rocks, and then crushing them in its jaws. *Placodus* belonged to a group of reptiles called placodonts, which were protected by reinforced skeletons, or sometimes bony shells (page 202). The placodonts became extinct before the Triassic came to an end.

MAXIMUM LENGTH 2m
TIME Early Triassic
FOSSIL FINDS Europe (France)

△ Nothosaurus *was one of the larger members of its family, with a seal-like lifestyle. Because it was cold-blooded – like its relatives – its oxygen consumption would have been relatively low, enabling it to stay submerged for several minutes at a time. Its nostrils were positioned halfway down its muzzle, and would have been closed by flaps of skin when it dived.*

REPTILES IN THE SEA

PLESIOSAURS

Plesiosaurs first appeared in the Late Triassic, but had their heyday in the Jurassic. There were two basic forms: species with long necks and small heads, the 'true' plesiosaurs, and species with short necks and large heads, the pliosaurs (page 190). Both types had four flipper-like fins, and they swam by beating these up and down like wings, instead of by waving their tails. All of them were ocean-going carnivores that returned to land only when they laid their eggs. Compared to early marine reptiles, some of them were enormous, even rivalling modern whales in size.

△ Plesiosaurus *would have fed by powering through the water with its paddles, while using its flexible neck to lunge after fish and squid. Its head was triangular with a pointed snout – an efficient shape for slicing through the water.*

PLESIOSAURUS
Some of the earliest *Plesiosaurus* fossils were discovered by the English fossil-collector Mary Anning in the 1820s (page 197). The specimens she found were well-preserved and remarkably complete – a result of rapid burial by a soft blanket of marine sediment, which prevented the remains being disturbed. Her finds, and many others, show that there were several species of *Plesiosaurus*, all of them variations on the same successful 'design'. They had narrow heads, slender necks and tails, and two pairs of paddles roughly equal in size. Their teeth were numerous, pointed and slightly curved – a shape that evolved for catching fish that would then be swallowed whole. *Plesiosaurus'* large paddles and robust build make it likely that it pursued its prey, instead of waiting for fish to come within range.

MAXIMUM LENGTH	3m
TIME	Early Jurassic
FOSSIL FINDS	Europe (England, France, Germany)

RHOMALEOSAURUS
With its relatively long neck and large head, *Rhomaleosaurus* looked like

▷ Rhomaleosaurus *was the early Jurassic equivalent of a killer whale, hunting fish and perhaps other reptiles with its well-armed jaws. Unlike small-headed plesiosaurs, it could have torn large animals to pieces by tossing them in the air.*

a halfway stage between true plesiosaurs and the pliosaurs. Its classification is still a matter of debate, and at times it has been allotted to both these groups. Its lifestyle is more certain, because fossils clearly show a powerful body, two pairs of roughly equal paddles and crocodile-like jaws, sometimes nearly 1m long, armed with large protruding teeth. Some recent research suggests that *Rhomaleosaurus* and its relatives may have swum with their jaws slightly ajar, allowing water to go in through the mouth, and out through the nostrils. This unusual arrangement – a reversal of the normal water flow – would have allowed them to track down prey by smell rather than by sight.

MAXIMUM LENGTH	7m
TIME	Early Jurassic
FOSSIL FINDS	Europe (England, Germany)

CRYPTOCLIDUS
A large plesiosaur with a 2m long neck, *Cryptoclidus* had a number of evolutionary refinements for life at sea. Its flippers were much larger than those of earlier plesiosaurs, giving it more power underwater, and its teeth were long, pointed and interlocking, so that they formed a cage-like trap for fish, shrimp and squid. Fossils of this animal are often very well preserved, and some of the best came from clay quarries in England at a time when clay was dug out by hand. This kind of quarrying is now carried out by machine, so complete fossil skeletons are a much rarer find today.

MAXIMUM LENGTH	8m
TIME	Late Jurassic
FOSSIL FINDS	Europe (England, France), Asia (Russia)

MURAENOSAURUS
Muraenosaurus – 'moray eel lizard' – belonged to a group of reptiles called elasmosaurs, renowned for their extraordinarily

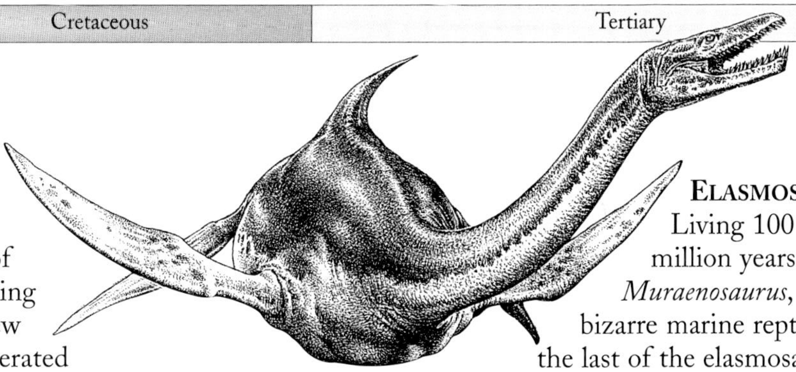

long necks. It was one of the early examples of the neck-stretching trend, which grew ever more exaggerated as time went by. It had up to 44 neck vertebrae, and altogether, they accounted for over half its entire body length. Its head was relatively tiny – just 40cm long – and it also had relatively small flippers for its size, and stubby tail. This combination of features suggests that *Muraenosaurus* was not an active hunter. Instead, it probably rested on the seabed in shallow water, where it could attack fish either from beneath the surface, or from above. To feed, it would have drawn its neck back into a curve, and then suddenly straightened it to grab its prey. Its small head would also have allowed it to extract fish from crevices among rocks.

MAXIMUM LENGTH 6m

TIME Late Jurassic

FOSSIL FINDS Europe (England, France)

ELASMOSAURUS
Living 100 million years after *Muraenosaurus*, this bizarre marine reptile was the last of the elasmosaur line. It had up to 71 neck vertebrae, contributing to a snake-like neck up to 6m long. The central part of its body was also much larger than in *Muraenosaurus*. *Elasmosaurus'* feeding technique was probably similar to its earlier relatives, although its increased neck length would have given it a greater reach. The theory that it was a sit-and-wait predator has been bolstered by the discovery of stomach stones, or gastroliths, which it may have used as a kind of ballast.

MAXIMUM LENGTH 14m

TIME Late Cretaceous

FOSSIL FINDS North America (Wyoming, Kansas), Asia (Japan)

◁ *Powered by its well-developed paddles,* Cryptoclidus *would have 'flown' through the water.*

▽ Elasmosaurus *homes in on a shoal of fish. This plesiosaur is often portrayed as a sea monster, but its narrow head meant it could tackle only quite small prey.*

189

PLIOSAURS

Descended from plesiosaurs, pliosaurs became the top marine predators from the early Jurassic into the Cretaceous. With short necks, massive heads and viciously armed jaws, they could attack animals almost their own size, ripping off chunks of flesh like today's sharks or killer whales. They probably hunted alone, and they may have relied partly on their sense of smell to track down food. In pliosaur evolution, natural selection favoured increasing size. After more than 60 million years, the outcome of this process was *Liopleurodon*, perhaps the largest predator ever to have existed on this planet.

△ Kronosaurus' *head accounted for about a third of its entire body length, and its jaws ran almost the entire length of the skull, giving them a depth of nearly 3m. It had two other distinguishing features that set it apart from other pliosaurs: the top of its head was unusually flattened and its ribs were thicker.*

MACROPLATA
A relatively primitive pliosaur from the early Jurassic, *Macroplata* still had features in common with its plesiosaur ancestors: a long neck with 29 vertebrae, and a fairly small head. Two specimens from England, dated about 15 million years apart, highlight the trends in pliosaur evolution – the more recent species had a longer head, as well as a slightly larger body. In pliosaurs as a whole, the limbs also became larger and stronger than those of plesiosaurs, allowing them to power through the water after their prey.

MAXIMUM LENGTH 5m

TIME	Early Jurassic
FOSSIL FINDS	Europe (England)

SIMOLESTES
Simolestes was slightly larger than *Macroplata*, and had a more typical pliosaur shape, with a short neck, massively built head and large paddle-like legs. Its neck contained only 20 vertebrae – far fewer than many plesiosaurs, but still more than pliosaurs of later times.

Its jaws had blunt ends, giving it a snub-nosed appearance, and the lower one was equipped with half a dozen extra-large teeth, which stabbed upwards into prey. It would have killed small prey outright, but with larger animals, it probably attacked and then circled at a distance, waiting for the moment when its victim was too weak to fight back. Sharks use the same technique.

MAXIMUM LENGTH 6m

TIME	Mid Jurassic
FOSSIL FINDS	Europe (France), Asia (India)

PLIOSAURUS
First identified in the 1840s, the 'original' pliosaur has proved a difficult animal to classify. Many palaeontologists believe that it is actually a form of *Liopleurodon*, because their remains look so similar. Among the few differences are the teeth – *Liopleurodon*'s were round in cross-section while *Pliosaurus*' were triangular. *Pliosaurus* had about 20 neck vertebrae, and its skull was up to 2m long.

MAXIMUM LENGTH 12m

TIME	Mid Jurassic
FOSSIL FINDS	Europe (England), South America (Argentina)

PELONEUSTES

A compact late Jurassic pliosaur, *Peloneustes* shows the developing trend in the family for a larger head and shorter neck, as well as a more streamlined shape. Its hind paddles were slightly larger than its front ones – the reverse of the situation in many plesiosaurs. However, as in plesiosaurs, both pairs of flippers were used in swimming, although the rear pair are likely to have done more of the work.

Each flipper would have twisted as it beat up and down through the water, creating a backward thrust that drove the animal forwards (page 194). The remains of suckers, preserved as fossils in *Peloneustes*' stomach, show that squid formed an important part of its diet. Its teeth were relatively small, making it unlikely that it attacked large prey.

MAXIMUM LENGTH 3m

TIME Late Jurassic

FOSSIL FINDS Europe (UK, Russia)

LIOPLEURODON

Once it reached maturity, this colossal pliosaur was so large that it had no enemies apart from its own kind. Estimates of its length range from about 12m to as much as 25m – a figure that suggests it might have weighed over 100 tonnes. This is much bigger than the sperm whale, which is the largest living predator that tracks down and attacks individual prey. *Liopleurodon* would have fed on any marine animal large enough to attract its attention. Although it was fully equipped for life in the open sea, it may also have swum into shallow water, where it could pick off dinosaurs foraging near the shore. It relied mainly on vision and smell, lunging forwards to make the kill with an array of widely spaced, dagger-like teeth. These were conical in shape, and up to 30cm long – twice the length of those of *Tyrannosaurus*. They projected from the front of its jaws, which hinged at a point close to the back of its skull – a distance of up to 4m. Given its size, *Liopleurodon* would have been able to travel immense distances, but little is known of its breeding behaviour. On land, it would have been as helpless as a beached whale, which suggests that it gave birth to live young instead of laying eggs.

MAXIMUM LENGTH 25m

TIME Late Jurassic

FOSSIL FINDS Europe (UK, France, Germany)

KRONOSAURUS

The first pliosaur fossil finds in Australia were made in Queensland, and date back to the 1880s. In 1990, cattle ranchers in the same area stumbled across another set of fossilized bones protruding from the ground like a tree stump. They turned out to belong to *Kronosaurus*, or a similar animal, and are among the most complete pliosaur remains currently known. Although *Kronosaurus* was only generally a little over half the size of *Liopleurodon*, it was still larger and heavier than most land-based predators of the Cretaceous, with a head measuring 2.5m.

MAXIMUM LENGTH 10m

TIME Early Cretaceous

FOSSIL FINDS Australia (Queensland), South America (Colombia)

◁ Liopleurodon *was a terrifying marine predator of enormous size and power. Armed with murderous projecting teeth, and protected by plate-like bones on its underside, it would have reigned supreme in the seas of the Jurassic.*

▽ *Although a midget compared to some of its relatives,* Peloneustes *was still a substantial predator, the size of a large modern dolphin. It would have been a fast and agile swimmer, powered by its four paddles, and catching fish and squid in its narrow, toothed mouth.*

REPTILES IN THE SEA

ICHTHYOSAURS

Ichthyosaurs, or 'fish lizards', were the first reptiles that were fully adapted to life in the sea. These reptiles had streamlined bodies and four paired flippers, and most had crescent-shaped tails. Hundreds of ichthyosaur fossils have been found, and many are superbly preserved. Some fossilized ichthyosaurs died with embryos inside their bodies, or even while they were giving birth – proof that they did not lay eggs.

▷ *Like other ichthyosaurs,* Mixosaurus *had four paired flippers, and a single upright fin on its back. The flippers acted as stabilizers and rudders, while the tail provided the power for swimming.*

MIXOSAURUS

Mixosaurus, meaning 'mixed lizard', lived about 230 million years ago, when ichthyosaurs were already well established. Although it was fully adapted to life at sea, it still had several primitive features. The most obvious one was its tail, which ended in a point, instead of having two vertical lobes. *Mixosaurus* fed on fish, and its distribution – in warm, shallow seas worldwide – show that it was very successful.

LENGTH 1m

TIME Mid Triassic

FOSSIL FINDS North America (Nevada, Alaska), Europe (France, Germany, Norway), Asia (China), New Zealand

ICHTHYOSAURUS

Looking like a small dolphin, *Ichthyosaurus* is one of the best known marine prehistoric reptiles, with hundreds of fossils having been found. A powerful swimmer, it could probably have reached speeds of 40km/h, powered by its vertical two-lobed tail. Its snout was long and narrow, and was armed with small but sharp teeth – ideal for gripping squid and other animals with slippery bodies.

LENGTH 2m

TIME Early Jurassic to early Cretaceous

FOSSIL FINDS North America (Alberta), Greenland, Europe (England, Germany)

▷ *Compared to most ichthyosaurs, Shonisaurus was a vast and bulky animal. At one fossil site in Nevada, the remains of more than 30* Shonisaurus *have been found close together, suggesting that these giant reptiles lived in schools, like many of today's whales.*

▽ *With its streamlined body and long jaws, Temnodontosaurus was shaped for catching fast-moving prey. Fish made up most of its diet, but it also ate squid and other cephalopod molluscs. Their hard remains have been found inside Temnodontosaurus skeletons.*

TEMNODONTOSAURUS

Also known as *Leptopterygius*, this large ichthyosaur had a long snout, a barrel-shaped body and a powerful two-lobed tail. Most ichthyosaurs had good eyesight, but this one's eyes were the biggest of any known animal, alive or extinct. They measured up to 26cm across, and as in most ichthyosaurs, were surrounded by a ring of thin, overlapping bony plates, which helped to protect them during dives. *Leptopterygius'* large eyes may have been an adaptation for hunting at night.

LENGTH 9m

TIME Late Jurassic

FOSSIL FINDS Europe (England, Germany)

SHONISAURUS

With a body as long as a bus, *Shonisaurus* is the largest ichthyosaur that has yet been discovered. It appeared relatively early in ichthyosaur evolution, and had some unusual features that set it apart from its relatives. Among these were a deep, bulky body; long, equally-sized flippers; and teeth only in the front of its jaws. Its diet is uncertain, but its size alone means that it would have been a formidable predator, capable of tackling many other sea animals.

LENGTH 15m

TIME Late Triassic

FOSSIL FINDS North America (Nevada)

▷ *Ichthyosaurs, plesiosaurs and turtles all had different swimming styles. Ichthyosaurs were the most fish-like of the three, swimming with side-to-side undulations. Plesiosaurs used a complex swimming technique with two pairs of paddles moving in alternate directions. Turtles swim with their front legs, with very little push coming from the pair at the rear.*

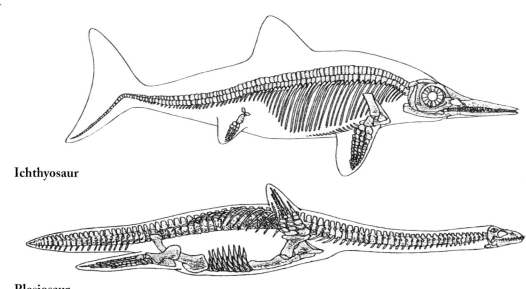

Ichthyosaur

Plesiosaur

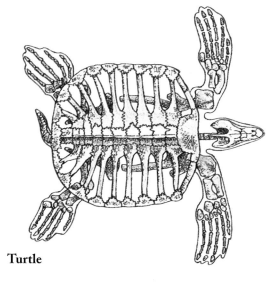

Turtle

SWIMMING STYLES

WHEN REPTILES TOOK UP LIFE IN WATER, THEY EVOLVED DIFFERENT METHODS OF SWIMMING. SOME SWAM LIKE FISH, BUT OTHERS MOVED IN WAYS THAT HAVE NO DIRECT EQUIVALENT IN LIVING ANIMALS.

To swim, an animal has to push against the water around it. This backward push drives the animal forwards, in the same way that the push from a propeller moves a boat. Reptiles evolved swimming styles with modified versions of two quite different body parts: tails and limbs. Tail propulsion is the common swimming style in fish, and was the method evolved by ichthyosaurs. Limb propulsion is used by seals and penguins, but reptiles evolved some versions of it that were uniquely their own.

POWER AT THE REAR
To swim efficiently, an animal has to push against the water with the minimum of turbulence. This creates a smooth water flow as the animal moves – the exact opposite of what happens when somebody splashes about as they learn to swim. Tail propulsion is ideal for this, and it is no accident that most fish use their tails to swim instead of 'rowing' with their other fins.

The earliest marine reptiles, such as *Placodus* (page 187), had long webbed tails that they rippled from side to side, in conjunction with the rest of their bodies. For animals that originated on land, this way of swimming needed relatively few physical changes, but it had the disadvantage of being fairly slow. Ichthyosaurs, on the other hand, evolved shorter, blade-like tails, much more like those of fish. Most of their body movement took place at the tail end, while their paddle-like limbs acted as rudders and stabilizers, keeping them on course. This swimming style is almost exactly the same as the one used by the fastest fish today.

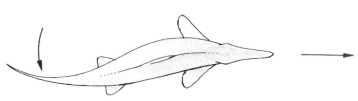

△ *In fish and ichthyosaurs, the body and tail push against the water as they bend from side to side.*

△ *The side-to-side movements generate a force that drives the animal forwards through the water.*

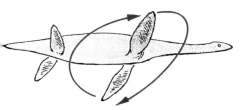

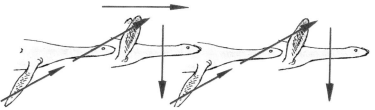

△ *In plesiosaurs, the tip of each flipper follows a roughly elliptical path (assuming the animal is still).*

△ *The backward push comes during the downstroke. The flipper then twists to move upwards edge-on.*

△ *Turtles move both sets of flippers together, but the front pair does the work.*

△ *The flippers work like oars, although they can also 'glide' like wings.*

△ *To push the turtle forwards, the flippers move downwards and backwards.*

PADDLES AND FLIPPERS

In most other marine reptiles, evolution followed a different course. These animals also developed paddle-like limbs, but instead of being fairly immobile, their limbs kept some of the movement they had on land. For some of these reptiles, the tail helped in propulsion, but in others, particularly turtles, it became so small that it played no part in swimming at all.

Evolution often exaggerates differences between front and back legs, and this is exactly what happened with turtles. Their forelimbs became longer and more powerful, beating up and down like a pair of wings to push the animal through the water. The back legs were much smaller and used mainly for steering and stability. But in plesiosaurs, the four paddles stayed roughly similar in size. Plesiosaurs probably swam with all four limbs working simultaneously, a highly unusual swimming style that has not been seen either before, or since.

THE PLESIOSAUR PUZZLE

For stability, plesiosaurs' two pairs of legs would almost certainly have beaten in opposite directions, but the exact path of each paddle is not easy to work out. They may have pushed horizontally, like oars, or diagonally, or vertically up and down. From studies of plesiosaur skeletons, the second theory is generally accepted as the most likely of the three. Each flipper generated a backward push as it came down, and then twisted so that it could slide back into the 'up' position with minimal resistance against the water. The upstroke was aided by the animal's spine, which bent rhythmically as it swam.

▽ *Plesiosaurs used their flippers for steering and braking, as well as for building up speed. Here, an* Elasmosaurus *carries out a sharp turn to pursue a shoal of fish.*

FAMILY GROUP
Guarded by their mother, two young Temnodontosaurus *swim past a rocky reef in search of food. Because female ichthyosaurs gave birth to live young, they had small families. The females probably looked after their offspring, and showed them how to hunt.*

FOSSIL-HUNTING IN EUROPE

EUROPE WAS THE BIRTHPLACE OF PALAEONTOLOGY. EUROPEAN FOSSIL FINDS HAVE INCLUDED A NUMBER OF SIGNIFICANT ONES, BEGINNING WITH THE DISCOVERY OF FOSSIL REPTILES, OVER 250 YEARS AGO.

Fossils are common objects in some parts of Europe. During the medieval period, they were thought to be the remains of animals that had perished in the biblical Great Flood – something that some people still believe today. But by the 1700s, fossils of truly gigantic animals started to come to light, making scientists increasingly doubtful about the traditional version of Earth's history. They gradually realized that the Earth was far older than previously supposed, and that a wide range of animals had lived in the distant past, only to become extinct.

▷ *Carefully splitting open thin sheets of limestone, quarry workers in Germany reveal well-preserved fossils of Jurassic fish that have been entombed in limestone for over 150 million years.*

▷ *This is a fossil shrimp from the famous Solnhöfen limestone quarries in southern Germany. Because the rock particles are so fine, all the details of its body have been preserved. Solnhöfen has also yielded fossils of soft-bodied animals, such as jellyfish.*

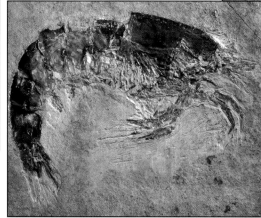

BROUGHT TO THE SURFACE
In the early days of palaeontology, most fossils were discovered by accident, often by workers in Europe's quarries. One of the most spectacular of these early finds was the 'Beast of Maastricht' – a giant crocodile-like skull that was found in a chalk quarry in the Netherlands in 1776. The 'Beast' was actually a mosasaur (page 200), but scientists of the time imagined that it must belong

Born in 1799, Mary Anning was the world's first professional collector of fossils. Her home town, Lyme Regis in England, is flanked by seacliffs of Jurassic shale and mudstone, and it was here, in 1811, that she found the first known remains of an ichthyosaur, which had fallen out of the cliffs onto the shore. Thirteen years later, she discovered another first: the almost complete fossil skeleton of a plesiosaur.

to an animal that still existed, probably either a crocodile or a whale.

The confusion over this animal was understandable, because the tooth-filled jaws of a mosasaur do look distinctly crocodilian.

But, in 1784, an Italian naturalist published an account of an even more remarkable fossil that he had found in the Solnhöfen limestone quarries in southern Germany. Unlike the Maastricht mosasaur, this animal was small, but it looked unlike anything that scientists had ever seen or heard of before. Resembling a mixture between a bat and a bird, it was actually a pterosaur – the first one to be studied in a systematic way. This fossil was the scientific equivalent of front-page news, and as interest in palaeontology mushroomed, quarry workers kept a keen lookout for interesting specimens, which by now were fetching record prices.

During the early 1800s, quarries like Solnhöfen generated a steady stream of fossil remains. At this time, a young woman called Mary Anning became the first person to collect fossils for a living. Mary Anning lived on the coast of Dorset in England, in an area where fossil-filled cliffs are being steadily eroded by the sea, and her finds included an almost complete ichthyosaur, which was identified as an extinct marine reptile. The idea of extinction was becoming widely accepted and this helped to prepare the way for more momentous discoveries in the years that followed.

THE FIRST DINOSAURS

The first dinosaur fossil to be formally described was found in 1676 by the English museum curator Robert Plot. At the time, Plot's discovery – the 'knee end' of a giant thigh bone – was thought to be from a large mammal, perhaps even a giant human being. Over 140 years passed before more remains of the animal were found in an Oxfordshire quarry. These fossils were examined by a pioneering geologist, William Buckland, who recognized that they belonged to a carnivorous reptile, which he named *Megalosaurus*. The following year, another English geologist, Gideon Mantell, identified the remains of *Iguanodon*, again correctly deducing that they were from a reptile, rather than a mammal.

The name *Megalosaurus* means 'giant lizard', and shows that nineteenth-century geologists were still trying to squeeze their newly discovered animals into known branches of the reptile world. But this situation was not to last for long. In 1841,

the leading English anatomist Richard Owen showed that *Megalosaurus* and *Iguanodon* were different from living reptiles in many ways, quite apart from their size. He proposed a new name for this extinct group of reptiles – 'the dinosaurs'.

MAMMALS AND PEOPLE

After this breakthrough, European palaeontology began to move at a rapid pace. The first fossil of *Archaeopteryx* was found at the Solnhöfen quarries in 1861, and as the nineteenth century drew to a close, European fossil-hunters began to send back fossils from other parts of the world. These formed the basis of magnificent museum collections in cities such as London, Paris and Berlin. At home, palaeontologists continued to unearth a wide range of reptiles, particularly marine forms, such as ichthyosaurs and plesiosaurs, but their finds also included extinct mammals – mammoths, bears and rhinoceroses – which flourished in Europe during Ice Age times.

In the last 150 years, Europe has also been an important source of fossils and artefacts belonging to early humans, which spread northwards through the continent after moving out of Africa. The finds include the remains not only of our direct ancestors, but also those of Neanderthal Man (page 216).

◁ *The crumbling cliffs of Lyme Regis, on the south coast of England, are a fossil-hunter's paradise. Their layered rock formed from seabed sediment in Jurassic times, and contains the remains of a wide variety of animals, from ichthyosaurs to ammonites.*

△ *The Solnhöfen quarries in southern Germany produce limestone with an extremely fine grain. The rock was built up by tiny specks of sediment that settled out in coral reef lagoons during the late Jurassic. The quarries are famous for being the source of* Archaeopteryx *and half a dozen kinds of pterosaur, but they have also yielded many fish, and over 100 kinds of fossil insect.*

REPTILES IN THE SEA

MOSASAURS

△ Mosasaurus *and its relatives were alive when the ichthyosaurs had died out, making them among the largest marine reptiles in the late Cretaceous.*

Mosasaurs were latecomers to the ranks of Mesozoic marine reptiles, appearing late in the Cretaceous Period, and disappearing when it came to a close. Unlike other sea-going reptiles, they belonged to the same line of animals as today's monitor lizards. They had scaly, lizard-like skin, and they swam by rippling their long bodies, which ended in a flattened fin-bearing tail. Some of them grew to a great size, and they had unusual jaws which could bend sideways to engulf and crush their prey.

of widely spaced fin-like paddles, containing many more toe bones than in its land-dwelling ancestors. Its tail was vertically flattened, and this – together with its wedge-shaped skull – made it look like a fish crossed with a crocodile. Like all mosasaurs, its jaws had a joint about halfway along their length, allowing them to extend sideways, and they were equipped with a battery of sharply pointed teeth. It probably fed on fish, squid and turtles, but it also ate ammonites. This is known because fossilized ammonites have been discovered with bite marks that match *Mosasaurus'* teeth.

MAXIMUM LENGTH 10m

TIME Late Cretaceous

FOSSIL FINDS Europe (Holland, Belgium), North America (Texas, South Dakota)

▽ Tylosaurus (below) *had the sinuous shape, small limbs and narrow head characteristic of the mosasaur family.*

▷ Platecarpus (right) *had an extra-large number of 'finger' and 'toe' bones, a typical feature of marine reptiles.*

MOSASAURUS

Mosasaurus has a unique place in the study of prehistoric life. When the first skull came to light, in a Dutch quarry in 1776, it was assumed to belong to an unknown animal – perhaps a crocodile or whale – that was still alive somewhere on Earth. But as the decades went by without a living *Mosasaurus* being found, scientists began to grasp a crucial fact: animal life in the past included species that have become extinct. The creature that triggered this breakthrough was one of the deadliest marine predators of the late Cretaceous. Its limbs had evolved into two pairs

TYLOSAURUS

Similar in form to *Mosasaurus*, although slightly smaller, *Tylosaurus* would have been an equally formidable predator of the late Cretaceous seas. Like *Mosasaurus*, it drove itself through the water with its tail, using its paddle-shaped flippers for steering, and perhaps for stabilizing itself when it rested inshore. Its teeth were up to 5cm long and 3cm wide at the base,

200

and would constantly have been replaced throughout its lifetime. It also had a sclerotic ring around its eyes – a circle of small, flattened bones that acted as a protective shield in front of the eyeball. In common with other mosasaurs, *Tylosaurus* lived in shallow seas. But although hundreds of mosasaur fossils have been found, unlike ichthyosaurs none shows signs of carrying embryos. This makes it probable that most mosasaurs laid eggs, hauling themselves onto sandy beaches like turtles. Their flippers would have been ineffective on land, so they may have writhed their way up the shore.

MAXIMUM LENGTH 8m

TIME Late Cretaceous

FOSSIL FINDS North America (Texas, Kansas), New Zealand

PLATECARPUS

Remains found on both sides of the Atlantic show that *Platecarpus* was a fairly common marine reptile in the late Cretaceous. Although quite small compared to other mosasaurs, it was about the same size as many of today's open-water sharks, and its long jaws would have made it an effective predator. It probably fed on fish and squid, but exactly how it hunted is unclear. It may have fed in the same way as modern seals, cruising through the shallows close to the shore, and catching animals frightened by its approach.

MAXIMUM LENGTH 6m

TIME Late Cretaceous

FOSSIL FINDS North America (Manitoba, Northwest Territories, Kansas, Colorado, Alabama, Mississippi), Europe (Belgium)

GLOBIDENS

When *Globidens* first came to light in Alabama in 1912, it was given its name because of its remarkable teeth. They had rounded crowns, and looked like a row of golfballs set in the animal's jaws. Teeth like these were clearly no use for grasping fish or squid, and instead *Globidens* probably fed on seabed molluscs and crustaceans, cracking open their shells and body cases with its jaws. Only a handful of *Globidens* skulls have been found – all in North America – but isolated teeth have been found in other parts of the world.

MAXIMUM LENGTH 6m

TIME Late Cretaceous

FOSSIL FINDS North America (Alabama, Kansas, South Dakota)

PLOTOSAURUS

One of the largest of about 20 mosasaurs so far discovered, *Plotosaurus* had a long body, and a snake-like tail with a flattened vertical fin. Its small flippers were widely spaced, making them ineffective for propulsion but good for steering and stability. Skin impressions found near some *Plotosaurus* fossils show that it was covered in small scales, like today's monitor lizards. With its sleek shape and sharp teeth, it would have been a major threat to fish and squid in shallow seas as the Cretaceous neared its end.

MAXIMUM LENGTH 10m

TIME Late Cretaceous

FOSSIL FINDS North America (Kansas)

△ With its jaws gaping open, Globidens *(top)* reveals a mouth full of bulbous and extremely hard teeth. The main teeth were up to 3cm across; the ones at the front of the jaw were smaller and peg-like.

△ Plotosaurus *(above)* was so well-adapted to marine life that it would have had difficulty moving on land. This suggests that it gave birth to live young, unlike some of its relatives.

REPTILES IN THE SEA

SHELLED REPTILES

During the Mesozoic Era, two quite different groups of marine reptiles evolved shells as a protection against predators. One group, the placodonts, were relatives of some of the earliest reptiles in the seas (page 197). They emerged in the Triassic, but were extinct before it came to an end. The other group were the chelonians – animals that also appeared in the Triassic and were the ancestors of the tortoises and turtles alive today. Although they lived at different times, these two groups evolved similar adaptations to suit similar ways of life.

△ *With its streamlined shell and huge 'wingspan', Archelon (top right) roamed vast distances throughout the seas of the Late Cretaceous.*

▷ Placochelys *(right) is a combination name that means 'placodont-turtle' – a fitting description of this remarkably turtle-like animal.*

▽ Henodus *(below) had a rectangular shell. Its legs were relatively short and stumpy, suggesting that it spent most of its time crawling across the seabed.*

ARCHELON
Chelonians first appeared on land, and although tortoises remained there, turtles took up life in freshwater or the sea. By the late Cretaceous, one marine species – *Archelon* – became the largest sea turtle that has ever lived. It weighed about 3 tonnes, and swam by beating its wing-like front flippers, which were 4.5m from tip to tip. Its shell was formed by an open lattice of struts, instead of a complete shield of bone, and it probably had a rubbery surface, like the shells of leatherback turtles today. Like other chelonians, *Archelon*'s jaws formed a toothless beak, and it fed on jellyfish and other soft-bodied animals. Despite its great weight, it reproduced by hauling itself onto beaches and laying eggs.

MAXIMUM LENGTH	4m
TIME	Late Cretaceous
FOSSIL FINDS	North America (Kansas, Dakota)

HENODUS
Long before *Archelon* appeared in the seas, *Henodus*, a placodont, – had evolved a shell for self-defence. Unlike a turtle's shell, this one was made up of several hundred bony plates, which fitted together like a mosaic. The edges of the shell were drawn out into a pair of rigid flaps, giving a flattened shape. *Henodus* had a blunt mouth, without any teeth, and it fed on molluscs and other slow-moving animals in shallow water.

MAXIMUM LENGTH	1m
TIME	Late Triassic
FOSSIL FINDS	Europe (Germany)

PLACOCHELYS
The shell of this placodont was shallow and almost rectangular, and was covered with a scattering of bony plates that made it harder to attack.

It had flat-toothed jaws, ending in a narrow beak that was ideal for prising molluscs from rocks. It had flattened legs which worked like flippers, and their size meant that it was probably a good swimmer. However, like a marine turtle, it could not pull its legs within its shell if it was attacked. *Placochelys* almost certainly reproduced by laying eggs, and it would have had no difficulty crawling out onto land.

MAXIMUM LENGTH	90cm
TIME	Late Triassic
FOSSIL FINDS	Europe (Germany)

THE AGE OF MAMMALS

During Earth's long history, most of the changes involving animal life have been extremely slow. But, 66 million years ago, something happened that had an abrupt and disastrous effect on the world's dominant animals. The 150-million-year reign of dinosaurs came to an end, and many other reptiles, including pterosaurs and plesiosaurs, also disappeared. The surviving reptiles never completely recovered from this setback, but for mammals it brought new opportunities. The Mesozoic Era had ended, ushering in the Cenozoic – the era in which we live today.

THE END OF THE DINOSAURS

BEFORE THE AGE OF MAMMALS BEGAN, SOME DINOSAUR FAMILIES HAD ALREADY BECOME EXTINCT, BUT WITHOUT THE CATASTROPHE THAT OCCURRED 66 MILLION YEARS AGO, DINOSAURS MIGHT STILL BE DOMINANT TODAY.

In the Earth's crust, only the thinnest of lines separates the last rocks of the Age of Reptiles from the first ones formed during the Age of Mammals. But this geological turning-point – known as the K-T boundary – has been studied by scientists in minute detail, in places all over the world. The reason is that it holds the secret to what happened at the end of the Cretaceous Period, when as many as fifty per cent of all the world's animal and plant species became extinct. Those studies point to one likely culprit – an object from outer space.

▷ *Terrified by the light released by a giant meteorite, a tyrannosaur reacts by running for its life. It has only seconds to live, because the impact has already set off an atmospheric shock wave which will burst over the horizon, sweeping away almost anything that can be moved, from animals and plants to boulders weighing many tonnes.*

THE EVIDENCE

Dozens of theories have been put forward for the extinction of the dinosaurs, often without any evidence. But in the 1980s, two American scientists, Luis Alvarez and his son Walter, published research showing that a massive meteorite, up to 15km across, might have smashed into the Earth, causing devastation on an unimaginable scale. Their evidence was the unusually high level of iridium that they found in the K-T boundary. Iridium is a chemical element, and is normally ten times more rare than gold. The most likely explanation for the raised level, according to the Alvarez team, was that it had come from a giant meteorite that had vapourized on impact about 66.4 million years ago.

When they first proposed this idea, the site of the impact was unknown. But, in the 1990s, geologists investigated the remnants of a huge crater off Mexico's Yucatán Peninsula and found that its age almost exactly matched the time of this event. The crater is about 300km across, indicating that the meteorite that made it would have sent shock waves right around the world.

THE IMPACT

Some scientists are not convinced by the meteorite theory, and think that, as with the Permian extinction (page 66), the true causes might have been volcanic eruptions and other natural events. If a giant meteorite did crash into the Earth, the results would have been incredibly destructive immediately after, as well as in the weeks and months that followed. In the second or so that it took to fall through the atmosphere, its outer surface would have melted, creating a burst of light brighter than thousands of Suns. Once it struck the Earth and vapourized, shock waves would have reverberated throughout the planet, triggering off landslides and earthquakes. Millions of tonnes of dust would been blasted into the air, replacing the intense light of the impact itself with day after day of deep gloom. Choked by dust and deprived of light, plant plankton would soon have died in the sea, followed by plants on land. And without plants, animals would have had no food.

VICTIMS AND SURVIVORS

The few remaining species of sauropods would have soon died out, followed by other plant-eating dinosaurs. Predatory theropods might have been able to hold out for longer by scavenging, but the disintegration of food chains would have made life increasingly difficult. Eventually, after perhaps centuries or millennia, the last dinosaurs would have disappeared. Small animals fared better, perhaps because they were less exposed, but the checklist of survivors raises some puzzling questions. Why did pterosaurs vanish, while birds managed to pull through? What physical features allowed crocodiles to survive, while most other aquatic reptiles perished? More than 60 million years after the K-T event, answers to these questions will probably never be known.

THE AGE OF MAMMALS

EARLY TERTIARY

The Tertiary Period (meaning 'third') was given its name in the 1700s, when it was thought to be the third major interval in Earth's distant past. The Tertiary began after the Cretaceous mass extinction, and it continued until 1.6 million years ago, which means that it includes almost all of the Age of Mammals. During the early Tertiary – often known as the Paleogene – some of the continents were close to the positions they occupy today, but Australia was still in the process of becoming an island, and North and South America were separated by the sea.

▷ Pakicetus *(top right) is the earliest known cetacean – a founder member of the group of mammals that includes today's whales and dolphins. About 2m long, it had long jaws with flesh-tearing teeth.*

▽ Pristichampus, *a land-dwelling crocodile, attacks a* Hyracotherium, *one of the earliest known members of the horse family.* Hyracotherium *stood just 20cm at the shoulders.*

CHANGING DIETS

When the Tertiary Period began, mammals had already existed for at least 150 million years, and two major lines – the placental mammals and the marsupials – were well established. However, during this long phase in their history, neither of these lines played a major role in Earth's animal life. They were about the size of today's mice and voles, and they emerged under the cover of darkness to feed. Most of them ate insects, earthworms and other small animals, cutting up their prey with tiny but sharp teeth.

With the disappearance of the dinosaurs and many other groups of animals, mammals were confronted with new opportunities on an extraordinary scale. Practically all of the large plant-eaters had disappeared, leaving a huge and largely untapped source of food. There were no large meat-eaters at all. From modest beginnings, mammals went through an astounding surge of evolution. They eventually filled both these gaps, becoming the most important plant-eaters and hunters on land, and even spreading into the air and sea.

Some of the first large carnivorous mammals were the creodonts, a group of placental mammals that included species that looked like weasels, cats and hyenas. Creodonts flourished for several million years, but became extinct before the early Tertiary came to an end. Marsupial meat-eaters were important predators in Australia and South America, but another group of placental mammals, the carnivores, or meat-eaters, became the leading predators in all other parts of the world.

Early Tertiary carnivores included the ancestors of all the main families of mammalian hunters, including cats, dogs and mustelids (animals that include today's badgers, otters and skunks). One feature that all these animals shared was a set of teeth shaped for gripping and slicing flesh. Their gripping teeth, or canines, were near the front of their jaws, ideally placed for stabbing into prey. As carnivores evolved, some species developed very long canines, a feature that reached its high point in the sabre-toothed cats. These were equipped with two stabbing teeth up to 15cm long, which were flattened from side to side. True sabre-toothed cats were all placentals, but some marsupials – for example, *Thylacosmilus* (page 208) – developed in a similar way, an example of convergent evolution.

THE RISE OF THE PLANT-EATERS

For mammals that fed on insects, the switch to eating plants was more complicated than the switch to hunting larger prey. They gradually evolved front incisors to harvest their food, and grinding teeth or molars to reduce it to a pulp. More importantly, they developed complex digestive systems, filled with micro-organisms, that enabled them to break down the food. Many of these animals developed long legs and hooves, which meant they could run for safety if attacked.

During the early Tertiary, several lines of hoofed placental mammals developed in different parts of the world. They included the early ancestors of today's elephants, as well as tapirs and rhinoceroses. Horses evolved in the northern hemisphere, but they were mirrored by convincing horse lookalikes, litopterns, which developed in isolation in South America. The most impressive of these plant-eaters would have been the brontotheres, animals that looked like giant rhinoceroses with head-shields and horns. One of the largest, *Brontotherium*, lived in North America, had a forked horn and weighed up to 2 tonnes.

REPTILES AND BIRDS

Apart from the mammals, other survivors from the Cretaceous extinction made the most of new opportunities in a dinosaur-free world. Among them were the reptiles that emerged from the extinction unscathed: lizards and snakes, turtles and tortoises, and – largest of all – the crocodilians. Most crocodilians kept to their original watery habitats, but some, such as *Pristichampus*, abandoned this kind of life and took up hunting on land, running on powerful legs that ended in hoof-like claws.

For birds, the disappearance of pterosaurs meant less competition for fish. But on land, the extinction of their immediate relatives – the predatory theropods – opened up some new and different ways of living. Giant flightless hunters evolved, capable of running down other animals and tearing them apart with their beaks. One of the best known examples of these feathered predators was *Diatryma*, which lived in North America and Europe about 50 million years ago. Standing about 2m tall, it probably fed on mammals, but declined when predatory mammals became larger and more widespread. Similar birds survived for much longer in South America, perhaps because large predatory mammals were rare on this island continent, which was cut off from the rest of the world.

◁ *Crouched in shallow water,* Moeritherium *feeds on waterplants. This portly, pig-sized animal was an early proboscidean – a relative of today's elephants, and of extinct mammoths and mastodonts. Its ears, eyes and nostrils were in a line along the top of its head, allowing it to float with most of its body submerged.*

▽ *With its long legs and powerful beak,* Diatryma *was well-equipped for making sudden raids among herds of small grazing mammals. Small animals were swallowed whole, but larger ones were torn up by the hook at the beak's tip.*

THE AGE OF MAMMALS

LATE TERTIARY

The late Tertiary – or Neogene – began about 23 million years ago. Life had fully recovered after the great Cretaceous extinction, with mammals continuing to flourish, reaching a peak of diversity as the global climate became cooler and drier. The continents were less scattered than they were in early Tertiary times and, towards the end of this period, a momentous event occurred in the western hemisphere: North and South America became joined by a narrow isthmus of dry land.

▷ *Hapalops was a ground sloth which lived in South America about 20 million years ago. It was about 1.2m long – a modest size compared to some of its later relatives, such as* Megatherium *(page 213).*

▽ *The South American marsupial sabre-toothed 'cat'* Thylacosmilus *attacked its prey with a pair of enormous canine teeth. True placental cats evolved similar weapons independently –* Smilodon *is one well-known example (page 212).*

SEPARATION AND CONNECTION

Marsupial mammals first appeared during the late Cretaceous Period, when many of the continents were still connected. Fossils show that they spread across Europe, North America and South America, reaching Australia in the Tertiary. Marsupials and placental mammals lived side by side, with marsupials proving just as successful as their relatives in the struggle to survive. But, during the Tertiary Period, continental drift caused great changes in these two mammal lines. Some of the continents began to separate, carrying their mammals with them. Marsupials died out in Europe and North America, but in South America and Australia – now both islands – they thrived.

Today, Australia is well-known for its marsupials, but South America had almost as many kinds in Tertiary times, including opossums – rodent-like insect-eaters that spent their life in trees – and ground-based predators that looked like hyenas and bears. The largest of the South American predators were the sabre-toothed marsupial 'cats'. One of these, *Thylacosmilus*, had the longest canine teeth of any hunting mammal.

In Australia, marsupials remained in isolation until humans arrived, perhaps 60,000 years ago. There were no placental mammals to compete with, so they evolved into an extraordinary array of forms. In South America, things were different partly because placental mammals existed on the continent as well. But as the Tertiary neared its end, the Central American land-bridge allowed mammals from North and South America to mix. For some of South America's marsupials, particularly the opossums, this brought a chance to spread north, but for plant-eating species and placentals, it meant extra competition as hoofed mammals, such as horses and deer, spread south.

UNLIKELY PARTNERS

During the late Tertiary, as the world's climate grew drier, grassy plains became a major animal habitat for the first time. Plant-eating mammals gradually adapted to this, switching from a diet based on leaves of trees and shrubs to one based on grass.

Grasses grow from the bottom up, rather than at their tips. As a result, they can grow back if they are eaten down to the ground, whereas other plants, such as tree saplings, become stunted and die. By killing the plants that grasses compete with, mammalian grazers help grass to spread.

This improbable partnership proved to be one of the great success stories in mammal evolution, particularly in the interior of northern continents. In North America, larger and faster horses evolved, as well as the antelope-like pronghorns. In Europe and Asia, the main grazers were bovids – animals that include today's cattle and sheep.

OUT OF THE TREES

The Late Tertiary was an important time for primates, a group of mammals that adapted to life in trees. The earliest remains – just five teeth – date back to the Late Cretaceous. By the Early Tertiary, ancestors of monkeys and apes make their first appearance in the fossil record. Primates had hands that could grip, forward-facing eyes and large brains – features that helped them to judge distances and to jump from branch to branch.

Throughout the Tertiary, primates in the Americas remained forest-dwellers, just as they are today. But in Europe, Africa and Asia, an increasing number of species took up life on the ground, probably because forests were giving way to grassland. These ground-dwellers included the ancestors of today's baboons, as well as hominids – animals related to today's chimpanzees and gorillas, and also to ourselves. Unlike monkeys, hominids did not have tails, and most could stand on their back feet to get a better view of their surroundings. This upright posture freed their hands for other tasks, such as carrying food or even making tools. It was a major development, and one that would have unimaginable consequences for the whole of the living world.

◁ Merychippus *was a late Tertiary member of the horse family, about 1m high at the shoulder. Compared to* Hyracotherium *(page 206), it was larger, and its weight was supported by just one toe on each foot, rather than three or four. As horses evolved, all traces of their other toes disappeared.*

▽ *Keeping a careful lookout for danger, a troop of* Ankarapithecus *forage on the ground.* Ankarapithecus *lived in the Near East about 10 million years ago – well before the split between the line that led to today's great apes, and the one that led to human beings.*

THE AGE OF MAMMALS

QUATERNARY

Upheavals caused by climate change have been a common feature in the history of life, but few periods have seen such abrupt swings as the last 1.6 million years. The Quaternary Period is divided into two geological epochs: the Pleistocene, which spanned the whole of the last Ice Age, and the Holocene, which began about 10,000 years ago, when the ice staged its most recent retreat. For land animals the Quaternary has been a challenging time.

▷ *The woolly mammoth evolved in Europe and Asia, but spread to North America via the land-bridge that formed across the Bering Sea (page 23). The hump on its head contained a store of fat that acted as a food reserve.*

▽ *The European cave bear is one of several Ice Age species that are known from the fossilized remains of animals hibernating in caves underground.*

EBB AND FLOW
Ice Ages are much more than periods of intense and long-lasting cold. During a typical Ice Age, average temperatures swing up and down, and with each steep drop, or glaciation, the world's polar ice caps advance, and glaciers creep further down mountains in other parts of the world. During the warm intervals, or interglacials, the reverse happens, and the ice goes into retreat. We are currently experiencing an interglacial – one that started when the Holocene Epoch began.

Ice Ages are impossible to predict, although they are almost certainly linked to variations in Earth's orbit around the Sun. As well as changing average temperatures and ice cover, they have other effects on plant and animal habitats. One of these is a drop in sea levels, caused by more water being locked up as ice. Another is changes in rainfall patterns, which can make some areas drier than they are in warmer times.

For plant life during the Pleistocene, climate changes were often problematic, particularly in the far north and south where the ground was bulldozed by slowly moving ice. But for land animals, falling sea levels sometimes proved useful, as they allowed species to migrate across land bridges to areas that they had not been able to reach before.

MAMMOTHS AND MASTODONTS
At their maximum spread, the ice caps of the Pleistocene stretched as far south as present-day London and New York. To the south of these giant ice sheets was tundra – a bleak and vast expanse of boggy grassland, crisscrossed by icy rivers carrying meltwater to the sea. It was a hostile landscape, but despite the cold, summer brought a rich supply of plant food. For warm-blooded mammals, it was a good place to be.

The most celebrated of the Ice Age mammals were the mammoths and the mastodonts, two groups of animals belonging to the elephant line. The steppe mammoth, *Mammuthus trogontheri*, which lived in Europe about 500,000 years ago, was one of the first species to become adapted to severe cold by developing a coat of long, thick fur. Unlike today's elephants, it had a high-crowned head and sloping back, and in males, the tusks were sometimes more than 5m long. The more familiar woolly mammoth, *Mammuthus primigenius*, was a more compact animal, measuring less than 3m high. Its tusks were also smaller, and it probably used them to scrape away snow as it searched for food. The American mastodont, *Mammut americanum*, looked very similar, and roamed the coniferous forests on the tundra's southern edge.

The steppe mammoth died out long ago, but the woolly mammoth and American mastodont survived into the relatively recent past. The mastodont is thought to have died out about 8,000 years ago, while the woolly mammoth clung on for another two millennia. Human hunters were probably responsible for making both species extinct.

ICE AGE RHINOS
The northern tundra was also home to the woolly rhinoceros, *Coelodonta antiquitatis*, another animal whose modern relatives live in much warmer parts of the world. Standing about 2m high, it had a pair of solid horns made of matted hair – a family feature that distinguishes rhinos from other hoofed mammals. Its thickset shape and long coat were characteristic of Ice Age mammals, because large bodies can generate

plenty of heat from their food, while thick fur helps to keep it in. Woolly rhinos lived in Europe and in Siberia, and survived until the ice retreated at the end of the Pleistocene. Specimens have been found frozen in permafrost, but some have also been recovered from naturally occurring oil seeps in parts of central Europe.

Another Ice Age species, *Elasmotherium*, had what was probably the largest horn of any member of the rhino family. It was about the same size as a white rhino – the largest species alive today – but its horn was up to 2m long, with a spreading base that covered nearly all its forehead and muzzle.

SURVIVING THE WINTER
For plant-eaters on the tundra, summer may have been a season of plenty but winter was a testing time. Many grazing mammals migrated south, heading for forested regions were there was some shelter, and food in the form of bark and buds. These included reindeer and the so-called Irish elk, whose remains have been found in many parts of northern Europe and Asia. Reindeer follow their traditional migration routes today, but the Irish elk is no more. In some remote parts of Europe, the species may have lasted until 500BC.

Unlike grazing animals, Ice Age bears spent the winter in a dormant state, which meant that they did not have to search for food. In some caves in Europe, mud deep in caves still carries scratch marks made by bears travelling to and from their hibernation dens.

◁ *Unlike the woolly mammoth, the woolly rhinoceros did not manage to spread from Asia to North America, but it did have a wide distribution from the northern tundra to the grasslands further south. As with modern rhinos, its horns evolved partly for impressing rivals, and partly for self-defence.*

▽ *With its enormous antlers, the male Irish elk would have been one of the most spectacular animals in Europe and northern Asia during Ice Age times. There were several species of these remarkable deer, all with extravagant antlers that were shed and regrown each year.*

THE AGE OF MAMMALS

▽ In Ice Age California, 20,000 years ago, an imperial mammoth lies in a tar pit, while a sabre-toothed tiger fights off scavengers that have already gathered in the hope of feeding on the mammoth's remains. The scavengers include storks and vultures, and also the dire wolf – the largest known member of the dog family. Most of the animals in this scene died out about 10,000 years ago.

DEATH AT RANCHO LA BREA

Some of the most vivid evidence of life in Pleistocene times comes not from the far north, but from the heart of modern Los Angeles in the USA. This is the unlikely setting for one of the world's most remarkable fossil sites – the famous tar pits of Rancho La Brea. Here, pools of sticky asphalt existed in Ice Age times, creating traps for animals on a massive scale.

For much of the late Pleistocene, the climate of this part of California was cooler and wetter than it is today, and the well-watered landscape was home to a wide variety of animals, including mammoths, giant ground sloths and sabre-toothed tigers. The tar pits were often covered with the remains of dead plants, and in the winter, animals could walk across the surface in complete safety, because the asphalt was cold and firm. But, during the summer, the asphalt absorbed the Sun's heat, and started to liquefy like hot tar on the surface of a road. At this time of the year, animals walking across what looked like solid ground could suddenly find themselves falling into

sticky black pools, with no hope of getting out. As they struggled to save themselves, these trapped animals attracted predators and scavengers, which also became stuck.

After each summer's deadly toll, winter rains covered the victims with sand and sediment, and the process of fossilization began. Unlike most fossils, the ones at Rancho La Brea consist of original bones, rather than ones that have been mineralized, or 'turned to stone'. Impregnated with oily asphalt and cut off from oxygen in the air, they have escaped the normal processes of decay for over 10,000 years.

TREASURE IN THE TAR

Many of the tar pits have now been excavated, yielding fossils on a truly staggering scale. These late Pleistocene treasure chests have disgorged the remains of nearly 60 species of mammals, with over 2,000 skeletons of sabre-toothed tigers alone. The largest victims were mammoths, and the smallest included flying insects, which had made the mistake of settling on the surface of the tar, instead of flying on.

▷ *The giant moa*
Diornis maximus *was*
the largest of about two
dozen species whose
remains have been
found in New
Zealand. Until
Polynesian settlers
arrived about
1,000 years ago, it
lived in a world
entirely free of land
mammals apart from
bats. An adult giant
moa could hold up to
2.5kg of stones in its
gizzard, helping it to
grind up its food. Moas
laid just a single egg.

Birds feature in the catch. Their fragile skeletons break easily, but in the tar pits they were well preserved. The only animals that managed to avoid this black death were nocturnal species. This was because the surface of the asphalt hardened after sunset.

RULED BY BIRDS

Although mammals were the largest plant-eaters of Ice Age times, some remote islands, such as Madagascar and New Zealand, had no large land mammals of their own. Their largest animals were flightless birds, which grew to colossal sizes. In Madagascar, the biggest species were the elephant birds, some of which weighed almost half a tonne. One species, *Aepyornis maximus*, laid the world's largest known bird egg (page 16). New Zealand's counterparts, known collectively as moas, included one species, *Dinornis maximus*, that measured up to 3.7m high, making it the tallest bird ever.

Birds like this were able to evolve on remote islands because there were no predatory mammals to attack either them or their chicks. Most fed on seeds, berries and shoots, and they ground up their food with gizzard stones which were very like the gastroliths of dinosaurs (page 78). They survived the changes at the end of the last Ice Age, but sadly, they were not able to survive the arrival of human beings, their spears, bows and arrows, and dogs. Madagascar's last elephant bird probably died about 1,000 years ago, while the last of the moas is thought to have died out much more recently – perhaps as late as 1800.

THE PLEISTOCENE EXTINCTION

One of the tantalizing features about Ice Age animals is that – in geological terms – they existed not that long ago. Few of them lasted as long as the moas, but a whole host of large mammals were still alive and well about 10,000 years ago. However, as the last glaciation came to an end, hundreds of species abruptly died out. North America was one of the worst affected regions, losing three-quarters of all its large mammals, including many whose remains have been dug up at Rancho La Brea.

Why did this massive round of extinctions take place? Some palaeontologists believe that it was triggered mainly by the sudden change in climate as the ice retreated, and the world warmed up. According to this theory, rapid changes in plant life – such as the switch from tundra to forest – left many mammals without a source of food. But similar changes had happened in previous times, without the same widespread species loss. Many palaeontologists point the finger at a very different cause: the rapid spread of human hunters. According to this theory, migrating humans targeted large animals, killing so many that natural food chains began to collapse, and animals were unable to recover.

▷ *The giant ground*
sloth Megatherium *lived*
in South America during
Ice Age times. Almost as
big as a modern elephant,
it could stand on its back
legs to reach up into trees,
hooking down leafy
branches with its long
claws. Today's sloths
belong to the same group
of mammals, but rarely
set foot on the ground.

HUMAN EVOLUTION

The origin of our own species is one of the most closely studied areas of prehistory. Although humans are unique in many ways, palaeontologists have no doubt that we developed through evolution, just like all the other inhabitants of the living world. Our closest living relatives are the great apes, but our own ancestors were human-like animals called hominids, which split from the line leading to apes about 5 million years ago. Following that split, evolution produced a succession of hominid species, but today only one of them is left – ourselves.

THE FIRST HOMINIDS

At one time, experts believed that the ape and hominid lines parted company up to 20 million years ago, meaning that this was the time when our last shared ancestor was alive. Since then, human genes have been compared with those of other living primates. They show that our genes are remarkably similar to those of the great apes – particularly gorillas and chimpanzees. This connection has prompted some rethinking, and today most experts date the split between the apes and hominids at 4 to 5 million years ago.

At the beginning of the last century, many palaeontologists thought humans evolved in Asia, but today there is no doubt that Africa was the birthplace of the human line. The first known hominids belonged to the genus *Australopithecus*, which literally means 'southern ape'. With their long arms, short legs, and protruding jaws, australopithecines had many ape-like characteristics, but even the earliest of them walked upright on their back legs more than 4 million years ago.

△ *Australopithecus* afarensis *lived in East Africa between about 3 and 4 million years ago. Adults stood about 1.2m high, and had brains about one-third the size of ours. Because they stood upright, their hands were free to use sticks and stones as tools, but unlike later hominids, there is no evidence that they shaped them for particular tasks.*

THE 'SOUTHERN APES'

The first southern ape discovery was also one of the strangest. It was a child's skull, found in a South African quarry in 1924. Raymond Dart, the scientist who examined it, concluded that it belonged to an extinct species that linked humans and apes, which he named *Australopithecus africanus*. At the time, many other scientists strongly disagreed, preferring the idea that humans evolved in Asia. But with further discoveries, it became clear that Dart was correct, and that the 'southern apes' were very likely to have been among our ancestors.

Since the 1920s, experts have identified at least six separate species of australopithecines, from remains found at more than 20 sites in eastern and southern Africa. Most of these sites have been in Africa's Great Rift Valley, where periodic eruptions have engulfed hominids in volcanic ash. The remains often consist of no more than teeth or fragments of jaws, but in 1974, two American anthropologists stumbled across an amazing find – nearly half a female skeleton, belonging to a species called *Australopithecus afarensis*. Nicknamed 'Lucy', its owner lived nearly 3 million years ago. Trace fossils (page 19) have also been found. One of the most evocative, a trail consisting of three sets of footprints, was discovered in 1978. Left by two adults and a child, this family outing pre-dated Lucy by about 500,000 years.

THE TOOL-MAKERS

The last australopithecines died out between 1.6 and one million years ago. But long before they disappeared, they gave rise to a new group of hominids that lived alongside them for several hundred thousand years. These newcomers were our immediate ancestors, and had much more human-like features. They are classified in the genus

▷ *After a successful hunt, a group of* Homo heidelbergensis *set about cutting up a dead rhinoceros – a kill that will provide them with food for many days. This hominid was first found in Europe, but originally evolved in Africa perhaps 250,000 years ago. Thought by some experts to be a form of* Homo erectus, *it probably gave rise to our own species.*

Homo, the small group of primates to which modern humans belong.

Unlike australopithecines, these 'anatomical humans' were adept at making stone tools. One of the earliest species, *Homo habilis* or 'handy man', made simple tools by smashing stones to give them a sharp edge. *Homo erectus*, or 'upright man' was a later species that evolved at about the time the australopithecines disappeared. It had a more skilful technique, using the flakes chipped from stones, rather than the original stones themselves. These flakes were carefully shaped, creating spearheads and a wide range of other implements. *Homo erectus* was not

particularly good at inventing new designs, but as a stone tool-maker he (or she) would have been far more expert than almost anybody alive today.

No australopithecine remains have been found outside Africa, which makes it likely that the southern apes became extinct without spreading to other parts of the world. But *Homo erectus* was much more adventurous, and spread throughout Europe and Asia, taking with it the art of toolmaking, and also perhaps the knowledge of how to use fire. Shorter than modern humans, and with a brain slightly smaller than ours, it was the most successful hominid so far, and our direct ancestor.

◁ *'Peking man' was a form of* Homo erectus *that lived in the Far East. Excavations at caves at Zhoukoudian, in northeast China, have revealed layers of ash near its remains, showing that this hominid knew how to use fire. Peking man probably lit fires from natural blazes, and kept them going for weeks or months at a time.*

THE AGE OF MAMMALS

△ *A simple pebble tool (left) made by* Homo habilis *over 2 million years ago, contrasts with a superbly crafted spearhead (right) made by prehistoric people called Cro-Magnons. The Cro-Magnons date back to about 35,000 years ago, and lived in Europe and Asia.*

▽ *In this imaginary meeting somewhere in Ice Age Europe, a group of Neanderthalers (left) confront a hunting party of modern humans. Both sides are well-armed, and events threaten to turn violent, because the Neanderthalers sense that their home and livelihood is at stake. Whether scenes like this took place is unclear, but one fact is known – the Neanderthal species did not survive.*

MODERN HUMANS

Humans almost certainly evolved from *Homo erectus*, perhaps through the intermediate species *Homo heidelbergensis*, but there was no precise moment when modern humans suddenly stepped onto the prehistoric stage. Instead, our ancestors' features slowly changed, first going through an 'archaic' form, and then reaching a 'modern' form indistinguishable from ourselves. The first 'modern' humans probably appeared between 120,000 and 100,000 years ago. In geological terms this is remarkably recent, and it means that the family tree of modern humans stretches back no more than about 7,500 generations.

Modern humans are also thought to have evolved in Africa. Fossils show that they reached the Middle East by about 90,000ya, and the Far East by about 60,000ya. As a species, we have been spreading ever since.

EARLY MODERN HUMANS

In 1856, long before anything was known about hominids in Africa, workers in a German lime quarry found a collection of bones in the mud of a cave. The bones were heavily built and clearly very old, and among them was part of a skull, with large brown ridges over the eyes. When these remains were examined by anatomical experts, many concluded that they belonged either to a subnormal human or an ape-like animal.

Neanderthal Man, as it came to be called, turned out to be one of the most extraordinary discoveries in the search for our ancestors. Known only in Europe and the Middle East, this hominid lived between about 120,000 and 35,000 years ago, at a time when modern humans had already made the move out of their African birthplace. At the end of this period, the Neanderthalers disappeared without trace.

Anthropologists are still not certain who the Neanderthalers were and what happened to them. One theory is that they belonged to our own species and merged with modern human beings. A more likely possibility is that they were a separate species – one that lost out in the struggle for food and space, and eventually became extinct.

SUCCESS STORY

If sheer numbers are a guide, humans are the most successful large animals that have ever lived. At present, the human population totals about 6 billion, and it is expected to level off at about 11 billion at some point in the 21st century. Many factors have been

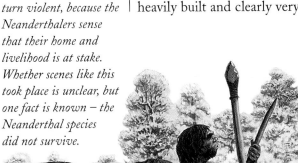

responsible for our success, including the invention of farming, about 10,000 years ago, and the rapid development of technology. However, first and foremost, it is due to something that makes humans unique – the ability to communicate, and to learn from other people's experiences as well as our own.

| urassic | Cretaceous | Tertiary | Quaternary |

GLOSSARY

Adaptation A feature of an animal that helps it to survive. Adaptations develop through evolution, and include physical features, and also different kinds of behaviour.

Aestivating Spending hot or dry times of the year dormant, or asleep. When cooler times return, an aestivating animal wakes up.

Algae Simple plant-like organisms that grow by collecting energy from sunlight. Most algae live in water. Many are microscopic, but the largest, the seaweeds, can be many metres long.

Ammonoids Extinct **molluscs** with tentacles, and spiral shells containing a row of separate chambers. Ammonoids lived in the sea, and were distant relatives of today's octopuses and squid.

Anapsids Reptiles without any skull openings behind their eye sockets. Living anapsids include tortoises and turtles.

Archosaurs The group of reptiles that includes pterosaurs and dinosaurs, as well as the crocodilians and birds. Archosaurs are often known as the 'ruling reptiles'.

Arthropods A huge and highly successful group of invertebrate animals that have a flexible body case, or exoskeleton, and legs that bend at joints. Living arthropods include insects, arachnids and crustaceans; extinct ones include **trilobites** and sea scorpions.

Bacteria The smallest, simplest and most ancient living things on Earth. Bacteria live in a variety of habitats, including on and in living animals. Most are harmless, but some – 'germs' – can cause disease.

Bipedal Standing and moving two legs, instead of four.

Camouflage Protective coloration that allows an animal to blend in with its background. Plant-eaters use camouflage to avoid predators; some predators are camouflaged to launch surprise attacks on prey.

Canine tooth A tooth with a single point, shaped for stabbing into prey. Enlarged canine teeth are a common feature in hunters such as sabre-toothed tigers.

Carnivore Any animal that lives by eating other animals. The word carnivore is also used for a particular group of mammals that includes today's cats, dogs and bears, together with their extinct ancestors.

Carnosaurs A group of giant, flesh-eating dinosaurs or **theropods**. Unlike smaller hunters, carnosaurs used teeth, not claws, to bring down prey.

Carrion The remains of dead animals.

Cenozoic Era The part of Earth's geological history that started after the extinction of the dinosaurs, 66 million years ago, and that continues today.

Cetaceans Whales, dolphins and their relatives. Cetaceans live in water, but they are air-breathing mammals, evolving from animals that lived on land.

Chelonians Tortoises, turtles and their relatives. Chelonians are an ancient group of reptiles, that have hardly changed in 250 million years.

Chordates Animals that have a reinforcing rod, a **notochord**, running the length of their bodies. Some are soft-bodied, but in most, the **vertebrates**, the notochord is enclosed inside a hard backbone, making up part of a complete internal skeleton.

Clade An ancestral **species**, together with all the other species that have evolved from it. Because the members of a clade share the same ancestor, they make up a complete and self-contained group in **evolution**. Dinosaurs and birds are examples of clades; fish are not, because they evolved from several different ancestors.

Cladogram A diagram that shows **clades**.

Cold-blooded See **Ectothermic**

Continental drift The gradual movement of continents across the Earth's surface. Continental drift is driven by heat from deep inside the Earth, which keeps the solid crust on the move.

Convergent evolution The **evolution** of similar features in animals that share similar ways of life. Convergent evolution can make unrelated animals difficult to tell apart.

Coprolites Fossilized animal droppings.

Cyanobacteria Bacteria that live in the same way as plants, by collecting the energy in sunlight. Also known as BLUE-GREEN ALGAE.

Cycads Cone-bearing plants, resembling small palm trees, that were a common food of dinosaurs. Cycads still exist.

Diapsids Reptiles with two skull opening on either side of the head, behind the eye sockets. The diapsids include the dinosaurs, as well as the crocodilians, snakes and lizards.

Ectothermic Having a body temperature that rises and falls in step with the temperature outside. Ectothermic animals include invertebrates, fish, amphibians and living reptiles.

Endothermic Having a body temperature that stays warm and steady whatever the conditions outside. Living ectothermic animals include mammals and birds; extinct ones included pterosaurs and some dinosaurs.

Evolution A gradual change in living things, as each generation follows the one before it. Evolution allows animals to adapt to changes around them.

Exoskeleton A hard case that protects an animal's body from outside, instead of supporting it from within. Exoskeletons are a common feature in **invertebrates**; **arthropods** have exoskeletons made of separate plates, which meet at flexible joints.

Extinct No longer alive anywhere on Earth.

Fossil The preserved relics of living things. Some fossils are formed by animal remains, but others are signs, such as footprints, which animals leave behind.

Gastralia Extra ribs that protect the part of the body containing the stomach and the intestines.

Gastroliths Stones swallowed by dinosaurs and other animals, and used to help grind up food.

Gastropods **Molluscs** that have a coiled shell and a single sucker-like foot.

Gondwana A giant continent that formed part of **Pangaea**. Gondwana eventually broke up to form South America, Africa, India, Antarctica and Australia.

Herbivore Any animal that lives by eating plants.

Hyperphalangy An evolutionary trend that increases the number of bones in an animal's feet. Hyperphalangy was a common feature of marine reptiles in prehistoric times.

Ichnologists Scientists who study fossilized footprints and tracks, and other trace fossils.

Ichthyosaurs A group of extinct marine reptiles that evolved fish-like bodies, and narrow, tooth-filled 'beaks'.

Incisor tooth A tooth at the front of the jaw, used for cutting into food. Incisors usually have a single, straight, cutting edge.

Invertebrates Animals that do not have a backbone, or a bony skeleton. Invertebrates were the first animals to evolve, and make up over 95 per cent of all the animal species on Earth.

Laurasia A giant continent that once formed part of **Pangaea**. Laurasia broke up to form North America, Europe and northern Asia.

Mesozoic Era The part of Earth's geological history that began 245 million years ago, and ended when the dinosaurs became extinct.

Microorganisms Living things that can be seen only with the help of a microscope. They include **bacteria**, as well as other forms of life. For several billion years, microorganisms were the only living things on Earth.

Molar tooth A tooth at the rear of the jaw, used for crushing and grinding food. Molars often have a flat surface, with raised bumps or ridges that grind against each other.

Molluscs Invertebrates that have a soft body which is often protected by a hard shell. Fossil molluscs are common, because their shells often fossilized when they settled on the seabed.

Nautiloids Extinct **molluscs** with tentacles, and straight or spiral shells containing a row of separate chambers. Like **ammonoids**, nautiloids lived in the sea, and were distant relatives of today's octopuses and squid.

Notochord A reinforcing rod that runs down an animal's body, allowing the animal to move by bending from side to side. Notochords are found only in **chordates**.

Ornithischians One of the two overall groups of dinosaurs. ornithischians had bird-like hip bones and were all plant-eaters.

Ornithopods A group of ornithischian dinosaurs that included

a range of small or medium-sized plant-eaters, such as iguanodonts and hadrosaurs.

Osteoderms Bony plates that form on the surface of the skin.

Palaeontology The study of fossil remains.

Paleozoic Era The part of Earth's geological history that saw the development of the first hard-bodied animals, approximately 540mya. During this era, living things made the transition from water to land.

Pangaea The supercontinent that existed during much of the **Mesozoic Era**, when reptiles ruled the land.

Placentals Mammals that give birth to well-developed young. The young develop inside their mother's womb or uterus, and are fed through a spongy pad called a placenta, which connects with their mother's blood supply.

Plankton Small or microscopic animals and plants that drift near the surface of the sea. Plankton is an important food for many marine animals.

Predators Animals that catch and eat other living animals – their prey. Predators are usually larger than their prey, unless they hunt in packs, and they are always less common.

Pterodactyls A group of short-tailed **pterosaurs**, or flying reptiles. The pterodactyls included the largest flying animals that have ever existed.

Pterosaurs Flying reptiles that lived at the same time as the dinosaurs. Pterosaurs had leathery wings, and bony beaks with or without teeth. Early forms had long tails.

Saurischians One of the two overall groups of dinosaurs. Saurischians had lizard-like hip bones, and they included predators as well as plant-eaters. The largest and heaviest dinosaurs belonged to this group.

Sauropods Plant-eating

dinosaurs with giant bodies, long necks and tails, and relatively tiny heads. The sauropods included the largest land animals to have existed.

Scavenger An animal that feeds on dead remains.

Species A group of living things that share the same features and that can breed with each other in the wild. Each species has its own two-part scientific name, for example *Tyrannosaurus rex*. The first part of the name indicates a genus, or collection of species, while the second name indicates one particular species in the genus.

Stromatolites Rock-like mounds produced by **microorganisms** growing in shallow water. Fossilized stromatolites are among the oldest signs of life on Earth.

Synapsids Reptiles and other animals that have a single skull opening on either side of the head, behind the eye sockets. The synapsids include today's mammals, and also their ancestors, the **therapsids**.

Tetrapods Animals with backbones and four legs. Most tetrapods use all their legs for moving although some (including many dinosaurs) stand on their back legs alone.

Therapsids A group of extinct animals that had features intermediate between reptiles and mammals. Also known as 'mammal-like reptiles'.

Theropods Predatory or omnivorous dinosaurs that usually walked on their back legs.

Trilobites A group of prehistoric arthropods, named after the three lengthways lobes of their bodies. Trilobites lived in the sea, and survived for over 250 million years.

Vertebrates Animals that have backbones. Vertebrates include fish, amphibians, reptiles, birds and mammals.

Warm-blooded See **Endothermic**

INDEX

Page numbers in **bold** refer to main sections.
Page numbers in *italic* refer to illustrations.

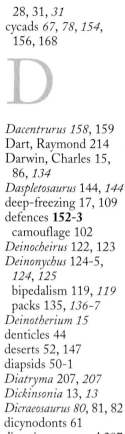

WEBSITES

www.dinodata.net
A giant compendium of facts and figures about dinosaurs

www.dinosauricon.com
One of the most comprehensive dinosaur sites on the web, with information on hundreds of genera

www.enchantedlearning.com/subjects/dinosaurs
A site that covers dinosaurs and other prehistoric animals, with up-to-the-minute news about excavations and discoveries

www.nhm.org
Website of the Natural History Museum of Los Angeles County. Contains extensive information about prehistoric animals from the tar pits at Rancho La Brea

www.ucmp.berkeley.edu
Website of the Museum of Paleontology at the University of California, Berkeley. Features a comprehensive guide to life at all stages in the Earth's past

www.ucmp.berkeley.edu/pin/pinentrance.html
An English-language website that provides access to the Russian Paleontological Institute (PIN) – the world's largest fossil collection.

www.fieldmuseum.org
Website of the Field Museum, Chicago, which features details of Sue – the world's most complete specimen of Tyrannosaurus rex

www.tyrrellmuseum.com
Website of the Royal Tyrrell Museum of Palaeontology, Alberta, Canada. Contains a virtual tour of fossil exhibits, including the Burgess Shale

www.pterosaurs.net
The most comprehensive guide to pterosaurs on the web

ACKNOWLEDGEMENTS

The publishers would like to thank the following for their contribution to this book:

Editorial assistance Sheila Clewley, Julie Ferris
Design assistance Mark Bristow
Picture reseach assistance Audrey Reynolds
Artbank assistance Wendy Allison, Steve Robinson

Photographs
Every effort has been made to trace the copyright holders of the photographs. The publishers apologise for any inconvenience caused.

(*t* = top; *c* = centre; *b* = bottom; *l* = left; *r* = right)
Front cover: *tc* (back cover) Ardea London/Francois Gohier; *tr* (back cover) Ardea London; *cl* (back cover) Ardea London; *b* (cover - spine) Ardea London; *co* (front flap) Ardea London; 3*c* Ardea London/Francois Gohier; 10*tr* Ardea London/Francois Gohier; 11*cl* Science Photo Library/Michael Abbey; *c* Science Photo Library/Sinclair Stammers; 12*tr* Ardea London; *cl* Geoscience Features Picture Library; 14*tl* NHPA/Daniel Heuclin; *clt* Ardea London/P Morris; *clb* Geoscience Features Picture Library; *bl* Geoscience Features Picture Library; 15 *br* The Natural History Museum, London/M Long; 16*tr* Ardea London/Masahiro Lijima; *cl* The Natural History Museum, London; 17*tr* Science Photo Library/Paul Zahl; *b* Novosti; 18*tr* Ardea London/Francois Gohier; *cl* Science Photo Library/Sinclair Stammers; 19*c* The Natural History Museum, London; 20*cl* Ardea London/Francois Gohier; *b* Geoscience Features Picture Library/Dinosaur Nat. Mon.; 21*tl* Geoscience Features Picture Library/Dinosaur Nat. Mon.; *tc* Geoscience Features Picture Library/Dinosaur Nat. Mon.; *tr* Geoscience Features Picture Library/Dinosaurs Nat. Mon.; *c* Geoscience Features Picture Library/Dinosaur Nat. Mon; *cr* Science Photo Library/Peter Menzel; 25*tc* /www.osf.uk.com/Phil Devries; TR Still Pictures/Bryan & Cherry Alexander; 30*tr* Science Photo Library/Louise K Broman; *bc* Frank Lane Picture Agency; *br* Ardea London; *br* Science Photo Library/Jim Amos; 56*c* Science Photo Library/Sinclair Stammers; 64*tr* NHPA/Dan Griggs; 78*tr* Corbis; 84*tr* Ardea London/Francois Gohier; *bl* Ardea London/Francois Grohier; 86*tr* The Field Museum/#GEO85673_2c; *bl* Science Photo Library/Carlos Goldin; 87*tc* Derek Hall; CR Science Photo Library; 103*tr* Ardea London; 108*tr* The Natural History Museum, London; *cl* Ardea London; *bc* Ardea London; 109*tr* Humboldt University, Berlin; *c* Frank Spooner Pictures; 110*tr* National Geographic Society/O. Louis Mazzatenta; *cl* Frank Spooner Pictures; *bc* Frank Spooner Pictures; 111*tr* National Geographic Society/O. Louis Mazzatenta; *b* The Natural History Museum, London; *c* Ardea London; 146*tr* Science Photo Library/Simon Fraser; *cl* The Natural History Museum, London; *bc* Science Photo Library; 147*tr* Geoscience Features Picture Library; *cr* Ardea London/Francois Gohier; *bc* Frank Spooner Pictures/J.M.Giboux; 148*c* Ardea London/Peter Steyn; *bc* BBC Natural History Unit Picture Library; 149*tl* Quarto/Dr Reed; 150*bl* Bruce Coleman Collection; 152*tr* Ardea London/Francois Gohier; 153*c* Ardea London/Francois Gohier; 160*tr* University of Chicago; *cl* University of Chicago; *br* University of Chicago; 161*tl* Humboldt University, Berlin; *tc* Humboldt University, Berlin; *c* The Natural History Museum, London; 162*l* Quarto; BR NHPA; 168*cl* Ardea London/P.J.Green; 170*tr* Ardea London; 171*tr* Quarto; *b* Quarto; 184*bl* Quarto; 194*tr* Quarto; 195*t* Quarto; 198*tr* The Natural History Museum, London; BC Geoscience Features Picture Library; 210*c* The Natural History Museum, London; *bl* The Natural History Museum, London/M Long; 211*tl* The Natural History Museum, London/M Long; 213*tl* The Natural History Museum, London; 216*tl* Michael Holford; *tc* Michael Holford